D0848406

CONRAD
THE NOVELIST

CONRAD
THE NOVELIST

ALBERT J. GUERARD

HARVARD UNIVERSITY PRESS
Cambridge, Massachusetts

Fifth Printing, 1969

Distributed in Great Britain by Oxford University Press, London

Library of Congress Catalog Card Number: 58-8995
Printed in the United States of America

FOR COLLOT

PREFACE

THE true purpose of this book (that true purpose one discovers only upon writing the last line) is to express and define my response to a writer I have long liked and admired. But the book also completes a series of three related studies of which two — *Thomas Hardy* (1949) and *André Gide* (1951) — have already been published. The general aim of the series was to "throw some light on the development of the modern novel, and on the modern novelist's perplexities," and to examine Hardy, Conrad, and Gide as "roughly representative of the progress of the novel" from 1875 to 1925. Treating the three, it seemed to me, one could "record the impulse away from orthodox realism, classical psychology, and conventional structure; or, the impulse toward the somber and ironic distortions, the psychological explorations, the dislocations in form of many novelists writing in the middle of the twentieth century."

My original ambition, as it happens, was even more sweeping than this. It was to write "a book on the contemporary novel seen against the background of certain nineteenth-century intellectual and literary tendencies." In that *Summa,* as I recall, Conrad was to be given one of many chapters, while Hardy and Gide were to be disposed of even more briefly. Luckily I discovered before long that I preferred the intensive study of a few novelists to a panoramic survey of many names and trends. Ten years ago I promised that my enterprise would become more historical; obviously it has become less so. The grouping of the three names and several modes of fiction still strikes me as useful and provocative.

But my concern is now frankly with the single novelist and with the individual novel.

The rash promise of a book on the contemporary novel was made in a brief monograph, *Joseph Conrad,* published by New Directions in 1947. The present volume also fulfills, in a sense, a moral obligation to examine Conrad less hurriedly than I did in that 75-page monograph, and with more attention to his value as a novelist. But this is not an "expansion" of that pamphlet, and in fact I refrained from rereading my earlier study while writing the first draft of this entirely different one. I have reread it now, with a shock of amused recognition as of a friend who has greatly changed yet remains in certain fundamentals the same. The changed and receding personage is not so much Conrad as myself. I find looking back, as one does on such wild oats, that in 1947 I was still noticeably bemused by the attitudes of Irving Babbitt, and was obviously pleased to find some of Babbitt's austerities in Conrad. I suggested, almost, that Conrad wrote certain books in order to express an ethical view of life. The truth of the matter is that an ethical and conservative view of life was second nature in Conrad, holding in check a strong skeptical bent and strong rebellious drive. But the objective of "final utterance" was probably less commanding, and less intellectual, than I made it out to be.

This is a matter of emphasis. A more serious naïveté appeared in my failure to give Conrad his full due as a psychological novelist — partly because I expected and did not find much concern with abnormal psychology, partly because I was simply unequipped to understand some of his richest intuitions. I thus joined a fairly long line of critics who, because they were ignorant of certain psychological processes, misread crucial pages and then went on to describe Conrad as a simple classical psychologist. I take this occasion to recognize that Gustav Morf, whose *The Polish Heritage of Joseph Conrad* I treated rather severely in 1947, was often closer to the truth than I. And I am now more willing to agree with Morton D. Zabel that Conrad was an important spiritual historian, exceptionally aware of the destructive violence of the modern age. I had naïvely undervalued Conrad as a psychological novelist because I did not find, for instance, more and better "Freudian" dreams. So in the political area I undervalued Conrad because I found so few concrete references to the specific issues and conflicts of his time. It has taken the full aftermath of the Second World War to make me recognize the political insights of *Nostromo, The Secret Agent,* and *Under Western Eyes,* and their pertinence for our own time.

Certain other peculiarities of my monograph require no apology: the emphasis given, for instance, to Conrad's concern with spiritual and moral isolation, or the summary and analysis of "The Secret Sharer"—then a "little known" story. These matters (the preoccupation of so many college freshmen today) were then unfamiliar enough, and it is safe to say that in 1947 the large majority of critics in America did not read Conrad at all. I wrote that there were "signs that Conrad is about to be 'rediscovered,' " and that the most encouraging of these was a single essay by Zabel in the Winter 1945 issue of *The Sewanee Review.* The ten years have brought a more substantial rediscovery than I dared hoped for, by new critics and by old. The striking if uncautious essays of Robert W. Stallman and Vernon Young have undoubtedly brought Conrad new readers. From the various recent books and essays I would single out as "indispensable" Zabel's introductions to *The Portable Conrad,* to *The Nigger of the "Narcissus"* (Harper), and *Under Western Eyes* (New Directions); Robert Penn Warren's introduction to the Modern Library Edition of *Nostromo;* Dorothy Van Ghent's chapter on *Lord Jim* in *The English Novel: Form and Function;* and Thomas C. Moser's *Joseph Conrad: Achievement and Decline.* (The reader of Moser's book will doubtless recognize, in this one, certain attitudes, arguments, and even examples. The fact is that Moser and I have been jointly interested in Conrad for so long, and have discussed him so many times both in and out of the classroom, that it no longer seems useful or even possible for us to determine priorities and footnote our indebtedness to each other. And of course it would have been foolish to try to avoid each other's tracks.) Douglas Hewitt's *Conrad: A Reassessment* strikes me as one of the best of several brief recent critiques, and may usefully be read with M. C. Bradbrook's *Joseph Conrad: Poland's English Genius.* Anyone seriously interested in Conrad will of course still turn to the works of the late G. Jean-Aubry and to John D. Gordan's meticulous *Joseph Conrad: The Making of a Novelist.* Jean-Aubry's *The Sea Dreamer* (1957, a translation of the *Vie de Conrad*) is in some ways less useful than his important *Joseph Conrad: Life and Letters* of 1927, since the later volume even more frequently blurs the distinction between fact and fiction or conjecture, is poorly documented, and offers few letters in full. For these reasons, and because it takes almost no notice of work done in the last twenty-five years, it cannot serve as a definitive biography for scholarly reference. But it remains an unpretentious and engaging introduction to the life. Kenneth A. Lohf's and Eugene P. Sheehy's *Joseph Conrad at Mid-Century* is an ample and seemingly reliable bibliography of editions and studies through 1955. A few corrections and additions of Polish material may be found in Ludwik Krzyżanowski, "Joseph Conrad: A Bibliographical Note," in *The Polish Review,* II (Spring and Summer 1957), 133–140. Finally, Robert Haugh's *Joseph Conrad* is a most pleasing appreciative introduction.

Time has changed more than the fortunes of Conrad in America. In 1949 I felt I had to make a case for certain "dangerous" procedures in my *Thomas Hardy;* had to argue the intentionalist issue more than once and assert the possibilities of unconscious creation. If I were to defend myself now (so much have times changed) it would perhaps be against those who consider me too conservative. This book proposes to be even less biographical than my study of André Gide, but still concerned with the creative temperament in its relation to subject and method. In a word I am sufficiently "intentionalist" myself to remain incorrigibly interested in the psychology of composition. It seemed reasonable to group and consider in a first chapter the two frankly autobiographical books and the important series of subjective short novels written in the first person. Two of these are early works, but one of them — *The Shadow Line* (1917) — is Conrad's last important work of fiction. I shall not apologize for the "psychologizing" emphasis given, but refer those who demand an apology to the preface of my *André Gide*. The reader is forewarned, however, of a first chapter both dark and difficult.

With the second chapter I return to Conrad's earliest stories and novels for a survey of his development and self-discovery in his first years as a writer. Thereafter the treatment remains chronological, and emphasizes the full-length novels rather than the short stories and novelettes. The chapters on *Lord Jim* and *Nostromo* attempt lengthy if not comprehensive analyses. They proceed from my feeling that the greatest novels (as compared with the greatest poems or plays) seldom receive the full technical analysis they deserve, and the full not casual rendering of theme. My aim is to talk as rigorously and fully about these novels as certain critics talk about poems. Thus these chapters frankly run the risk of excessive argument and quotation and allusion in their strong desire not to be superficial. I have been urged in the past to be more minute and more directly concerned with technique, and have also been urged to give myself elbow-room. In this volume I accede to these urgings ruthlessly.

The chapter on *The Nigger of the "Narcissus,"* while certainly as long meditated as the others, may seem very different in manner: more personal, and more elliptical in style. It reads in the assertive manner of an essay, and is "impressionistic" in the sense that it returns (incrementally, I trust) to the same point three and four times. The fact is that this essay-chapter was written, substantially as it stands and before any of the others, for publication in *The Kenyon Review* (Spring 1957). This may explain why it occasionally makes a familiar assertion as for the first time. I considered rewriting this chapter from beginning to end to bring it more in accord with the tone of the rest, adding for instance more proof and more quotation. But in the end I decided to leave the chapter as it stands as a very direct yet considered expression of my affection for Conrad's work.

One further matter may be mentioned in advance. The

names of Hardy and Gide appear very occasionally, as points of reference, and to help us place Conrad between the primitive generous story-telling of the one and the subtle fictional dialectic of the other. But the name of William Faulkner appears much more frequently, and I had better affirm at once that Conrad's affinities with Faulkner are closer than his affinities with either Hardy or Gide. The similarities of temperament and conviction and method and even style are striking. In 1946 I asked Mr. Faulkner whether he did not feel he had been influenced by Conrad, and mentioned *Nostromo* in particular. Faulkner replied, "I can see why you would think so." A good Faulknerian answer; and this lesser question of proving or disproving "influence" now interests me not at all. But the responses of kindred temperaments and major talents to similar problems of material and method could well prove illuminating; might at least help us to discover and define those problems. I believe that one of the best ways to understand the potentialities and limitations of Conradian impressionism is to observe what happens when Faulkner carries the same experiments much further. Thus I was often conscious of Faulkner as I watched Conrad meet and overcome obstacles, in the pages to follow, and in the end I stopped resisting the temptation to bring his name in. But I trust the frequent reference can be made without my seeming to argue that Faulkner is *ipso facto* a "greater Conrad" or *ipso facto* "another and lesser Conrad." Writers of this magnitude inevitably differ.

This book was completed with the aid of a fellowship from the John Simon Guggenheim Foundation, and of a grant for research expenses from the Milton-Clark Fund of Harvard University. I am indebted to J. M. Dent and Sons, Ltd., for permission to quote from Conrad's works, and to Mr. Jocelyn Baines for permission to quote (in my appendix) from the letter of Tadeusz Bobrowski.

Albert J. Guerard

December 1, 1957

CONTENTS

CONRAD
THE NOVELIST

Chapter One

THE JOURNEY WITHIN

THE purest criticism attends only to the text, which it conceives as floating in a timeless vacuum: a text and meaning immutable, created by no flesh-and-blood writer and without flesh-and-blood readers in mind. This book cannot hope to achieve such purity. For Joseph Conrad was one of the most subjective and most personal of English novelists. And his best work makes its calculated appeal to the living sensibilities and commitments of readers; it is a deliberate invasion of our lives, and deliberately manipulates our responses. With some effort we can ignore or dismiss the outward man — who at eleven witnessed the public funeral of his patriot father; who may have fought a duel with an American adventurer; who did or did not run illegal guns to Venezuela and probably did run them to Spain; who sailed on certain ships and commanded the *Otago* and went up the Congo. Or the man who having abandoned the sea nervously shaped pellets of bread and was periodically disabled by gout, or when interrupted in his proof-reading on the floor of a railroad compartment sprang at Ford Madox Ford's throat;[1] who earned large sums of money from his later books yet three days before his death made anguished appeal for a twenty-pound advance. The "life" was two distinct and desperate adventures, successfully achieved; one ignores that heroic life with reluctance.

But we cannot ignore the personality and temperament that pervade the best writings (and some of the worst) and largely determine their form. For we are concerned with a style that is unmistakably a speaking voice; with a certain way of constructing novels that may derive from temperamental evasiveness; above all with an intense conflict of novelistic judgment and sympathy presumably reflecting divisions in Conrad himself. By artistic intention he may belong, as he wished, to the race of Turgenev and Flaubert, or even to that of Marryat. But as writer and creative temperament he evokes rather Dostoevsky (whom he called "that haunted, grimacing creature") and Faulkner, the most distinguished of his direct successors. His work is built out of enormous will power and wide personal experience; and in justice the reader must try to remember in the unbiographical pages to follow that this withdrawn lonely meditative man *did* act, *had* been adventurous. But also the best work was built, nearly as much as Gide's best, out of conflict, anxiety, fear. Conrad too was a much divided man.

The "real" Conrad is doubtless as irrecoverable as the "real" Hardy or the "real" Gide. Of the shadowy being we can begin to recover, an obvious trait of temperament is an evasiveness bent on keeping distances. It is a trait too complex to be dismissed as mere pride and aristocratic aloofness. The evasiveness of the prefaces to the collected works is notorious: it is coy, clearly embarrassed, and at times rather tiresome. Conrad was wise not to supply too many clues to novels which are mysteries for the reader to explore. But also he obviously felt himself in a new and improper relationship to the public, in these prefaces, and protected his privacy as best he could. *This much you shall know of me, and no more.* Gide too was slippery and elusive, but he made a great and even compulsive effort to expose the secrets of his sexual and artistic life. With Conrad as with Faulkner we feel an equally strong reluctance to talk about personal matters. Except of course in fiction! Thus certain episodes remain for the biographer very dark indeed: Conrad's Marseilles adventure and his brief visit to South America[2] or Faulkner's wartime experience. The preposterous inventions of some Faulkner interviews suggest a humorous disdain for a public that had so long misread his work. There may be some of this in Conrad too, who granted almost no interviews, and whose professions of respect for the general public are wholly contradicted by his letters. But in both writers the object finally to be circled and concealed may be, simply, the self.

This evasiveness, however irritating to the biographer, can be one of the foundations of a high art. And Conrad's *A Personal Record* (1912) is a true work of art. It proposes to describe the beginnings of the two great adventures: the initiation to the sea, the initiation to the life of a writer. But the narrative begins with his writing of the tenth chapter of *Almayer's Folly* while landlocked in Rouen aboard the *Adowa* (which was to be his last ship) in the winter of 1893–94. And it ends with his first momentary contact with a British ship, in 1874 or 1875. Between this beginning which was really an ending and this end which was truly a beginning Conrad's memory flows freely in time and space: over his childhood and Polish heritage, over his first meeting with one Kaspar Almayer, over certain later experiences as a writer. The autobiography exploits, that is, the now perfected technique of impressionistic fiction; and the "free" flow of memory is in fact beautifully controlled to achieve certain startling transitions, and to play intimately with the sensibilities of readers. It is one of Conrad's most subtly and most deliberately constructed books. And it suggests that the technique chosen for a most evasive personal record was temperamentally suited to the writer of very personal novels. The experiments in a new novelistic form also respected a deep psychic need to control and modify one's distance from experience.

"Even before the most seductive reveries I have remained mindful of that sobriety of interior life, that asceticism of sentiment, in which alone the naked form of truth, such as one conceives it, such as one feels it, can be rendered without shame." [3] In this and a few more such passages Conrad reminds us of the great contradiction of his life: the dreamer, adventurer, audacious seaman, and innovating subjective writer was also a cool rationalist, political conservative, and withdrawn spectator. As factual autobiography *A Personal*

Record is exceptionally evasive — which makes it all the truer to the temperament it proposes to express. Doubtless it comes closest to essential conflicts and anxieties in the pages concerning Poland. One paradox is less severe than it might seem to certain modern readers, though more severe than Conrad pretended: that this conservative satirist of revolution and critic of social-democrat visionaries was the son of Apollo Korzeniowski, leader of the Red faction in the Polish uprising of 1863. Conrad makes short shrift of the critic who called him "son of a Revolutionist," [4] but there is some evidence that the father was in fact more revolutionary and more visionary than many of his colleagues.

A Personal Record contains affectionate evocations of adventurous forbears, as of the grand-uncle Nicholas who during the Napoleonic retreat from Moscow ate Lithuanian dog. He did it, Conrad comments, *pro patria;* "in that light it appears a sweet and decorous meal." The whimsical remark is important, and suggests that the paradoxes of Conrad are indeed similar to those of Faulkner — the two men belonging to an aristocratic tradition which yet professed sympathy for the underprivileged of the earth; recalling with amused envy and pride the fantastic military exploits of ancestors; belonging to lands that had been invaded and brutally occupied; and now watching with disdain a degraded present and the manipulation of the masses by propaganda. The key to the Faulkner social ethic is an aristocratic *noblesse oblige.* And as Faulkner falls into an exalted breathless rhetoric when making certain large affirmations, so too does Conrad in "Prince Roman," one of his most affirmative stories, whose subject is literally *noblesse oblige.* "But as soon as he found his voice he thanked God aloud for letting him live long enough to see the descendant of the illustrious family in its youngest generation give an example *coram Gentibus* of the love of his country and of valor in the field." These are the tones and this is the running rhythm of Conrad when he is deeply moved — whether in enthusiasm or contempt* — and

* The rhythm and at times the rhetoric are similar to those of (especially in France) the proclamation and manifesto. The issue of Polish nationality

his biographer would do well to attend to all such passages. Prince Roman, whom Conrad had seen as a child, led his score of cholera-ravaged soldiers to a fortress where the last stand of the 1831 revolution (the narrator himself uses the word) was made. And even Conrad must recognize that such action looks like the fanaticism he professes to abhor:

But fanaticism is human. Man has adored ferocious divinities. There is ferocity in every passion, even in love itself. The religion of undying hope resembles the mad cult of despair, of death, of annihilation. The difference lies in the moral motive springing from the secret needs and the unexpressed aspiration of the believers. It is only to vain men that all is vanity; and all is deception only to those who have never been sincere with themselves.[5]

Pro patria; and rationalism has its limits. The analogy with Faulkner is further significant, since Faulkner has not left the South. In *The Polish Heritage of Joseph Conrad* Gustav Morf insists too literally on the guilt-feelings attached to the "desertion" of Poland and to British naturalization. The echoes and reflections he finds in the novels seem too direct and undisguised. But the charge of a kind of desertion is one the young Conrad had to face in 1874 and later, and it is the most uncomfortable matter with which *A Personal Record* must deal:

. . . for why should I, the son of a land which such men as these have turned up with their ploughshares and bedewed with their blood, undertake the pursuit of fantastic meals of salt junk and hard tack upon the wide seas? On the kindest view it seems an unanswerable question. Alas! I have the conviction that there are men of unstained rectitude who are ready to murmur scorn-

provoked this style even in a cablegram of 1920. I quote the cablegram only as far as the first comma:

"For Poles the sense of duty and the imperishable feeling of nationality preserved in the hearts and defended by the hands of their immediate ancestors in open struggles against the might of three powers and in indomitable defence of crushing oppression for more than a hundred years is sufficient inducement to assist in reconstructing the independent dignity and usefulness of the reborn republic . . ." (G. Jean-Aubry, *Joseph Conrad: Life and Letters* [2 vols. New York, 1927], II, 239).

fully the word desertion. Thus the taste of innocent adventure may be made bitter to the palate. The part of the inexplicable should be allowed for in appraising the conduct of men in a world where no explanation is final. No charge of faithlessness ought to be lightly uttered.[6]

But for a boy between fifteen and sixteen, sensitive enough, in all conscience, the commotion of his little world had seemed a very considerable thing indeed. So considerable that, absurdly enough, the echoes of it linger to this day. I catch myself in hours of solitude and retrospect meeting arguments and charges made thirty-five years ago by voices now for ever still; finding things to say that an assailed boy could not have found, simply because of the mysteriousness of his impulses to himself. I understood no more than the people who called upon me to explain myself. There was no precedent. I verily believe mine was the only case of a boy of my nationality and antecedents taking a, so to speak, standing jump out of his racial surroundings and associations.[7]

One more passage takes us very close to the heart of this elusive book, and to the determination of Conrad as seaman. It refers to the sea appreciations given him by various captains:

It seems that it is for these few bits of paper, headed by the names of a few ships and signed by the names of a few Scots and English shipmasters, that I have faced the astonished indignations, the mockeries and the reproaches of a sort hard to bear for a boy of fifteen; that I have been charged with the want of patriotism, the want of sense, and the want of heart too; that I went through agonies of self-conflict and shed secret tears not a few, and had the beauties of the Furca Pass spoiled for me, and have been called an "incorrigible Don Quixote," in allusion to the book-born madness of the knight. For that spoil. They rustle, those bits of paper — some dozen of them in all . . . I do not know whether I have been a good seaman, but I know I have been a very faithful one.[8]

"Those who read me know my conviction that the world, the temporal world, rests on a few very simple ideas; so simple that they must be as old as the hills. It rests notably, among others, on the idea of Fidelity." [9] These sentences, coming from a writer so complex and subtle, and who dramatized betrayal so magnificently, have astonished various readers. But in a life whose two great events were "jumps" — the departure from Poland in 1874, the quitting of the sea in 1894 — the obligation to prove one's fidelity was great. So too was the obligation to succeed in a chosen hard task.

A Personal Record may thus be, in its secret burden, an attempt to prove such fidelity. Though slighter and more casual, *The Mirror of the Sea* (1906) reminds us of a less austere Conrad: of the man who had other insecurities and who had, in fact, engaged briefly in illegal activities. The autobiographical revelations are even fewer, and some of these are inadvertent. It is interesting to know that *Lord Jim*'s training-ship episode had a remote basis in observed experience, and Jim's period of inertia and stay in a "Far Eastern hospital" before shipping on the *Patna* a basis more direct.[10] Various passages talk about that untested sense of security Conrad would dramatize in several short novels. But the most interesting and most puzzling section concerns smuggling on behalf of the Carlists, the last voyage of the *Tremolino,* and the character and role of Dominic Cervoni. There are brief glimpses, too, of the Doña Rita and the J. M. K. Blunt who will appear in *The Arrow of Gold* of 1919, an admittedly autobiographical novel. (In that novel "M. George" becomes Doña Rita's lover, and is wounded by Blunt in a duel.) As for the smuggling, Conrad does not, in *The Mirror of the Sea,* try to justify this enterprise on moral or political grounds. He puts the experience down for what it must have been, a young man's romantic adventure.

And he does not conceal his awed liking for the "astute and ruthless" Cervoni, "this modern and unlawful wanderer with his own legend of loves, dangers, and bloodshed" — prototype of the manly aggressive hero to be watched in more than one novel with mingled sympathy and distrust. Cervoni's crime was to kill his traitorous nephew César with one blow of his fist in the very moment of the *Tremolino*'s sinking — the nephew plummeting to his death because he wore gold stolen from Conrad around his waist. Safe ashore, Dominic Cervoni left the party: feeling less guilt for the drowning than shame for the nephew's treason. And he "takes his place in my memory by the side of the legendary wanderer on the sea of marvels and terrors, by the side of the fatal and impious adventurer, to whom the evoked shade of the soothsayer predicted a journey inland with an oar on his shoulder, till he had met men who had never set eyes on ships and oars." *The Mirror of the Sea* — as much by its essays on seamanship as by such personal memories — would suggest that the dream into which Conrad fell when he went to Marseilles in October 1874 was an active and adventurous dream.

But what actually happened in Marseilles? Conrad himself speaks of the relationship of the two books, *The Mirror of the Sea* and *The Arrow of Gold,* in his Author's Note to the later one, and there he goes out of his way to repudiate any suspicion "of facts concealed, of explanations held back, of inadequate motives." It is all true history, "a complete record"; and has so been accepted by biographers, notably by Jean-Aubry and, with even greater recklessness, by E. H. Visiak in his *The Mirror of Conrad.* Those trips to the Gulf of Mexico and South America, and the possible gun-running there, are another story. But in Marseilles (we are asked to believe) Conrad was introduced to Carlist circles, and there met a "Rita de Lastaola," who may at one time have been the mistress of Don Carlos himself and was now working on his behalf. "The possibility of raising Catalonia in the interest of the *Rey netto,* who had just then crossed the Pyrenees, was much discussed there." [11] Thus *The Mirror of the Sea.*

The historical reference is obscure — since Don Carlos entered Spain on July 16, 1873, more than a year before Conrad came to Marseilles — but less obscure than certain other dates and matters to follow. With Blunt and two others, we are told, Conrad formed a syndicate owning the *Tremolino* (a ship of which no other record has yet been found), to be used for the smuggling of messages and arms. And he hired Dominic Cervoni the *padrone.* Much later, in a letter to J. C. Squire in 1919, Conrad spoke of the experience prosaically. "All this gun-running was a very dull, if dangerous business . . . But in truth, the Carlist invasion was a very straightforward adventure conducted with inconceivable stupidity and a foredoomed failure from the first." [12] Yet the account in *The Mirror of the Sea* is exciting: the *Tremolino* is driven onto a rock to avoid capture. Even the picture drawn by the incautious Jean-Aubry becomes vague at this point. His assumption was that Conrad, now ruined, was at last accepted by Doña Rita as a lover, and that they lived that idyll in the Alpes-Maritimes enjoyed by Rita and M. George in the novel. Conrad is thereupon insulted by Blunt, fights the duel with him, and is wounded in the left side. We know as historical fact that a Blunt existed, an American adventurer attached to the Carlist cause; also that Conrad's uncle Thaddeus Bobrowski arrived in Marseilles late in February 1878, in answer to a telegram announcing that Conrad was wounded. Did the real Doña Rita (whose prototype has never been identified) possess those riches inherited, in the novel, from a worldly painter and former lover? In any event Bobrowski presumably found the improvident Conrad as penniless as usual.

This, briefly, has been the accepted Marseilles story, and even the trustful Jean-Aubry was disturbed by certain discrepancies in it.* It is entirely possible, as Jocelyn Baines

* The great problem is to establish when the *Tremolino* voyages could have occurred. The chief discrepancy is that Dominic Cervoni was recorded as employed as mate on the *Saint Antoine* from June 14, 1875, until October 14, 1877, and therefore would have found it difficult to be with Conrad on the *Tremolino* prior to Don Carlos' withdrawal from Spain on February 28, 1876. There is thus evidence to suggest that the *Tremolino* voyages occurred late in 1877. But it is possible that the records of Cervoni's employment on the *Saint Antoine* are incorrect, and possible too that Cervoni served on the *Tremolino* between journeys of the *Saint Antoine*. Another plausible alternative exists: that Conrad and the other youthful conspirators did not acknowledge that the Carlist cause was dead (and in fact there were isolated outbreaks until 1888) and were working to further the cause of a *second* invasion. In that event the puzzling words of *The Mirror of the Sea*—"had just then crossed the Pyrenees"—would refer to the defeated Don Carlos' crossing into France in 1876, rather than to his crossing into Spain in 1873. We do know that Bobrowski refers as late as October 14, 1876, more than seven months after Don Carlos' withdrawal, to Conrad's "determination to join the Carlist forces," and of course it is known that the vacillating Pretender long nourished the idea of returning to Spain. Thus conceivably

suggests in a recent article,[13] that the *Tremolino* was engaged, late in 1877 and early in 1878, in smuggling which had little to do with the Carlist adventure. But this same article, based on a long-lost letter from Bobrowski to Stefan Buszczynski (friend and eulogist of Conrad's father) raises a possibility still more startling: that Conrad was not wounded in a duel with J. M. K. Blunt but instead shot himself near the heart after losing all his money in Monte Carlo. (See the Appendix for partial text of this letter.) What are we to believe? It is a serious enough matter for a Polish Catholic to attempt suicide, one the solid substantial uncle might well want to conceal, if not Conrad himself. And a significant enough matter too, for a novelist who would come to dramatize guilt and concealment and self-destruction so powerfully. If the story given by the Bobrowski letter is true, then the clear and tempting correspondences between *The Mirror of the Sea* and *The Arrow of Gold* would constitute a most elaborate covering of traces: a web of proof (established even after Bobrowski and Blunt were dead) that one had been wounded in a duel, that one had not attempted suicide.[14]

During his lifetime, however, the uncle Thaddeus Bobrowski was extremely important; and Conrad's attitude toward him may be one key to the mystery. The possibility still exists (assuming the authenticity of the Bobrowski letter) that Conrad, after being wounded in a duel over a girl with whom he was living, and whom he had met in connection with the forbidden Carlist adventure, preferred to have his uncle think he had tried to kill himself. How better convey to guardian and substitute father how very desperate one's

---

the *Tremolino* could still in late 1877 be sailing on behalf of the Carlists; or, possibly, combining smuggling for profit with political enterprise. Two sentences from *The Mirror of the Sea* are hard to reconcile with this view, since they suggest that the royal headquarters were still in Spain: "Our hostess, slightly panting yet, and just a shade dishevelled, turned tartly upon J. M. K. B., desiring to know when *he* would be ready to go off by the *Tremolino*, or in any other way, in order to join the royal headquarters. Did he intend, she asked ironically, to wait for the very eve of the entry into Madrid?"

There is the further possibility that Conrad's memory of dates played him false after so many years.

plight had been, how acutely one had again needed money? How, at least, win further sympathetic concern? A duel over a youthful love affair can be dismissed casually, but not so attempted suicide. Did Conrad lie to his uncle? Or did he prefer to lie to posterity most intricately?

The matter remains very dark, and the question an open one. But we do know beyond cavil that Thaddeus Bobrowski's approval and disapproval were matters of the greatest concern to Conrad. Was he to such an extent an inhibiting substitute father that Conrad could do no good creative work, no successful externalizing of experience and fantasy, until his critical presence was out of the way? The idea — as we look back on Bobrowski's numerous expressions of doubt or distrust or disapproval — is plausible. Bobrowski died on February 11, 1894, and Conrad was stricken with grief. But still he could now write, in "a burst of energy, between January and May, 1894 . . . the last three chapters of *Almayer's Folly*." [15] That intractable first novel was at last finished rather easily.

Such at least are some of the questions raised by the two frankly autobiographical books, *A Personal Record* and *The Mirror of the Sea*. Not many of the questions are answered. The novels themselves, in fact, may give us fuller and more reliable answers.

I trust it is no longer necessary to argue the distinction between the "public man" or citizen holding certain convictions and charting certain artistic intentions (who writes autobiographies, prefaces, essays, letters) and the wayward dreamer who writes novels often very different from the ones he intended to write. We must go to those letters, prefaces, and essays for succinct expressions of Conrad's cosmic skepticism and extreme commitment to order: for his hard sayings and harsh allegiance to reason, law, tradition, and conservative political institution.[16] But the subtle interplay of order and anarchy in the novels takes us much closer to the artist who creates, possibly closer even to the man who suffers. And there is, after all — certain new critics to the contrary — some relationship between these very different beings: the citizen and the dreamer. Insofar as the citizen's convictions and intentions are importantly carried over into the dreamer's fictional world by an act of will — there to collide with his unconscious or half-conscious impulses — they may contribute no small share to the "novelistic temperament" and to the dreams it dreams. But even where this is true, as it certainly is with Conrad, there may remain important differences between the citizen's conceptual view of his own personality and the artist's intuitive view of it. The Conrad cautiously discovered by *A Personal Record* is not exactly the one reflected in *The Shadow Line,* which is subtitled "A Confession." And the multiple personality dynamically revealed in *Lord Jim* differs importantly from both of these.

It may be asked why we need concern ourselves with Conrad's "conception of himself," or need speculate on his inner conflicts. A criticism bemusing itself with such matters may not seem to have progressed so very far, after all, beyond the old biographical criticism that listed the drawing-rooms through which Thackeray passed and the ships on which Conrad sailed.[17] But the stubborn initial fact confronts us that Conrad had to live with it, the conception of himself, and this meant that he had to write about it at least obliquely. An important body of his fiction belongs frankly to the un-English genre of the spiritual autobiography, the fictional *examen-de-conscience* and confession, the rare precious genre of *The Autobiography of Mark Rutherford* and *Adolphe* and *The Immoralist.*

The questions of deliberateness and of factual accuracy are not very important, unless as explanations for failure. The late *Arrow of Gold* may well have set out to be the most autobiographical novel of all. But what it tells us of the Conradian temperament is either confused or distracting. Real names do not compensate for blurred feelings, and the subjective or autobiographical work which is not a work of art is irrelevant to our purpose. Our present concern is rather with five short novels closely or distantly based on personal experience and narrated either by Marlow or directly in the first person: "Youth," "Heart of Darkness," "The Secret Sharer," "A Smile of Fortune," and *The Shadow Line*. There is every reason to group them somewhere, as comparable and unusual achievements, rather than follow the accidents of chronology. And there is good reason to group them at the outset.

For these short novels are fairly direct intuitive expressions of the personality and temperament diffused through the longer novels, and of certain major conflicts and anxieties which remain shadowed in them. More controlled in form and style than the longer novels, they yet plunge deeper at times into the "lonely region of stress and strife." [18] And there are intricate relations among these books. We know that Conrad broke away from *Lord Jim* to write "Heart of Darkness," where he isolated more relentlessly the image of the benevolent dreamer possessed by what he hoped to possess. And "The Secret Sharer" of 1909 throws an intense light backward on *Lord Jim*'s dim drama of conflicting loyalties and crippling identifications.

These short novels should not be read as footnotes to the "major" ones, however. All five are not only works of art in their own right, but as a rule distinctly purer and less compromising works of art than the longer books. They are not to be taken as in any way peripheral. Nor should we consider them mere pretexts for a discussion and definition of some "real" or quintessential Conradian personality and creative temperament. They are interesting to us not primarily because they reveal this or that about the long-suffering Conrad who died in 1924, but because their evocations and definitions of human dilemma and of spiritual change are so moving, so artful, and so true. These stories bring to fiction some of the concentration and gravity of great reflective lyric poetry. And they take the reader — whatever the mildly neurotic and courageous Conrad did or did not actually suffer — through human experiences of major importance. However, these experiences are truly introspective. Thus to discuss the stories in terms of personality change and conflict does not take them out of their own area of discourse, since this is what they are about.*

The Nigger of the "Narcissus," based on a real voyage and certainly one of Conrad's most personal books, must for various reasons be treated separately. "Amy Foster," on the other hand, may be added to the group as the best symbolic expression of Conrad's sense of isolation, and although it is little concerned with the narrator of the story. The other five are about the narrator first of all, whether we regard him as projection of the author or not, and though many critics have misread the stories as travelogues or adventure yarns. We call them personal novels and spiritual autobiographies not so much because of their basis in concrete personal experience and actual voyages, as because they clearly attempt to convey with precision the nuances of spiritual crisis and change. All five are serious and sincere expressions of at least one author-personality: the voice that speaks to us is unmistakably authentic. "Heart of Darkness" is a slightly overembroidered exercise in Conrad's most elaborate style; "The Secret Sharer" and *The Shadow Line* perhaps his two great triumphs of a style plain and pure. Of the five, at least these two maintain exquisite control over their materials without preventing the unconscious from coming into important play. (Only "Youth" does not enlist the devil's share of unconscious creation.) "A Smile of Fortune" and even the charming "Youth" may not belong with the best of Conrad. But "Heart of Darkness" and "The Secret Sharer" and *The Shadow Line* belong not only with that best. Historically speaking, they are among the first and best — one is tempted to say only —

* The reader whose interest in Conrad was primarily psychiatric would not necessarily begin with these short novels. As a rule though not always, the richer the dream and the less self-conscious it is, the more reliable is its evidence concerning personality and temperament. Thus *Nostromo* certainly tells us more about the "real Conrad" than does the highly autobiographical "Youth," as *Our Mutual Friend* tells us more about Dickens than *David Copperfield,* or *Light in August* more about Faulkner than *Mosquitoes.* On the other hand the spare, controlled, deliberately introspective "The Secret Sharer" may have more to say than the diffuse and unself-conscious Malayan novels. Not all valuable revelations are unconscious.

symbolist masterpieces in English fiction. The sea voyages and the one great Congo journey are unmistakably journeys within, and journeys through a darkness.

The matter may come to seem dark indeed, so a brief forewarning is necessary. The term and concept of the *night journey,* borrowed from anthropology and now gaining some currency in criticism, will appear several times in the following pages. By it I refer to the archetypal myth dramatized in much great literature since the Book of Jonah: the story of an essentially solitary journey involving profound spiritual change in the voyager. In its classical form the journey is a descent into the earth, followed by a return to light. Sometimes the dream is literally an illuminating dream (as with Don Quixote's experience in the well); more often it is dramatized through an actual voyage and movement through space. A familiar variant concerns passage through a tunnel or other dark place; another describes descent to the depths of the sea. It is assumed that this myth, like any powerful and universal dream, has some other meaning than one of literal adventure, though this other meaning is often unintended. *We dream this dream because we are the people we are; because our conscious and unconscious lives alike have certain psychic needs.* The nature of the vision may vary; so too may vary the nature of the change and rebirth experienced.

But very often the dream appears to be about the introspective process itself: about a risky descent into the preconscious or even unconscious; about a restorative return to the primitive sources of being and an advance through temporary regression. Psychologists have their different geographies of the unconscious, they too using or creating myths and symbolic figures to suggest unseen realities. Not all would agree that the male shadow, female anima, and occult mandala have as definite an existence as Jung implies, and not all would agree with him that integration of the personality is impossible without a full descent into the unconscious. But nearly all would agree that an unconscious exists.

It therefore should go without saying that a powerful successful dreaming of the night journey is itself likely to be unconscious to some extent; the dreamer may have no clear awareness of the nature of his dream. I suspect the myth of the night journey is unusually conscious in "The Secret Sharer," slightly less conscious in "Heart of Darkness," still less conscious in *The Shadow Line*. Psychologically speaking, "Youth" offers no real night journey at all.

The subtleties and symbolisms of "The Secret Sharer," *The Shadow Line,* and *The Nigger of the "Narcissus,"* and all the controversies over their meaning, tempt us to forget that these are also stories of actual voyages, important to their author as voyages. The navigational maneuvers were literally matters of life and death, not merely symbolic vehicles. Conrad wanted us to see and know these ships and their crews, vanishing before the rush of time. "My task which I am trying to achieve is, by the power of the written word, to make you hear, to make you feel — it is, before all, to make you *see*." And the intensity of the mature Conrad's response to his youthful captains — the fact that he could still become so involved in their trials and initiations — may lead us to forget how far he had left them behind, at least in time and flesh. But it is starkly there and should not be overlooked or minimized, the great break in his life: the turn to the sedentary convict labor of converting "nervous force into phrases" [19] after twenty years of adventure and practical work on the stubborn seas. Thus the least interesting of the autobiographical short novels, "Youth" (1898), may be the closest to the author's ordinary waking experience in its nostalgic backward glance. It exists first of all as the feat of memory Conrad claimed it to be: a literal and vivid rendering of his voyage in the doomed *Palestine*. And it dramatizes the most obvious personality conflict (youthful seaman–landlocked meditator) in such simple terms that there seems to be no conflict at all.

There is, rather, a total separation and twenty years' gulf in time between the second mate's ignorant "youth" (the eagerness with which he courts danger, his vanity and youthful illusion of omnipotence, his discovery of romance in disaster, his blindness to the old captain's tragedy) and the narrator's disenchanted maturity. In *Lord Jim* Marlow is proxy for the intellectual, probing, moralistic side of a divided self, yet is intimately involved with a side both romantic and vulnerable. In "Youth" the division is the ordinary one imposed by time upon ordinary men; Marlow looks back on the still untested twenty-year-old with some affection and no little irony. But that earlier self is truly dead. It can be evoked only by the feat of memory, and does not involve him morally. In *The Mirror of the Sea,* under the title "Initiation," Conrad recalls his own loss of romantic illusion concerning the sea. He was elated by the chance to head a lifesaving crew, then shocked into an awareness of reality by the haggard appearance of the survivors.[20] In "Youth," no such important change occurs. The reason for the story's serenity, almost unique in Conrad's work, is thus simple enough: it is the only personal story in which the would-be initiate learns nothing, being still too young to learn. The brilliant nautical detail of "Youth," the thinness of its psycho-moral content, the clear but slightly mannered style, the recurring sentimentality of Marlow ("Pass the bottle!") — these suggest what Conrad's work would have been like, had it not involved important conflicts and anxieties. The temperamental condition of his greater books is that the conflicts are still very alive and real. They must still be struggled with and lived through and appeased.

"You fellows know there are those voyages that seem ordered for the illustration of life, that might stand for a symbol of existence." So Marlow forewarns his hearers at the outset of "Youth." Yet the story requires no interpreting. It seems more than any other of Conrad's to invite a simple enjoyment of its surface charm. The physical rendering of the *Judea*'s misadventures is always vivid; the absurd ship becomes heroic, as the absurd often does. And the pages on her death escape the story's cloying mannerism of breathless parallel clauses. The fine visualization is supported by rhythms exactly suited to the action:

Half an hour passed. Suddenly there was a frightful racket, rattle, clanking of chains, hiss of water, and millions of sparks flew up into the shivering column of smoke that stood leaning slightly above the ship. The cat-heads had burned away, and the two red-hot anchors had gone to the bottom, tearing out after them two hundred fathom of red-hot chain. The ship trembled, the mass of flame swayed as if ready to collapse, and the fore top-gallant-mast fell. It darted down like an arrow of fire, shot under, and instantly leaping up within an oar's length of the boats, floated quietly, very black on the luminous sea.[21]

Such a passage usefully reminds us, at the outset, that although psychological process was a major concern for Conrad the writer, so too was the remembered visible world.

There are certain moments in our lives, or clusters of experience, to which the unappeased imagination returns again and again, endowing them with significances no one could have seen at the time. Conrad's first voyage on the *Otago* in 1888, in command of a ship for the first time, with the events and months surrounding that voyage, clearly represents such a core of experience, to be valued and revalued by art. The long-delayed then extremely difficult trip from Bangkok to Singapore with a cholera- and dysentery-weakened crew was as severe a test as any insecure man could ask for. The trip took three weeks. But in retrospect, and as the imagination kept returning to it, that trip became the culminating episode in a whole period of emotional crisis. It would ultimately evoke, in addition to certain important pages of *Lord Jim* and a large share of the novelette "Falk," two of Conrad's most personal short novels: "The Secret Sharer" and *The Shadow Line*. It is interesting to observe Conrad move, over the years, toward a more and more personal account of that voyage. In the "Falk" of 1901 only a few paragraphs[22] refer directly to the sickness of the crew and to the narrator-captain's ignorance of his ship. Much of the rest is anecdote. But *The Shadow Line* of 1917, if we are to believe Conrad, is in part straight autobiographical record. And its preoccupations are certainly subjective.

The material facts, to be sure, are not very important. The spiritual ones are. Jean-Aubry says of this period that physically and morally Conrad "was passing through one of those transformations which are common enough in the lives of men, but differ in each case according to temperament and imagination and in being either restrained or explosive." [23] The comment may seem abnormally vague, but such crises are always exceedingly hard to define. An injury on the *Highland Forest* in the summer of 1887 was followed by "inexplicable periods of powerlessness, sudden accesses of mysterious pain," [24] and some weeks in a Singapore hospital. Conrad then served four and a half months as second mate on the *Vidar,* and made the Malayan voyages that were to supply him with so much material for his early work. On January 5, 1888, he suddenly gave up this berth which he would long afterward remember with pleasure. But fourteen days later he was given, as unexpectedly, the command of the *Otago.* (Lord Jim goes through a telescoped version of these experiences: a disabling accident and period of demoralizing ease in a hospital, at the end of which he suddenly gives up the idea of going home and takes a berth as chief mate of the *Patna.* The *Patna* is, like the *Vidar,* owned by an Arab, and hence free from the severe discipline of the home service.)[25] Perhaps Conrad was tired of the *Vidar*'s monotonous round of island voyages, as Jean-Aubry suggests. Or perhaps he feared and resisted that demoralization by an easy billet which he would later dream for Lord Jim. There is another and doubtless more remote possibility: that he was already obeying the writer's instinct to separate himself from material the unconscious has recognized as destined to be "used." But any more exact awareness of Conrad's fears and preoccupations must come from our reading of the stories themselves.*

* Conrad was twenty-nine to thirty-one during the period in question. But a highly subjective work of art necessarily reflects, even more, the time when it was written. Conrad wrote "The Secret Sharer" in November 1909 (at the age of fifty-one) at Hythe, where he found his house an "odious" hole; 1908 had been a bad year, during which he feared a breakdown (Jean-Aubry, *Life and Letters,* II, 5). And 1909 too. *The Shadow Line* was begun in 1914, immediately after the Conrads had escaped from Poland and the Continent,

We shall see, presently, how Conrad's imagination associated two famous crimes — the abandonment of the *Jeddah* by its officers and the killing of a rebellious member of the crew on the famous *Cutty Sark* — with this first testing voyage. The gravest issue at crucial moments in *Lord Jim* and throughout "The Secret Sharer" is what attitude to take toward one's brother or "double" who has committed a crime. In the diffuse and otherwise uninteresting "Falk," Conrad seems to be groping toward this central subject and conflict. And in so doing he associates a third major crime of the sea — cannibalism on a drifting ship, murder in order to survive — with his own period of immobilization at Bangkok while preparing for that first voyage. The new captain's problem is to get his ship out of the river, but Falk, who has the only tugboat on the river, refuses to take him. He regards Falk as his enemy, and for some pages the story promises to deal with or at least express neurotic feelings of gratuitous persecution. But in fact the persecution is real and is not gratuitous. A misunderstanding over a girl is presently cleared up; and, in order to get his ship taken down the river, the captain agrees to help Falk win her.

Thus far the story has touched upon but failed to develop the materials of *The Shadow Line*. The land has not yet become, symbolically, a paralysis of the spirit, and the menace of unreason has not yet become a conscious subject in its own right. But meanwhile — with the suspect bargain and with the act of commitment to a man not really known, and who in fact turns out to have committed a crime — we are entering another familiar area of Conradian discourse. Do circumstances excuse? The story, upon exposing Falk's crime, asks this familiar Marlovian question, to which Conrad's

---

and was finished amid wartime anxieties, in March 1915, according to Jean-Aubry (*ibid.*, 8, 164). Conrad's Author's Note says that it "was written in the last three months of the year 1916. Of all the subjects of which a writer of tales is more or less conscious within himself this is the only one I found it possible to attempt at the time." It is not unreasonable to connect the visit to Poland with this renewed preoccupation with his first command. Only major and solid success, as a seaman or as a writer, could silence the accusing Polish voices of his sixteenth year.

answers are usually hesitant if not equivocal. And the narrator remains loyal to the guilty man who refuses to commit suicide because he had committed a "marginal" crime, to *the man who wants to go on living* — as Marlow will remain loyal to Lord Jim, and the narrator of "The Secret Sharer" to Leggatt; as Captain Wallace of the *Cutty Sark* was loyal to his mate who had killed a man.

These then — as we look at "Falk" and momentarily look ahead to the two other short novels and to *Lord Jim* — are some of the feelings and real or imagined situations associated with Conrad's first voyage as captain: an untested man who does not have the feel of his ship and who has made insufficient or improper preparations for his first voyage, and who is so belabored by bad luck that he is driven close to paranoid unreason; an immobilized ship that cannot get started on its voyage or cannot reach the winds of the open sea, and that presently passes through an intense preternatural darkness and over a sea containing submerged hazards; and, of course, a man who either bargains with a criminal or actually identifies with him as brother and double. And the crimes themselves: the crimes of courageous or well-meaning men (except in *The Shadow Line*), yet each one a breach of trust.

So much for the "core of experience" and cluster of recurrent dreams. We may now look at the fictions themselves, though not in the order they were written.

"On my right hand there were lines of fishing-stakes resembling a mysterious system of half-submerged bamboo fences, incomprehensible in its division of the domain of tropical fishes . . ." The strange first paragraph of "The Secret Sharer," with its dream landscape of ill-defined boundaries between land, air and sea, prepares us for this most frankly psychological of Conrad's shorter works. Even at a quite explicit level it is the story of a personality test: "I wondered how far I should turn out faithful to that ideal conception of one's own personality every man sets up for himself secretly." The narrator-captain is insecure at the start; he looks forward to leaving "the unrest of the land."

The story moves from his sense of being stranger to his ship, and to himself, to a final mature confidence and integration: "And I was alone with her. Nothing! no one in the world should stand now between us, throwing a shadow on the way of silent knowledge and mute affection, the perfect communion of a seaman with his first command." This is the end of the experience. But he must give up, almost at its beginning, his illusion of the sea's great security and "untempted life." For the temptation appears on the very next page in the guise of Leggatt, fugitive from the *Sephora* because he had killed a member of his crew. Whatever test occurs, or whatever change in the narrator's personality, must be due to his relationship with Leggatt. For that relationship is the whole story.

He knows that the test must be faced in solitude: "far from all human eyes, with only sky and sea for spectators and for judges." Hence, in marked defiance of custom, he takes the anchor-watch himself, sending the other officers and men below. The direct result of this departure from routine is that the rope side-ladder is left hanging: the ladder up which Leggatt will climb moments later. The captain sees at the bottom of the ladder, when he tries to haul it up, a "headless corpse," "ghastly, silvery, fishlike." There is no way of knowing whether Conrad here intended the sea from which Leggatt climbs as a symbol of the unconscious, or whether he intended a reflexive reference to his opening sentence. What the scene does insist upon is that the captain is *responsible* for the dangling ladder and for Leggatt's coming. He has in a sense summoned Leggatt, who later remarks that it was "as if you had expected me." Even before the fugitive has a chance to reveal his crime, a "mysterious communication was established" between the two. The captain fetches a sleeping-suit, which is just the right size, and on the next page refers to Leggatt as his "double" for the first of many times.* "It was,

* The excellent motion picture based on the story handles the "double" situation with great tact by making Leggatt a slightly coarser, more brutal version of the captain. At one point it underlines the theme of sympathetic identification as Conrad does not: by having the narrator reënact in dream Leggatt's crime.

in the night, as though I had been faced by my own reflection in the depths of a sombre and immense mirror." He at once leaps to the most charitable interpretation of Leggatt's crime. He suggests it was due to a fit of temper.

It would be improper to forget, while preoccupied with the psychological symbolism, that Leggatt is substantial flesh and blood. The story dramatizes a human relationship and individual moral bond at variance with the moral bond to the community implicit in laws and maritime tradition. The narrator at once makes his decision to hide and protect the fugitive and at no time remotely considers betraying him. Leggatt must be hidden from the captain's own crew. And he must be kept hidden from the captain of the *Sephora* (with his fidelity to the law) on the following day:

> To the law. His obscure tenacity on that point had in it something incomprehensible and a little awful; something, as it were, mystical, quite apart from his anxiety that he should not be suspected of "countenancing any doings of that sort." Seven-and-thirty virtuous years at sea, of which over twenty of immaculate command, and the last fifteen in the *Sephora,* seemed to have laid him under some pitiless obligation.[26]

We do not need to go to the biography and letters to discover Conrad's respect for "immaculate command" and "pitiless obligation," or for such a traditional figure; it is implicit in much of his fiction. The narrator's sympathy, however, is wholly for the criminal Leggatt.

The reader too incorrigibly sympathizes with Leggatt. But it is well to recall that Leggatt appears to be a rather questionable seaman: a man who had got his post because his "people had some interest" with the owners, who was disliked by the men, who "wasn't exactly the sort for the chief mate of a ship like the *Sephora*." His crime was, like most crimes in Conrad, a marginal one. His order and his actions had saved the ship in a crisis; the same "strung-up force" had within the same hour fixed the foresail and killed a man. But still more essential (from an officer's point of view) is his contempt for law, his feeling that innocence and guilt are private matters. "But you don't see me coming back to explain such things to an old fellow in a wig and twelve respectable tradesmen, do you? What can they know whether I am guilty or not — or of *what* I am guilty, either?" It is entirely wrong to suppose, as some readers do, that Conrad unequivocally *approves* the captain's decision to harbor Leggatt. The reasons for the narrator's act are defined as "psychological (not moral)." Who knows what Conrad the responsible master-mariner might not have done, had he so connived in a fugitive's escape? The excellent captain of the *Cutty Sark* committed suicide four days after letting Leggatt's prototype go free.

This then is the situation in its purely human and material terms — a situation Conrad will dramatize again and again: the act of sympathetic identification with a suspect or outlaw figure, and the ensuing conflict between loyalty to the individual and loyalty to the community. It is, at our first response, a dramatic outward relationship. But as double Leggatt is also very inwardly a secret self. He provokes a crippling division of the narrator's personality, and one that interferes with his seamanship. On the first night the captain intends to pin together the curtains across the bed in which Leggatt is lying. But he cannot. He is too tired, in "a peculiarly intimate way." He feels less "torn in two" when he is with Leggatt in the cabin, but this naturally involves neglect of his duties. As for other times — "I was constantly watching myself, my secret self, as dependent on my actions as my own personality, sleeping in that bed, behind that door which faced me as I sat at the head of the table." He loses all "unconscious alertness," his relations with the other officers become more strained, and in the navigational crisis of Kohring he realizes that he does not know how to handle his ship. He has been seriously disoriented, and even begins to doubt Leggatt's bodily existence. "I think I had come creeping quietly as near insanity as any man who has not actually gone over the border." The whispering communion of the narrator and his double — of the seaman-self and some darker, more interior, and outlaw self — must have been necessary and rewarding, since the story ends as positively as it does. But it is obvious to both men that the arrangement cannot be permanent. Nor would it do for Leggatt *to come back to life* in his own guise.

The narrator therefore takes his ship close to the land, so that Leggatt can escape and swim to the island of Koh-ring. But he takes the ship much closer to that reefed shore than necessary. He is evidently compelled to take an extreme risk in payment for his experience. "It was now a matter of conscience to shave the land as close as possible . . . perhaps he [Leggatt] was able to understand why, on my conscience, it had to be thus close — no less." Before they separate he gives Leggatt three pieces of gold and forces his hat on him, to protect him from the tropic sun. And this act of "sudden pity for his mere flesh" saves the ship. At the critical moment when the captain must know whether the ship is moving, in that darkness as of the gateway of Erebus, he sees his hat, a saving mark, floating on the water. Now he can give the order to shift the helm; the ship at last moves ahead and is saved. The final sentence refers to Leggatt: "the secret sharer of my cabin and of my thoughts, as though he were my second self, had lowered himself into the water to take his punishment: a free man, a proud swimmer striking out for a new destiny." Leggatt is perhaps a free man in several senses, but not least in the sense that he has escaped the narrator's symbolizing projection. He has indeed become "mere flesh," is no longer a "double." And the hat floating on the black water now defines a necessary separateness.

"The Secret Sharer" is at once so closeknit in texture and so large in suggestion as to discourage interpretation. We know that in Jungian psychology a hat, in dreams, represents the personality, which can be transferred symbolically to another. But what are we to make of this hat floating on the night sea — that a wished transference of personality has luckily failed? In psychological terms the positive end of the introspective experience is incorporation not separation and split. But such an end would have required Leggatt to remain on board indefinitely, an absurdity in dramatic if not psychological terms. The truer significance of the ending would seem to lie in a desperate hope that both sides of the self might live on and go free, neither one destroyed. In Jungian terms, again, integration of personality cannot occur until the unconscious has been known, trafficked with, and in some sense liberated. And we do feel this to be the general burden of the story, whatever the logic or illogic of the ending. The outlaw has had his innings, yet the captain has emerged a stronger man.

In any event, general deductions are more rewarding than dogmatic paraphrase. What can we say in very general terms? First, I think, that the story reflects insecurity and a consequent compulsion to test the self; or, a willingness to engage in the "heroism of self-analysis." In broad terms "The Secret Sharer" concerns the classic night journey and willed descent into the unconscious. But even broader terms may be as true: that Conrad apparently detected in himself a division (possibly damaging, possibly saving) into a respectable traditional rational seaman-self and a more interior outlaw-self that repudiated law and tradition; and again, a division into a seaman-self operating from "unconscious alertness" and an introspective, brooding-self of solitary off-duty hours. In *Dejection: An Ode* Coleridge would doubtless have liked to prove that the introspective "abstruse researches" had not crippled his faculty for feeling. But he couldn't. Does not the positive ending of "The Secret Sharer" seek to prove that the self-analytic, introspective bent (reflected on every page of the story itself) has *not* crippled the seaman and active human being? The great danger of introspection is neurotic immobilization, and this is still another area "The Secret Sharer" touches upon. But Conrad deals with it more directly in *The Shadow Line*.

It might be objected that such an interpretation pays scant attention to the "work of art." On the contrary, the art of "The Secret Sharer" consists in its having conveyed so much human material so briefly and with such absolute authenticity. Its triumph is to have made one uninterrupted human relationship and story render so much: the suspenseful and sympathetic plight of Leggatt, the insecure narrator's resolution of his conflict, the deep human communion between the two men, the profound human experience (incorporating all the preceding) of the introspective night journey. We can say after the fact that a story attempting so much would be likely to split apart into its several themes. What holds it together? Partly, I think, a rigid economy and willed art of omission. The narrator, aside from his insistence that Leggatt is his "double," almost never adopts the language of psychological abstraction. He wisely makes no attempt to convey the hysterical immediacy of near-insanity (as Marlow in "Heart of Darkness" does); he avoids, as wisely, reporting the conversations of the two men at length. But most of all the story is saved and held by the narrator's grave, quiet, brooding voice, by the meditative seriousness of his tones. That voice commits us, from the beginning, to the interior resonance of the story. The point of view is not, as it happens, Conrad's usual one when employing the first person. His normal manner is to employ a retrospective first person, free to move where he wishes in time, and therefore free to foreshadow his conclusion. "The Secret Sharer," which carries us consecutively from the beginning of the experience to its end, is Conrad's most successful experiment by far with the method of nonretrospective first-person narration. The nominal narrative past is, actually, a harrowing present which the reader too must explore and survive.

(We may note, parenthetically, the way in which Conrad associates a famous crime with his first voyage as a captain — two crimes to be exact — and from the association derives this most subjective of his stories. And the story of the *Cutty Sark* suggests one of the reasons why *Lord Jim* and "The Secret Sharer" — in their marginal crimes, sympathetic identifications, and introspective concerns — belong to the same fictional and moral worlds.

The incidents on which the two stories were based — the abandonment of the *Jeddah,* the killing of a rebellious member of the crew on the famous *Cutty Sark* — both occurred in the summer of 1880. The chapter "A Hell Ship Voyage" in

Basil Lubbock's *The Log of the "Cutty Sark"* [27] provides certain details on the prototype of Leggatt, a "bucko mate" named Sidney Smith. He had vented his spite on three Negroes and especially on the incapable John Francis. When Francis refused to obey an order and the mate rushed upon him, the Negro raised a capstan bar. Smith wrested it away and struck the Negro with it, who on the third day afterward died. The mate persuaded "his kind-hearted captain" to let him escape, and at Anjer he was passed secretly to the American ship *Colorado.* Apparently only the crew of the *Cutty Sark,* though disliking both Francis and the mate, wanted to see justice done. The near-mutiny on board the *Narcissus* shows this pattern. Some years later Smith was apprehended, tried for murder on the high seas, and sentenced to seven years' hard labor.

Conrad's use of this material in "The Secret Sharer" and elsewhere suggests how an imagination both moral and sympathetic transforms a raw reality:

1. The character of Leggatt is made less brutal than that of Smith, but his crime has as much or as little justification.

2. The lawless act of sympathy was committed by the captain of the *Cutty Sark* — though he too, like the captain of the *Sephora,* had a fine reputation to uphold. He apparently regretted his act, for on the fourth day after leaving Anjer he committed suicide in a manner that reminds us of Brierly's suicide in *Lord Jim.* He called the helmsman's attention to the course, then jumped overboard. The apparent motive for Brierly's suicide was his sympathetic identification with Jim; though an assessor at the trial, he had wanted Jim to run away. Captain Wallace of the *Cutty Sark* thus enacted in real life one of the essential Conradian dramas: the torment of the conscientious man who has been guilty of a lawless sympathy, and of following an individual ethic in conflict with the "ethic of state."

3. The captain of the *Colorado* received Smith, according to Lubbock, because he was "only too glad to get hold of a manhandler of such reputation." Thus the narrator of "The Secret Sharer" combines both the sympathy of the *Cutty*

Sark's captain and the formal receiving role of the *Colorado*'s. Lubbock's book suggests, incidentally, that life on board the sailing-ships of that time could be at once more brutal and less disciplined than Conrad's novels and autobiographies indicate. At one time, earlier in the voyage, Francis and the mate had fought for fifteen minutes before being stopped by the captain.

4. However inhumane, Smith had "plenty of grit." He emerged from prison with his certificates gone but slowly worked his way up to command of an Atlantic tanker, and died in 1922, at the age of seventy-three. Did Conrad know what happened to Smith after the trial and imprisonment? In any event his sympathy must have been stirred, as it was with Lord Jim, by the spectacle of the man who wanted to go on living. One wonders, too, whether Sidney Smith read "The Secret Sharer" before he died?

The *Cutty Sark*'s trials were far from over, and some of them may have suggested other scenes to Conrad. The ship worked its way back to Anjer after the captain's suicide, encountering such difficulties that a seaman given to gloomy prophecies claimed she was bewitched, and would have no luck until the murderous mate was under lock and key — which reminds us of Mr. Burns in *The Shadow Line* and of Singleton in *The Nigger of the "Narcissus."* Some of the crew felt that the prophet himself was "the Jonah at the root of all the trouble." When the *Cutty Sark* reached Singapore on September 18, it was to find the city "already all agog with the *Jeddah* disaster" which lies behind *Lord Jim*.)

According to the Author's Note, *The Shadow Line* concerns "the change from youth, care-free and fervent, to the more self-conscious and more poignant period of maturer life." The story itself speaks at first of the region of "early youth" that must be left behind; two pages later of "the green sickness of late youth." But the ennui described by the narrator in the first two chapters often seems closer to the *démon de midi* experienced by so many men in early middle age: a "rebellious discontent" and "obscure feeling of life being a waste of days"; a "spiritual drowsiness" and "feeling of life-emptiness"; generally, a directionless longing for change. One might refer again to those "inexplicable periods of powerlessness" after an accident and the subsequent stay in a hospital. But I prefer a general but strong subjective impression: *The Shadow Line* is, in part, about the living through and throwing off of an immobilizing neurotic depression. If we are to hazard any guesses at all (looking forward to Conrad's many immobilized heroes and apathetic underlings) we must hazard this one: that he radically feared paralysis of will and spiritual dryness, the "calme plat, grand miroir/ De mon désespoir." [28] How much of this anxiety goes back to remembered periods of fitful apathy and how much reflects contemporary difficulties as a writer (the *stérilité des écrivains nerveux*) is impossible to say. But the preoccupation with immobilization, together with the various explicit statements that action alone can save us, is one of the important Conrad recurrences.

The Shadow Line, while written in part in the pure unpretentious prose of "The Secret Sharer," is distinctly less perfect. It gets underway very slowly and uncertainly. To make the two stories truly analogous we need only cut out the first two chapters of *The Shadow Line:* need only begin with the two untested narrator-captains on board for the first time, communing with themselves. Conrad apparently conceived of *The Shadow Line* as dealing with the passage from ignorant and untested confidence through a major trial to the very different confidence of mature self-command. So conceived the story ought logically to have reflected, in its first pages, a naïve and buoyant confidence. What it really presents is a neurotic immobilization onshore, for which the opportunity of a first command is expected to provide a cure. But the dead calm of the Gulf of Siam simply mirrors in intensified form the same "moral dissolution" to be lived through, faced out, survived. The narrator comes closer to the phase he is leaving, much closer to the narrator of "The Secret Sharer," and doubtless much closer to Conrad himself, when he speaks of that "strange sense of insecurity in my past. I always suspected that I might be no good." Again I think we are very close to Conrad himself whenever the story makes a distinction between a seaman-self and a self more introspective and vulnerable. "The seaman's instinct alone survived in my moral dissolution." The conclusion is simply that of "The Secret Sharer": we cannot be good seamen, alone with our ships, until we have faced out, recognized, and subdued those selves which interfere with seamanship (i.e., action). We cannot achieve wholesome integration of the personality until we have made the archetypal journey into self.

The night journey (as in "The Secret Sharer") is described in symbolic terms. The narrator-captain relies on panaceas, as the inexperienced do. "My education was far from being finished, though I didn't know it." He assumes that mere movement from land to sea will solve all his troubles (including the fevers of his men), but ship and men are "snared in the river . . . as if in some poisonous trap." Later, the panacea is quinine. But his dead predecessor had sold the quinine and stuffed the bottles with a useless powder. The deranged chief mate attributes their material difficulties and even the strange calms of the Gulf to the malevolent spirit of the captain, buried in its depths. And at the very crisis of the story, immediately before the healing rain falls and the saving wind blows, the narrator-captain momentarily shares his superstitious fancy. Mr. Burns insists that the spirit of the dead, like Coleridge's Polar Spirit, controls their navigation. Is this the narrator's extreme peril of the soul: that he should come to believe these atavistic fantasies? The great experience of the story is not the saving rain and wind but the intense dead calm, the preternatural stillness of the air and preternatural blackness of the critical night, "the closing in of a menace from all sides." Critical night: the facing of a crisis and final saving break through the "creeping paralysis of a hopeless outlook." Like the Ancient Mariner, the narrator must surmount despair as well as apathy. And he too must live with his "sense of guilt," materially attached to his seaman's failure to verify the quinine. The end suggests that one must live with it, the sense of guilt, but also face it out. "A man should stand up to his bad luck, to his mistakes, to his conscience, and all that sort of thing."

The drama of integration in "The Secret Sharer" is classically, and neatly, conveyed through the mechanism of the double. We shall see more than once that Conrad, like Dostoevsky, finds this the best way to dramatize the schisms of the spirit: to objectify in a physical outsider a side of the self we sympathize with yet condemn. In "The Secret Sharer" the process is quite explicit. In *The Shadow Line* it exists as a subtle and possibly unintended nuance, and the division of the soul is into three not two. The sick Mr. Burns in his irrational fears, and confined through most of the voyage to his cabin, recalls the primitive Nigger of the *Narcissus*. He comes on deck only at the blackest moment of the decisive night; the narrator stumbles over him and momentarily takes him for the ghost of the dead captain. The rational Ransome, fearful of his weak heart yet of a saving extrovert temperament, represents an almost opposite force. At the end of the voyage both Mr. Burns and Ransome leave the ship, and the narrator is alone with it. He no longer needs either.

Published between the diffuse and often sentimental *Victory* and the minor, radically imperfect *Arrow of Gold, The Shadow Line* is Conrad's final important achievement as an artist. It represents his last and largely successful effort to make a minutely rendered material world serve symbolic ends: the real and the symbolic in perilous balance, neither toppling or violating the other. And it is the last work to offer few peripheral entertainments. Once again the narrating voice is authentic and moving. The unpretentious "spoken" prose is capable of evoking, richly, the daylight calms and the menacing black of the night. But the first two chapters are seriously defective, perhaps because they are so dependent on literal recall: of the material difficulties involved in getting the *Otago* underway, of a period of undefined anxiety. The irritability of the narrator at last becomes irritating to the reader.

In these chapters the author is groping toward discovery of his subject. Did he ever wholly discover it? Even the later chapters suffer from uncertainty. The novel is in no important sense that tribute to a crew Conrad wanted it in part to be: a record of sailors "worthy of my undying regard." And the narrator's sense of guilt is not attached, as it was in "The Secret Sharer," to a significant human action. It is instead a state of being — which may be true enough to life but is unrewarding for fiction. Uncertainty, too, clouds the crisis, and if there are many novels weakened because the novelist has too clear a conceptual view of his theme, there are others that suffer because he does not see that theme clearly enough. Briefly, *The Shadow Line* professes to deal with a physical experience so trying that it tempts the narrator to share Mr. Burns's paranoid unreason;* or, again, to deal with the passage from youth to maturity. But at its best the novel dramatizes rather the experience of immobilizing depression. Such a subject is humanly important, for all the dangers Matthew Arnold saw in it. But perhaps only a rich environing fantasy, as in Kafka, or a frame of environing action, as here with a sea voyage, can save it for fiction.†

"Heart of Darkness" is the most famous of these personal short novels: a *Pilgrim's Progress* for our pessimistic and psychologizing age. "Before the Congo I was just a mere animal." [29] The living nightmare of 1890 seems to have affected Conrad quite as importantly as did Gide's Congo experience thirty-six years later. The autobiographical basis of the narrative is well known, and its introspective bias obvious; this is Conrad's longest journey into self. But it is

* Various readers have detected resemblances to *The Ancient Mariner.* The climax should be compared with that of Yvor Winters' great and little-known short story "The Brink of Darkness," available in Alan Swallow's anthology of psychological fiction, *Anchor in the Sea.*

† We can understand Conrad's exasperation because some readers took *The Shadow Line* to be a story of the supernatural, or because Sidney Colvin hesitated to review it because he was unacquainted with the Gulf of Siam. Between the two positions a reader might argue this one: If *The Shadow Line* is faithfully based on an actual voyage delayed by sickness and by unusual calms on the Gulf of Siam, *why should it be regarded as being about anything more than that?* The answer is given by the narrator's tone of voice, and by his insistent preoccupation with his own states of mind.

well to remember that "Heart of Darkness" is also other if more superficial things: a sensitive and vivid travelogue, and a comment on "the vilest scramble for loot that ever disfigured the history of human conscience and geographical exploration." * The Congo was much in the public mind in 1889, when Henry Stanley's relief expedition found Emin Pasha (who like Kurtz did not want to be rescued), and it is interesting to note that Conrad was in Brussels during or immediately after Stanley's triumphant welcome there in April 1890.[30] This was just before he set out on his own Congo journey. We do not know how much the Georges Antoine Klein who died on board the *Roi des Belges* resembled the fictional Kurtz, but Stanley himself provided no mean example of a man who could gloss over the extermination of savages with pious moralisms which were very possibly "sincere."

"Heart of Darkness" thus has its important public side, as an angry document on absurd and brutal exploitation. Marlow is treated to the spectacle of a French man-of-war shelling an unseen "enemy" village in the bush, and presently he will wander into the grove at the first company station where the starving and sick Negroes withdraw to die. It is one of the greatest of Conrad's many moments of compassionate rendering. The compassion extends even to the cannibal crew of the *Roi des Belges*. Deprived of the rotten hippo meat they had brought along for food, and paid three nine-inch pieces of brass wire a week, they appear to subsist on "lumps of some stuff like half-cooked dough, of a dirty lavender color" which

* *Last Essays*, p. 17. In "Heart of Darkness" Conrad makes once his usual distinction between British imperialism and the imperialism of other nations. On the map in Brussels there "was a vast amount of red — good to see at any time, because one knows that some real work is done in there." His 1899 letters to E. L. Sanderson and to Mme. Angèle Zagórska on the Boer war express his position clearly. The conspiracy to oust the Briton "is ready to be hatched in other regions. It . . . is everlastingly skulking in the Far East. A war there or anywhere but in S. Africa would have been conclusive, — would have been worth the sacrifices" (Jean-Aubry, *Life and Letters,* I, 286). "That they — the Boers — are struggling in good faith for their independence cannot be doubted; but it is also a fact that they have no idea of liberty, which can only be found under the English flag all over the world" (*ibid.*, I, 288).

they keep wrapped in leaves. Conrad here operates through ambiguous suggestion (are the lumps human flesh?) but elsewhere he wants, like Gide after him, to make his complacent European reader *see:* see, for instance, the drunken unkempt official met on the road and three miles farther on the body of the Negro with a bullet hole in his forehead.* "Heart of Darkness" is a record of things seen and done. But also Conrad was reacting to the humanitarian pretenses of some of the looters precisely as the novelist today reacts to the moralisms of cold-war propaganda. Then it was ivory that poured from the heart of darkness; now it is uranium. Conrad shrewdly recognized — an intuition amply developed in *Nostromo* — that deception is most sinister when it becomes self-deception, and the propagandist takes seriously his own fictions. Kurtz "could get himself to believe anything — anything." The benevolent rhetoric of his seventeen-page report for the International Society for the Suppression of Savage Customs was meant sincerely enough. But a deeper sincerity spoke through his scrawled postscript: "Exterminate all the brutes!" The conservative Conrad (who found Donkin fit to be a labor leader) speaks through the journalist who says that "Kurtz's proper sphere ought to have been politics 'on the popular side.' "

Conrad, again like many novelists today, was both drawn to idealism and repelled by its hypocritical abuse. "The conquest of the earth, which mostly means the taking it away from those who have a different complexion or slightly flatter noses than ourselves, is not a pretty thing when you look into it too much. What redeems it is the idea only. An idea at the back of it; not a sentimental pretence but an idea; and an unselfish belief in the idea . . ." Marlow commits himself to the yet unseen agent partly because Kurtz "had come out equipped with moral ideas of some sort." Anything would seem preferable to the demoralized greed and total cynicism

* Compare "The Congo Diary," *Last Essays,* p. 163. Conrad did not use the skeleton tied to a post that he saw on Tuesday, July 29 (*ibid.,* p. 169). It might have seemed too blatant or too "literary" in a novel depending on mortuary imagery from beginning to end.

of the others, "the flabby devil" of the Central Station. Later, when he discovers what has happened to Kurtz's moral ideas, he remains faithful to the "nightmare of my choice." In *Under Western Eyes* Sophia Antonovna makes a distinction between those who burn and those who rot, and remarks that it is sometimes preferable to burn. The Kurtz who had made himself literally one of the devils of the land, and who in solitude had kicked himself loose of the earth, burns while the others rot. Through violent not flabby evil he exists in the moral universe even before pronouncing judgment on himself with his dying breath. A little too much has been made, I think, of the redemptive value of those two words — "The horror!" But none of the company "pilgrims" could have uttered them.

The redemptive view is Catholic, of course, though no priest was in attendance; Kurtz can repent as the gunman of *The Power and the Glory* cannot. "Heart of Darkness" (still at this public and wholly conscious level) combines a Victorian ethic and late Victorian fear of the white man's deterioration with a distinctly Catholic psychology. We are protected from ourselves by society with its laws and its watchful neighbors, Marlow observes. And we are protected by work. "You wonder I didn't go ashore for a howl and a dance? Well, no — I didn't. Fine sentiments, you say? Fine sentiments, be hanged! I had no time. I had to mess about with white-lead and strips of woolen blanket helping to put bandages on those leaky steam-pipes." But when the external restraints of society and work are removed, we must meet the challenge and temptation of savage reversion with our "own inborn strength. Principles won't do." This inborn strength appears to include restraint — the restraint that Kurtz lacked and the cannibal crew of the *Roi des Belges* surprisingly possessed. The hollow man, whose evil is the evil of *vacancy,* succumbs. And in their different degrees the pilgrims and Kurtz share this hollowness. "Perhaps there was nothing within" the manager of the Central Station. "Such a suspicion made one pause — for out there there were no external checks." And there was nothing inside the brickmaker, that papier-maché Mephistopheles, "but a little loose dirt, maybe."

As for Kurtz, the wilderness "echoed loudly within him because he was hollow at the core." Perhaps the chief contradiction of "Heart of Darkness" is that it suggests and dramatizes evil as an active energy (Kurtz and his unspeakable lusts) but defines evil as vacancy. The primitive (and here the contradiction is only verbal) is compact of passion and apathy. "I was struck by the fire of his eyes and the composed languor of his expression . . . This shadow looked satiated and calm, as though for the moment it had had its fill of all the emotions." Of the two menaces — the unspeakable desires and the apathy — apathy surely seemed the greater to Conrad. Hence we cannot quite believe the response of Marlow's heart to the beating of the tom-toms. This is, I think, the story's minor but central flaw, and the source of an unfruitful ambiguity: that it slightly overdoes the kinship with the "passionate uproar," slightly undervalues the temptation of inertia.

In any event, it is time to recognize that the story is not primarily about Kurtz or about the brutality of Belgian officials but about Marlow its narrator. To what extent it also expresses the Joseph Conrad a biographer might conceivably recover, who in 1898 still felt a debt must be paid for his Congo journey and who paid it by the writing of this story, is doubtless an insoluble question. I suspect two facts (of a possible several hundred) are important. First, that going to the Congo was the enactment of a childhood wish associated with the disapproved childhood ambition to go to sea, and that this belated enactment was itself profoundly disapproved, in 1890, by the uncle and guardian.[31] It was another gesture of a man bent on throwing his life away. But even more important may be the guilt of complicity, just such a guilt as many novelists of the Second World War have been obliged to work off. What Conrad thought of the expedition of the Katanga Company of 1890–1892 is accurately reflected in his remarks on the "Eldorado Exploring Expedition" of "Heart of Darkness": "It was reckless without hardihood, greedy without audacity, and cruel without courage . . . with no more moral purpose at the back of it than there is in burglars breaking into a safe." Yet Conrad hoped to obtain command of the expedition's ship even after he had returned from the initiatory voyage dramatized in his novel. Thus the adventurous Conrad and Conrad the moralist may have experienced collision. But the collision, again as with so many novelists of the second war, could well have been deferred and retrospective, not felt intensely at the time.

So much for the elusive Conrad of the biographers and of the "Congo Diary." Substantially and in its central emphasis "Heart of Darkness" concerns Marlow (projection to whatever great or small degree of a more irrecoverable Conrad) and his journey toward and through certain facets or potentialities of self. F. R. Leavis seems to regard him as a narrator only, providing a "specific and concretely realized point of view." [32] But Marlow reiterates often enough that he is recounting a spiritual voyage of self-discovery. He remarks casually but crucially that he did not know himself before setting out, and that he likes work for the chance it provides to "find yourself . . . what no other man can ever know." The Inner Station "was the farthest point of navigation and the culminating point of my experience." At a material and rather superficial level, the journey is through the temptation of atavism. It is a record of "remote kinship" with the "wild and passionate uproar," of a "trace of a response" to it, of a final rejection of the "fascination of the abomination." And why should there not be the trace of a response? "The mind of man is capable of anything — because everything is in it, all the past as well as all the future." Marlow's temptation is made concrete through his exposure to Kurtz, a white man and sometime idealist who had fully responded to the wilderness: a potential and fallen self. "I had turned to the wilderness really, not to Mr. Kurtz." At the climax Marlow follows Kurtz ashore, confounds the beat of the drum with the beating of his heart, goes through the ordeal of looking into Kurtz's "mad soul," and brings him back to the ship. He returns to Europe a changed and more knowing man. Ordinary people are now "intruders whose knowledge of life was to me an irritating pretence, because I felt so sure they could not possibly know the things I knew."

On this literal plane, and when the events are so abstracted from the dream-sensation conveying them, it is hard to take Marlow's plight very seriously. Will he, the busy captain and moralizing narrator, also revert to savagery, go ashore for a howl and a dance, indulge unspeakable lusts? The late Victorian reader (and possibly Conrad himself) could take this more seriously than we; could literally believe not merely in a Kurtz's deterioration through months of solitude but also in the sudden reversions to the "beast" of naturalistic fiction. Insofar as Conrad does want us to take it seriously and literally, we must admit the nominal triumph of a currently accepted but false psychology over his own truer intuitions. But the triumph is only nominal. For the personal narrative is unmistakably authentic, which means that it explores something truer, more fundamental, and distinctly less material: the night journey into the unconscious, and confrontation of an entity within the self. "I flung one shoe overboard, and became aware that that was exactly what I had been looking forward to — a talk with Kurtz." It little matters what, in terms of psychological symbolism, we call this double or say he represents: whether the Freudian id or the Jungian shadow or more vaguely the outlaw. And I am afraid it is impossible to say where Conrad's conscious understanding of his story began and ended. The important thing is that the introspective plunge and powerful dream seem true; and are therefore inevitably moving.

Certain circumstances of Marlow's voyage, looked at in these terms, take on a new importance. The true night journey can occur (except during analysis) only in sleep or in the waking dream of a profoundly intuitive mind. Marlow insists more than is necessary on the dreamlike quality of his narrative. "It seems to me I am trying to tell you a dream — making a vain attempt, because no relation of a dream can convey the dream-sensation, that commingling of absurdity, surprise, and bewilderment in a tremor of struggling revolt . . ." Even before leaving Brussels Marlow felt as though he "were about to set off for the center of the earth," not the center of a continent.[33] The introspective voyager leaves his familiar rational world, is "cut off from the comprehension" of his surroundings; his steamer toils "along slowly on the edge of a black and incomprehensible frenzy." As the crisis approaches, the dreamer and his ship move through a silence that "seemed unnatural, like a state of trance"; then enter (a few miles below the Inner Station) a deep fog. "The approach to this Kurtz grubbing for ivory in the wretched bush was beset by as many dangers as though he had been an enchanted princess sleeping in a fabulous castle."* Later, Marlow's task is to try "to break the spell" of the wilderness that holds Kurtz entranced.

The approach to the unconscious and primitive may be aided by a savage or half-savage guide, and may require the token removal of civilized trappings or aids; both conceptions are beautifully dramatized in Faulkner's "The Bear." In "Heart of Darkness" the token "relinquishment" and the death of the half-savage guide are connected. The helmsman falling at Marlow's feet casts blood on his shoes, which he is "morbidly anxious" to change and in fact throws overboard.† (The rescue of Wait in *The Nigger of the "Narcissus"* shows a similar pattern.) Here we have presumably entered an area of unconscious creation; the dream is true but the teller may have no idea why it is. So too, possibly, a psychic need as well as literary tact compelled Conrad to defer the meeting between Marlow and Kurtz for some three thousand words after announcing that it took place. We think we are about to meet Kurtz at last. But instead Marlow leaps ahead to his meeting with the "Intended"; comments on Kurtz's meg-

* The analogy of unspeakable Kurtz and enchanted princess may well be an intended irony. But there may be some significance in the fact that this once the double is imagined as an entranced feminine figure.

† Like any obscure human act, this one invites several interpretations, beginning with the simple washing away of guilt. The fear of the blood may be, however, a fear of the primitive toward which Marlow is moving. To throw the shoes overboard would then mean a token rejection of the savage, not the civilized-rational. In any event it seems plausible to have blood at this stage of a true initiation story.

alomania and assumption of his place among the devils of the land; reports on the seventeen-page pamphlet; relates his meeting and conversation with Kurtz's harlequin disciple — and only then tells of seeing through his binoculars the heads on the stakes surrounding Kurtz's house. This is the "evasive" Conrad in full play, deferring what we most want to know and see; perhaps compelled to defer climax in this way. The tactic is dramatically effective, though possibly carried to excess: we are told on the authority of completed knowledge certain things we would have found hard to believe had they been presented through a slow consecutive realistic discovery. But also it can be argued that it was psychologically impossible for Marlow to go at once to Kurtz's house with the others. The double must be brought on board the ship, and the first confrontation must occur there. We are reminded of Leggatt in the narrator's cabin, of the trapped Wait on the *Narcissus.* The incorporation and alliance between the two becomes material, and the identification of "selves."

Hence the shock Marlow experiences when he discovers that Kurtz's cabin is empty and his secret sharer gone; a part of himself has vanished. "What made this emotion so overpowering was — how shall I define it? — the moral shock I received, as if something altogether monstrous, intolerable to thought and odious to the soul, had been thrust upon me unexpectedly." And now he must risk the ultimate confrontation in a true solitude and must do so on shore. "I was anxious to deal with this shadow by myself alone — and to this day I don't know why I was so jealous of sharing with anyone the peculiar blackness of that experience." He follows the crawling Kurtz through the grass; comes upon him "long, pale, indistinct, like a vapor exhaled by the earth." ("I had cut him off cleverly . . .") We are told very little of what Kurtz said in the moments that follow; and little of his incoherent discourses after he is brought back to the ship. "His was an impenetrable darkness. I looked at him as you peer down at a man who is lying at the bottom of a precipice where the sun never shines" — a comment less vague and rhetorical, in terms of psychic geography, than it may seem at a first reading. And then Kurtz is dead, taken off the ship, his body buried in a "muddy hole." With the confrontation over, Marlow must still emerge from environing darkness, and does so through that other deep fog of sickness. The identification is not yet completely broken. "And it is not my own extremity I remember best — a vision of grayness without form filled with physical pain, and a careless contempt for the evanescence of all things — even of this pain itself. No! It is his extremity that I seem to have lived through." Only in the atonement of his lie to Kurtz's "Intended," back in the sepulchral city, does the experience come truly to an end. "I laid the ghost of his gifts at last with a lie . . ."

Such seems to be the content of the dream. If my summary has even a partial validity it should explain and to an extent justify some of the "adjectival and worse than supererogatory insistence" to which F. R. Leavis (who sees only the travelogue and the portrait of Kurtz) objects. I am willing to grant that the unspeakable rites and unspeakable secrets become wearisome, but the fact — at once literary and psychological — is that they must remain *unspoken.* A confrontation with such a double and facet of the unconscious cannot be reported through realistic dialogue; the conversations must remain as shadowy as the narrator's conversations with Leggatt. So too when Marlow finds it hard to define the moral shock he received on seeing the empty cabin, or when he says he doesn't know why he was jealous of sharing his experience, I think we can take him literally . . . and in a sense even be thankful for his uncertainty. The greater tautness and economy of "The Secret Sharer" comes from its larger conscious awareness of the psychological process it describes; from its more deliberate use of the double as symbol. And of the two stories I happen to prefer it. But it may be the groping, fumbling "Heart of Darkness" takes us into a deeper region of the mind. If the story is not about this deeper region, and not about Marlow himself, its length is quite indefensible. But even if one were to allow that the final section is about Kurtz (which I think simply absurd), a vivid pictorial record of his unspeakable lusts and gratifications would surely have been ludicrous. I share Mr. Leavis' admiration for the heads on the stakes. But not even Kurtz could have supported many such particulars.*

"I listened on the watch for the sentence, for the word, that would give me the clue to the faint uneasiness inspired by this narrative that seemed to shape itself without human lips in the heavy night air of the river." Thus one of Marlow's listeners, the original "I" who frames the story, comments on its initial effect. He has discovered how alert one must be to the ebb and flow of Marlow's narrative, and here warns the reader. But there is no single word; not even the word *trance* will do. For the shifting play of thought and feeling and image and event is very intricate. It is not vivid detail alone, the heads on stakes or the bloody shoes; nor only the dark mass of moralizing abstraction; nor the dramatized psychological intuitions apart from their context that give "Heart of Dark-

* The reader irritated by the hallucinated atmosphere and subjective preoccupation of "Heart of Darkness" should turn to Robert Louis Stevenson's short novel, *The Beach of Falesá* (1892). A new trader, Wiltshire, takes a native mistress, and finds himself — thanks to a rival trader (Case) — virtually excommunicated. The situation distantly resembles that of Willems in *The Outcast of the Islands.* Later, Wiltshire goes inland to discover the source of Case's power over the natives; he has heard stories that his rival worships or traffics with devils. He finds an Æolian harp in a tree (to simulate ghostly voices) and presently the place of worship:

"Along all the top of it was a line of queer figures, idols or scarecrows, or what not. They had carved and painted faces, ugly to view, their eyes and teeth were of shell, their hair and their bright clothes blew in the wind, and some of them worked with the tugging . . .

"Then it came in my mind that Case had let out to me the first day that he was a good forger of island curiosities, a thing by which so many traders turn an honest penny. And with that I saw the whole business, and how this display served the man a double purpose: first of all, to season his curiosities and then to frighten those that came to visit him."

Had Conrad read *The Beach of Falesá* before writing "Heart of Darkness"? The question is unimportant. The important thing is to recognize the immense distance from Case's carved faces to the skulls on Kurtz's palisade; from Case's pretended traffic with devils to Kurtz's role as one of the devils of the land; from Wiltshire's canny outwitting of a rival trader to Marlow's dark inward journey; from the inert jungle of Stevenson's South Pacific to the charged symbolic jungle of Conrad's Congo. The nighttime meeting of Case and Wiltshire is merely an exciting physical struggle. *The Beach of Falesá* is a good manly yarn totally bereft of psychological intuition.

ness" its brooding weight. The impressionist method — one cannot leave this story without subscribing to the obvious — finds here one of its great triumphs of tone. The random movement of the nightmare is also the controlled movement of a poem, in which a quality of feeling may be stated or suggested and only much later justified. But it is justified at last.

The method is in important ways different from that of *Lord Jim,* though the short novel was written during an interval in the long one, and though Marlow speaks to us in both. For we do not have here the radical obfuscations and sudden wrenchings and violent chronological ambiguities of *Lord Jim.* Nor are we, as in *Nostromo,* at the mercy of a wayward flashlight moving rapidly in a cluttered room. "Heart of Darkness" is no such true example of spatial form. Instead the narrative advances and withdraws as in a succession of long dark waves borne by an incoming tide. The waves encroach fairly evenly on the shore, and presently a few more feet of sand have been won. But an occasional wave thrusts up unexpectedly, much farther than the others: even as far, say, as Kurtz and his Inner Station. Or, to take the other figure: the flashlight is held firmly; there are no whimsical jerkings from side to side. But now and then it is raised higher, and for a brief moment in a sudden clear light we discern enigmatic matters to be explored much later. Thus the movement of the story is sinuously progressive, with much incremental repetition. The intent is not to subject the reader to multiple strains and ambiguities, but rather to throw over him a brooding gloom, such a warm pall as those two Fates in the home office might knit, back in the sepulchral city.

Yet no figure can convey "Heart of Darkness" in all its resonance and tenebrous atmosphere. The movement is not one of penetration and withdrawal only; it is also the tracing of a large grand circle of awareness. It begins with the friends on the yacht under the dark above Gravesend and at last returns to them, to the tranquil waterway that "leading to the uttermost ends of the earth flowed sombre under an overcast sky — seemed to lead into the heart of an immense darkness." For this also "has been one of the dark places of the earth," and Marlow employs from the first his methods of reflexive reference and casual foreshadowing. The Romans were men enough to face this darkness of the Thames running between savage shores. "Here and there a military camp lost in a wilderness, like a needle in a bundle of hay — cold, fog, tempests, disease, exile, and death — death skulking in the air, in the water, in the bush." But these Romans were "no colonists," no more than the pilgrims of the Congo nineteen hundred years later; "their administration was merely a squeeze." Thus early Marlow establishes certain political values. The French gunboat firing into a continent anticipates the blind firing of the pilgrims into the jungle when the ship has been attacked. And Marlow hears of Kurtz's first attempt to emerge from the wilderness long before he meets Kurtz in the flesh, and wrestles with his reluctance to leave. Marlow returns again and again, with increasing irony, to Kurtz's benevolent pamphlet.

The travelogue as travelogue is not to be ignored; and one of Roger Casement's consular successors in the Congo (to whom I introduced "Heart of Darkness" in 1957) remarked at once that Conrad certainly had a "feel for the country." The demoralization of the first company station is rendered by a boiler "wallowing in the grass," by a railway truck with its wheels in the air. Presently Marlow will discover a scar in the hillside into which drainage pipes for the settlement had been tumbled; then will walk into the grove where the Negroes are free to die in a "greenish gloom." The sharply visualized particulars suddenly intrude on the somber intellectual flow of Marlow's meditation: magnified, arresting. The boilermaker who "had to crawl in the mud under the bottom of the steamboat . . . would tie up that beard of his in a kind of white serviette he brought for the purpose. It had loops to go over his ears." The papier-maché Mephistopheles is as vivid, with his delicate hooked nose and glittering mica eyes. So too is Kurtz's harlequin companion and admirer, humbly dissociating himself from the master's lusts and gratifications. "I! I! I am a simple man. I have no great thoughts." And even Kurtz, shadow and symbol though he be, the man of eloquence who in this story is almost voiceless, and necessarily so — even Kurtz is sharply visualized, an "animated image of death," a skull and body emerging as from a winding sheet, "the cage of his ribs all astir, the bones of his arm waving."

This is Africa and its flabby inhabitants; Conrad did indeed have a "feel for the country." Yet the dark tonalities and final brooding impression derive as much from rhythm and rhetoric as from such visual details: derive from the high aloof ironies and from a prose that itself advances and recedes in waves. "This initiated wraith from the back of Nowhere honored me with its amazing confidence before it vanished altogether." Or, "It is strange how I accepted this unforseen partnership, this choice of nightmares forced upon me in the tenebrous land invaded by these mean and greedy phantoms." These are true Conradian rhythms, but they are also rhythms of thought. The immediate present can be rendered with great compactness and drama: the ship staggering within ten feet of the bank at the time of the attack, and Marlow's sudden glimpse of a face amongst the leaves, then of the bush "swarming with human limbs." But still more immediate and personal, it may be, are the meditative passages evoking vast tracts of time, and the "first of men taking possession of an accursed inheritance." The prose is varied, far more so than is usual in the early work, both in rhythm and in the movements from the general to the particular and back. But the shaped sentence collecting and fully expending its breath appears to be the norm. Some of the best passages begin and end with them:

"Going up that river was like traveling back to the earliest beginnings of the world, when vegetation rioted on the earth and the big trees were kings. An empty stream, a great silence, an impenetrable forest. The air was warm, thick, heavy, sluggish. There was no joy in the brilliance of sunshine. The long stretches of the waterway ran on, deserted, into the gloom of overshadowed distances. On silvery sandbanks hippos and alligators sunned themselves side by side." [34]

The insistence on darkness, finally, and quite apart from ethical or mythical overtone, seems a right one for this extremely personal statement. There is a darkness of passivity, paralysis, immobilization; it is from the state of entranced languor rather than from the monstrous desires that the double Kurtz, this shadow, must be saved. In Freudian theory, we are told, such preoccupation may indicate fear of the feminine and passive. But may it not also be connected, through one of the spirit's multiple disguises, with a radical fear of death, that other darkness? "I had turned to the wilderness really, not to Mr. Kurtz, who, I was ready to admit, was as good as buried. And for a moment it seemed to me as if I also were buried in a vast grave full of unspeakable secrets. I felt an intolerable weight oppressing my breast, the smell of the damp earth, the unseen presence of victorious corruption, the darkness of an impenetrable night."

It would be folly to try to limit the menace of vegetation in the restless life of Conradian image and symbol. But the passage reminds us again of the story's reflexive references, and its images of deathly immobilization in grass. Most striking are the black shadows dying in the greenish gloom of the grove at the first station. But grass sprouts between the stones of the European city, a "whited sepulcher," and on the same page Marlow anticipates coming upon the remains of his predecessor: "the grass growing through his ribs was tall enough to hide his bones." The critical meeting with Kurtz occurs on a trail through the grass. Is there not perhaps an intense horror behind the casualness with which Marlow reports his discoveries, say of the Negro with the bullet in his forehead? Or: "Now and then a carrier dead in harness, at rest in the long grass near the path, with an empty water gourd and his long staff lying by his side."

All this, one must acknowledge, does not make up an ordinary light travelogue. There is no little irony in the letter of November 9, 1891, Conrad received from his guardian after returning from the Congo, and while physically disabled and seriously depressed: "I am sure that with your melancholy temperament you ought to avoid all meditations which lead to pessimistic conclusions. I advise you to lead a more active life than ever and to cultivate cheerful habits." [35] Uneven in language on certain pages, and lacking "The Secret Sharer" 's economy, "Heart of Darkness" nevertheless remains one of the great dark meditations in literature, and one of the purest expressions of a melancholy temperament.

"Heart of Darkness" and "The Secret Sharer" are both stories of insecure and morally isolated men who meet and commit themselves to men even more isolated. The most important moments of these intimate relationships could not be reported successfully: those whispered conversations with Leggatt in the narrator's cabin, Marlow's conversations with Kurtz at the edge of the jungle and on board the *Roi des Belges*. On the final level of psychological symbolism, communication is with a deepest self; a symbolic descent into the unconscious results in immobilization and is followed by partial or full release. The double is exorcised, either to die or go free. But in the material terms of a relationship between flesh-and-blood men, these conversations are also important. Through them an act of communication has occurred, creating a bond of brotherhood and loyalty. In "Heart of Darkness" psychic needs most of all determine the loyalty to the "nightmare" of Marlow's choice, but in "The Secret Sharer" we have both loyalty to the outcast double within the self and loyalty to the flesh-and-blood outsider: "a free man, a proud swimmer striking out for a new destiny." The success or failure of such attempted communications between individuals (and the ensuing acts of loyalty or betrayal) is the subject and central preoccupation of Conrad's greatest books, most obviously of *Lord Jim* and *Under Western Eyes*. But failure to communicate is more frequent than success, and men are driven back to their crippling solitude and normal human condition: to "the tremendous fact of our isolation, of the loneliness impenetrable and transparent, elusive and everlasting; of the indestructible loneliness that surrounds, envelops, clothes every human soul from the cradle to the grave, and, perhaps, beyond." [36]

A long story, "Amy Foster" (1901), is Conrad's bitterest and most generalized statement of this sense of isolation. For the biographer it might seem one of the most personal of his works, since it dramatizes an obscurely unsuccessful marriage and the rejection of the Carpathian peasant Yanko Goorall by the British: in Morf's words, *"the tragedy of a man who could not acclimatise himself in a foreign country."* [37] Amy Foster, with her stolid inert mind and treacherous tenderness to suffering, may be a direct expression of Conrad's mysogyny. And of course it is plausible to see in Yanko Goorall a projection of Conrad's loneliness. The long years of solitude at sea, the "inexpressible melancholy" of tropic sunshine, the austere separateness of command, the years without legal nationality other than the unacceptable Russian, the arrival in England ("No explorer could have been more lonely"), the Congo experience and the year of sickness that followed it, the major uprooting which came with abandonment of the sea, the unreality and loneliness of a writer's life, the failure of even his literary friends to understand his intentions — all these may have conspired to determine the temperament revealed not merely in "Amy Foster."

The story is told by a Dr. Kennedy to the nominal writer of the story. Yanko Goorall is the sole survivor of the wreck of an emigrant ship; his one great need is "to get in touch with someone" in an English community that takes him for a madman. His pleas for help and food are answered by the lash of a carter's whip, the stones of children, a beating by a woman's umbrella. "He could talk to no one, and had no hope of ever understanding anybody." The "everyday material appearances" of this somber little town are nightmare oppressions, and even after he marries the dull-witted Amy Foster the community refuses to accept his rare outbursts of European gaiety. The doctor discovers that Yanko "longed for their boy to grow up so that he could have a man to talk with in that language that to our ears sounded so disturbing, so passionate, and so bizarre." In the end Amy herself, whose love was based on sexual excitation, becomes terrified of this stranger and his repulsive need to communicate. "Oh, I hope he won't talk!" She runs away in fright when, fevered, he calls for a glass of water. And he dies, "cast out mysteriously by the sea to perish in the supreme disaster of loneliness and despair."

All this may be intimately enough related to the Conrad who left Poland on an improbable adventure, and who carried a foreign accent to the end of his days. But in the reading "Amy Foster" appears to be a much less subjective work than "Heart of Darkness" and "The Secret Sharer." Its symbolism is moral and "cosmic," not psychological; its statement definitive not inconclusive. It is, simply, a generalized comment on the lonely, uncomprehended, absurd human destiny. And Yanko Goorall is more nearly an Everyman than any character in the rest of the work — this man who longs only for happiness and friendship, and is thrust upon a bleak shore; who has no "general notion" of his incomprehensible surroundings; who has something "striving upwards in his appearance" but ultimately surrenders his hopes; who almost to the end is like a "wild bird caught in a snare." The same words are used for the son at the very end of the story. Thus it is the human condition to be caught in a snare, and a very literal reader might well detect sacrilege in the bogus emigration agents who send Yanko on his journey. Yanko's brief passage through England is a whole life, as his arrival is a painful birth. He comes in the tossing hold of a ship where it always seems to be night; reaches shore he knows not how, and "crawling in the dark over the sea wall, [he] rolled down the other side into a dyke, where it was another miracle he didn't get drowned. But he struggled instinctively like an animal under a net, and this blind struggle threw him out into a field." Again it is impossible to know whether Conrad intended these images of birth and miry infancy as such. But they are there. Locked in Smith's wood-lodge, Yanko bites his fists with "rage, cold, hunger, amazement, and despair."

"Amy Foster" thus belongs, roughly, with such works as Kafka's *Amerika* and *The Trial* and Albert Camus' *The Stranger*. Its gravest weakness may lie in the fact that it is even more general than they: lacking at once the intimate claustrophobic imaginings of Kafka, and Camus' subtlety of understatement.

One further short novel (again in the guise of a first-person confession) remains to be considered: "A Smile of Fortune" (1912). The nameless narrator-captain is doubtless a less direct author-projection than the narrator of *The Shadow Line,* but we are nominally concerned with the same ship and Mr. Burns is still its chief mate. The story has at least some basis in the *Otago*'s stay in Mauritius, in November 1888, and Jean-Aubry took a cryptic remark made to him by Conrad as authority for assuming that the events — the attraction to Alice Jacobus as well as the cargo of potatoes — were autobiographical.[38] Further research led to the discovery, in 1931, that Conrad had asked the hand of one "Mademoiselle Eugénie" in marriage — she a pretty and lively orphan of a good French family — and been refused because she was already engaged. If this is true, "A Smile of Fortune" could represent a subtle form of fictional revenge on life, since the final rejection in the story is made by the captain. Jean-Aubry proceeds to assume that Conrad gave up the *Otago* because he did not want to return to Mauritius and the scene of his discomfiture.[39] It would be interesting to know with certainty. But "A Smile of Fortune" remains much the same interesting failure irrespective of its basis in fact: imagination is as revealing as memory! It is chiefly interesting, however, to the student of Conrad's temperament. What concerns us are the forms of clumsiness and evasion displayed in approaching the subject of sexual attraction. And, to be sure, Conrad's curious presentation and valuation of the experience itself. "A Smile of Fortune" is the only personal short novel to take up what proved to be his least congenial subject.

It is the story of a true seaman (not seaman-trader) corrupted by his stay on land. Through thirty-nine flat, unevocative pages (of the story's eighty-six) we watch and share his vague repugnance to the ship chandler Alfred Jacobus, and his discovery that Jacobus has an illegitimate daughter who never stirs from his house. The slow realistic reporting of these pages, so ill-suited to nonretrospective first-person narration, makes us regret Conrad's more meditative manner. This reporting shows some of the wearying characteristics of literal recall, and the "flabby devil" of this seaport has little intrinsic interest. The useless delays, an occasional awkwardness of transition, the commonplaceness of style — these may be attributed in part to an uncongenial technique, as well as to the fact that by 1912 Conrad had lost much of his stylistic power. But the very choice of an uncongenial method may suggest, too, an unwillingness to come to grips with one's subject. The narrator comes to grips with it only after the thirty-nine pages, when he consents to go to Jacobus' house (though vaguely forewarned) and there meets the daughter Alice.

The evasion of the sexual subject now and then leads, even in the later pages, to a major vulgarity: "Mere gratitude does not gnaw at one's interior economy in that particular way. Hunger might; but I was not feeling particularly hungry for Jacobus's food." But by and large the story picks up energy as soon as the slovenly and crouching Alice appears: "snarling and superb and barely clad in that flimsy, dingy, amber wrapper." The girl is associated from the beginning with her garden and its "voluptuous silence." The narrator stands "entranced," is fascinated by the girl's extraordinary rudeness, and begins to haunt the house. There is little conversation between them. He merely watches this girl who never stirs, "spell-bound" in her passivity, whose gaze is "so empty of thought." The captain's attraction could hardly be more voyeuristic. He enjoys looking at "her long immobilities," and wants only to *be there.*

> But I was not thinking of her. I was looking at the girl. It was what I was coming for daily; troubled, ashamed, eager; finding in my nearness to her a unique sensation which I indulged with dread, self-contempt, and deep pleasure, as if it were a secret vice bound to end in my undoing, like the habit of some drug or other which ruins and degrades its slave.[40]

The girl Alice, as ignorant of the world of men as the slovenly Miss Tina of James's *Aspern Papers,* suspects with some justice that she is the pawn of her father's commercial interests; even fears violent abduction. But the watching captain makes a sudden sexual advance only when his vanity is stung. He had assured her that he has no intention of doing anything, and is provoked by her obvious relief. The girl allows herself to be kissed, then slips away . . . and the father appears in the door. Had he seen anything or not? He does see the slipper the girl had lost in her flight, and blandly proposes once again a deal in potatoes. Desperately eager to see the girl once more, the captain agrees to buy the potatoes and hustles Jacobus out of the house. He is left free to pursue his embrace, and he calls the girl's name.

But he feels the evening closing upon him. And when she appears, as floating and shadowy as Kurtz rising from the grass, he has "the impression that she had come too late." He puts on her shoe (*which the father had held before him*), thus completing a ritual which becomes stereotyped in Conrad's love stories. He questions her on the fear she no longer feels, and kisses her forehead:

> This was the moment when I realised clearly with a sort of terror my complete detachment from that unfortunate creature. And as I lingered in that cruel self-knowledge I felt the light touch of her arms falling languidly on my neck and received a hasty, awkward, haphazard kiss which missed my lips. No! She was not afraid; but I was no longer moved.[41]

So he leaves the girl in her sinister garden, "odorous with the perfume of imprisoned flowers, which, like herself, were lost to sight in a world buried in darkness." Later he will feel guilty because he has aroused the love of a slovenly, pathetic, and unmarriageable creature. But that is not the cruel self-knowledge. What the scene rather brilliantly dramatizes is a voyeuristic impotence and the lonely collapse of desire.

The ironic ending of the story (the useless cargo of potatoes brings a large profit at the next and drought-stricken port) adds up with editorial neatness the menaces of sex and life on shore. The captain finds himself becoming a covetous trader, and learns that Jacobus looks forward to his return.

But how could he "go back to fan that fatal spark with my cold breath? No, no, that unexpected kiss had to be paid for at its full price." He resigns his command; he sees all his plans destroyed and his "modest future endangered." But the menace of sex was defined more precisely by the garden that "was one mass of gloom, like a cemetery of flowers buried in the darkness," and by the captain's entranced immobilization there.

"A Smile of Fortune," and Alice Jacobus' garden, furnish a sufficient introduction to the force of "love's tangled garden" in Conrad's world: to the importance of the sexual menace and the uncongeniality of the subject. Thomas Moser's *Joseph Conrad: Achievement and Decline,* the subtlest and most persuasive psychological critique of Conrad yet written, relieves us of any obligation to go into that dark matter at length. We need only summarize Moser's definitive analysis, which finds in love the clue to certain puzzling weaknesses in the early work and to the over-all inferiority of the last six full-length novels. Moser is not concerned with the biographer's Conrad (who showed signs of panic at the approach of his own late marriage) but with the uneasy misogynous temperament revealed in the books. And he makes a major distinction between the early Conrad, whose best work was concerned with moral failure and eschews love-interest, and the Conrad of 1912 and afterward, who tried to treat love affirmatively in six out of seven novels. The "apprentice work" and radical early failures dealt with love directly. But the early masterpieces did not.

The early Conrad's devaluation of women and of love is explicit in certain stories; in others, it is conveyed through imagery and through certain curious patterns of plot. Thus sex is implicitly a menace, repeatedly associated with a fecund destroying jungle or with thick grass, and the imminence of embrace or its consummation can call forth some of Conrad's gloomiest writing. A second early preoccupation is with impotence. A recurrent pattern finds hero and heroine menaced by an older rival, who may be a relative and who is frequently armed with an ineffective weapon, actual or symbolic. At a critical moment, the heroine disarms the rival and throws the weapon contemptuously at the lover's feet, thus accusing him of impotence. In a few stories both hero and rival seem impotent, and in many of them a voyeuristic undertone exists.

Such, according to Moser, is the Conrad of before 1912: showing comparatively little sympathy for his heroines, and dramatizing love as a destructive experience. But in the later novels he determined to present love as "the most important thing in life." Now he treats his heroines much more generously, and repeatedly proposes to dramatize Marlow's famous sermon on coupling in *Chance*. Moser is willing to agree with Paul Wiley (*Conrad's Measure of Man*) that Conrad *intended* to show the hero conquering the two unworthy motives of false chivalry and sensuality, in these later novels, and so make normality triumph over the abnormal. But he rightly observes that "the intended meanings . . . ran counter to the deepest impulses of his being."

Moser's book, hardly a welcome one to sentimentalists, goes very far into the dark area of those unconscious adjustments which may determine the success or failure of a novel. Or, even, determine whether it gets written at all. Is the uncongeniality of love as a subject, and Conrad's later determination to present it "affirmatively," the most important cause of his serious anticlimax, as Moser affirms? Perhaps. I should insist more than he does, however, on the understandable exhaustion following upon the astonishing creative labors of 1894–1903, on the turn to European settings and a more conventional realistic manner, above all on the effects of dictation. But I could not agree more warmly that the best work of Conrad is the work of a tragic pessimist, concerned with other kinds of masculine failure than sexual, and that his turn to "normality" was stultifying. Conrad's example exists as a glaring warning to the novelist who, today or in any age, tries to make himself into an "affirmative" writer. The betrayed imagination will collapse.

These preliminary comments, chiefly through their reading of a series of personal short novels, have tried to approach a complex and elusive creative temperament. Of necessity these pages have oversimplified matters: ignoring many of those digressions that reveal so much in any man's work, and drawing inference and abstract statement from intimate or oblique dream. There is no doubt that an authentic voice speaks to us in these short novels. But perhaps only an impressionistic novel with all the Conradian circlings could begin to clarify the personality behind it — as Conrad himself suggests by casting his *Personal Record* in the form he did.

And now it is necessary, still more roughly, to attempt a summing up:

There is first the always treacherous evidence of biography: of a gloomy childhood without childish companions, and the early loss of both father and mother; of a temperament which appeared to be melancholy and pessimistic even in late adolescence; of serious physical disability after the Congo journey, with gout, sickness, and nervous crises recurring for the rest of life; of periods of baffling creative sterility; of irritations stemming from marriage, debt, and long commercial failure as a writer; of declared religious skepticism and declared lack of sympathy for much in the modern world. There is, briefly, evidence for moderate neurosis and prolonged periods of depression, and it is doubtless wrong to dismiss as mere rhetoric the "fear of the Incomprehensible" and similar phrases expressing a dark undefinable menace. But let us recall again that this neurotic being was a manly personage who achieved honorable success in his two careers.

Biography and formal autobiography indicate two other matters of major importance: first, that Conrad's youthful departure from Poland precipitated much criticism, and that his uncle and others feared he was throwing his life away in an irresponsible adventure; second, that (after the radical "jump" away from Poland) Conrad's manhood breaks in two: the twenty years of active, adventurous life at sea, the thirty years of sedentary married life as a writer in a foreign language. At the dim threshold of biography we can safely detect an ambiguous loyalty to the father (in some sense a revolutionary dreamer) and to a glamorous family heritage. To become a British citizen was in no direct sense a betrayal of Poland, since it meant giving up legal Russian citizenship. But I think we can say, also safely enough, that Conrad's feelings toward Poland were never satisfactorily resolved.

All this is indeed vague and approximate. From the personal short novels — set against the more austere and conservative Conrad expressed in the prefaces, letters, and autobiographies — we may deduce a series of major inward conflicts. It is useful to enumerate these, so long as we remember that the categories are rough and often overlap:

A rationalist's declared distrust of the unconscious and rationalist's desire to be a sane orderly novelist — doubled by a powerful introspective drive that took the dreamer deeper into the unconscious than any earlier English novelist (except possibly Dickens);

A declared fear of the corrosive and faith-destroying intellect — doubled by a profound and ironic skepticism;

A declared belief that ethical matters are simple — doubled by an extraordinary sense of ethical complexities;

A declared ethic of simplicity, action, and the saving grace of work — doubled by a professional propensity to passive dreaming;

A declared distrust of generous idealism — doubled by a strong idealism (Conrad in very modern manner distrusting both the cynical "realist" and the professed "do-gooder" and disliking most intensely the complacency of those in between);

A declared commitment to authoritarian sea-tradition — doubled by a pronounced individualism (a conflict existing, according to Ford, even in the seaman, noted both for his risky maneuvers and for his meticulous attention to details of stowage);[42]

A declared and extreme political conservativism, at once aristocratic and pragmatist — doubled by great sympathy for the poor and disinherited of the earth (a conflict nominally resolved in the stance of *noblesse oblige*);

A declared fidelity to law as above the individual—doubled by a strong sense of fidelity to the individual, with betrayal of the individual the most deeply felt of all crimes;

Briefly: a deep commitment to order in society and in the self—doubled by incorrigible sympathy for the outlaw, whether existing in society or the self.

Such are some of the conflicts that divided this conscientious man and wayward imagination, and these are the psycho-moral foundations of the Conrad "world." The fear of sex and fear of impotence are undoubtedly important. Still more important is the fear of passivity, apathy, inertia; the concern with neurotic immobilization. But perhaps it is too presumptuous to establish an order among such perils of the soul. For we have still to sum up a more general insecurity, leading to a compulsion to test the self, or to dramatize such tests. The test of moral strength is the precondition of manhood; the "untested" have been disdained by destiny. But there is something equivocal about the test of the self-analytic night journey, with token or mortal payment to be made at its end. And we have still to sum up, too, the heart of the matter: guilt, the sense (at once conviction and feeling) that everything must be paid for. Sometimes guilt seems to inhere to the very fact of being alive in a world where "nobody is good enough." But guilt is no illusion. And if the fundamental human act is communication, so betrayal is the ultimate crime, to be dramatized again and again.

All this leads to (or at least corresponds with) Conrad's fictional world as we know it: with his repeated dramatization of moral "tests" in a menaced community and soulless unmoral cosmos; with his fine stories of self-analysis and self-discovery; with his constant return to the inconclusive case and marginal crime of the outlaw or failure of good intentions. And it leads still more importantly to the intense conflict of judgment and sympathy—of reason and feeling, detachment and intimacy—which is the very backbone of his work. In a crude version we can say (especially of "Youth") that a mature skeptical Marlow serves to embody and make concrete the area of judgment, reason, detachment. But the

Marlow of *Lord Jim,* aware of the conflict in himself and deliberately passing it on to his listeners and readers, is a truer projection of Conrad. For he too, if a double for the author, is haunted by his doubles. The Conradian double occasionally serves only to clarify a hero's plight. But more often he exists both as an actual fleshly human being to be saved or betrayed, and as a shadowy projection of a hidden self, also to be saved or betrayed.

These are the major matters. And, since technique is temperament and style the man, no small share of the Conradian technique owes something to these enumerated conflicts and fears. It is, as we shall see abundantly, a technique of evocation and evasion. The interposed narrator or interposed reporting witness, the careful manipulations of chronology, the vivid interruptive digressions, the sudden movements from the abstract to the concrete and back, the ebb and flow of a meditative wandering intellect, the constant narrowing and opening of the lens — all these are means of controlling the author's or narrator's distance from his subject. But also (and doubtless fairly soon in Conrad's career) they became conscious and deliberate means of controlling the reader's responses, of manipulating his feelings. And this is what sets Conrad apart from any earlier English novelist: his creation of conflict in the reader, and his fine control of that conflict. Thus the psychic necessity (or at least the technique which by trial and error proved congenial) became deliberate art. How Conrad worked toward this deliberateness — how he discovered his fictional world, his congenial material and method — will concern us in the chapter to follow.

Chapter Two

THE DISCOVERY OF A FICTIONAL WORLD

THE old rationalist conceptions of the creative process die hard. Among them is the assumption that a beginning novelist is always free to choose his fictional world: free to draw at will upon any part of his personal experience, and free to select (from the examples of the masters) the particular novelistic technique that will best dramatize his material. The misconception is much less common than it was twenty years ago, but it is present whenever a reviewer complains that a novelist perversely refuses to write the novels he "ought to write." No doubt it would be pleasant to dispose thus easily of what reason proposes, and so write at once and without fumbling the novels one ought, logically, to write. But the relationship of temperament to experience and method is entirely too intricate to permit this very often. From the large or small area of each man's experience and revery there are certain materials which seem to be richly usable in fiction, congenial to his temperament and talent; and others which ought to be but are not. And this is as true of technique. The beginning novelist may admire the methods of say Flaubert or Sherwood Anderson, yet be unable to use them; or, however much he admire Kafka or *Finnegans Wake,* be constrained to write traditional realistic fiction to the end of his days. Only by trial and error (and occasionally aided by criticism) can the novelist discover the particular combination of material and method that will energize his imagination and release his true "voice." For that voice — which, if he is a good writer, is not quite like anyone else's — is the expression of a creative temperament and possibly buried self, manifesting itself in "the shape and ring of sentences." In this sense style is indeed the man, though seldom the man that wife, friends, and biographer observe and know.

Thus the period of a novelist's apprentice work may be a period of unlearning and rejection of the seemingly suitable, as well as a period of learning. The little we know of Thomas Hardy's lost *A Poor Man and a Lady* ("By the Poor Man") suggests that he wanted to put his London experience and personal anxieties to use in a satire on urban corruption. But he would not become the true Hardy until he accepted Dorset as his background and distorted it into a fictional Wessex, or until he discovered his own blend of melodrama and realism. The example of William Faulkner, who in so many ways illuminates Conrad, is striking. In *Soldier's Pay* and *Mosquitoes* he wrote of things he knew well enough: of the emotions of flyers and the maladjustment of returning veterans, of airy flappers and sophisticated seductions, of artists and Bohemians in New Orleans. And he imitated writers as different as Swinburne, Cabell, Sherwood Anderson, Aldous Huxley. But we do not hear a true and sustained Faulknerian voice until we are well into *Sartoris*. Faulkner had first to discover the congenial material of ordinary life in a small town impinged upon and distorted by a romantic past, and the congenial material of masculine comradeship in the "big woods." So too he had to discover a method that would permit exaggeration, and a nameless narrator free to meditate on the action. Even in later books he would seldom write with distinction when dealing with intellectuals or flyers, or when confined to ordinary realistic modes. These materials and methods have remained uncongenial.

At least four clusters of personal and observed experience ought to have been available to Conrad in the 1890's, beginning to write but not yet committed to the life of a professional writer. One, obviously, was his own experience as seaman, officer, and master-mariner — this presently to be dramatized in the short personal novels of test and initiation, in

Typhoon, and in such lesser short novels as "Falk" and "The End of the Tether." A second was the Congo journey, with its vision of white men deteriorating in solitude or succumbing to their own rapacious folly. A third was the Malayan experience, the brief glimpses of savage apathy and of white men involved in native politics — this to be used in the first two novels of intrigue and betrayal, as well as in *Lord Jim*. All these were congenial materials. But a fourth and perhaps more immediate area of European experience — the trials and frustrations of a thinly disguised alter-ego as artist and lover, sexual maladjustment among educated Londoners, an observed tragedy of peasant life in Brittany — did not prove congenial at all.

As always, the history of discovering a method is more difficult to sum up briefly. On the one hand Conrad was attracted by the relative objectivity and detached realism of Flaubert and Maupassant, as well as by their cadences. And from the start of *Almayer's Folly* he experimented with interior monologue as a vehicle of narration. But in another direction he moved toward a more personal impressionism, and toward the techniques of evasion he would make truly his own. The crucial struggle, technically speaking, was to discover a narrator nominally not the author himself, not committed to consecutive reporting, and who could move where he wished in time, space, and thought.

It may be asked how the critic is to know which materials and methods are congenial, which ones not. Something may be inferred from the history of books: from the abandonment of *The Sisters* and from the long struggle with *The Rescue*. But here as with any critical method the best inferences are to be drawn from the presence or absence of energized, successful writing and of a genuine "voice." The critic, in other words, must be capable of distinguishing between good and bad prose, between (at least) the prose of *The Nigger of the "Narcissus,"*

Apart, far aft, and alone by the helm, old Singleton had deliberately tucked his white beard under the top button of his glistening coat. Swaying upon the din and tumult of the seas, with the whole battered length of the ship launched forward in a rolling rush before his steady old eyes, he stood rigidly still, forgotten by all, and with an attentive face. In front of his erect figure only the two arms moved crosswise with a swift and sudden readiness, to check or urge again the rapid stir of circling spokes. He steered with care.[1]

and the prose of the almost contemporary *Sisters:*

He would look to no one as teacher. He stood aloof from the world. But he took his stand in it. He had need of it. He had need to see the hollow enthusiasms and to hear the ring of empty words round him if for nothing else but to steady this wavering trust in his own convictions. Associating with many he communed with none. He was generally taciturn.[2]

It is reasonable to assume that for the first passage both material and method were congenial; for the second passage, neither.

In *A Personal Record* Conrad tells of the recollected Almayer appearing before him "in a hallucinated vision of forests and rivers and seas" — and of his sudden impulse, in 1889, to externalize and set down the dream. "The conception of a planned book was entirely outside my mental range when I sat down to write; the ambition of being an author had never turned up amongst these gracious imaginary existences one creates fondly for oneself at times in the stillness and immobility of a day-dream . . ." [3] In his early work Conrad was, at his best, a powerful and eccentric dreamer creating a method inadvertently, as opposed to the calculating craftsman who selects and executes stories with care. These are two ways of writing, deriving from two very different creative impulses, and *Lord Jim* would profit from both. But at the outset of Conrad's career, the dreamer produced interesting and idiosyncratic work; the cool planner did not. We may take, for the two extremes, two stories written in the summer of 1896, "An Outpost of Progress" and "The Lagoon." In a letter to Edward Garnett of August 14, 1896, Conrad spoke slightingly of "The Lagoon" as "a tricky thing with the usual forests, river — stars — wind — sunrise, and so on — and lots of secondhand Conradese in it." But his comment on "An Outpost of Progress," in the same letter, is even more significant:

The construction is bad. It is bad because it was a matter of conscious decision, and I have no discrimination — in the artistic sense. Things get themselves written — and you like them. Things get themselves into shape — and they are tolerable. But when *I* want to write — when *I* do consciously try to write or try to construct, then my ignorance has full play and the quality of my miserable and benighted intelligence is disclosed to the scandalized gaze of my literary father.[4]

"An Outpost of Progress" is chiefly interesting as a cold adumbration of "Heart of Darkness," and it is amusing to note that Conrad paid off old Congo scores by using real names for his miserable agents Kayerts and Carlier.[5] The two men are left in an isolated and unimportant company station for the collection of ivory and there quickly deteriorate. But the hard-won groping intuitions of "Heart of Darkness" are here presented by a detached omniscient author with essay-like explicitness. The two men are "left unassisted to face the wilderness." They are unequipped for lawless solitude, since society had forbidden them "all independent thought, all initiative, all departure from routine." Their surroundings are unintelligible, and in due time something is gone that "had kept the wilderness from interfering with their hearts." They do not, like Kurtz, write an essay on "the sacredness of the civilizing work." But they read such an essay and begin to think better of themselves. Soon enough, however, Carlier will speak of the necessity of "exterminating all the niggers." They are scandalized when a native assistant exchanges their servants for a rich supply of ivory. And they "believed their words." But presently they decide to keep the ivory and also to keep silent. Eventually the two men quarrel, and Kayerts (after shooting Carlier) falls into the madness and "wrong-headed lucidity" of Kurtz. "He seemed to have broken loose from himself altogether." On the arrival of the company steamer he hangs himself.

"An Outpost of Progress" thus offers a significant variant on "Heart of Darkness." Kurtz and even Marlow are vulnerable partly because they are intellectuals and individualists; Kayerts and Carlier because they are not. Otherwise, the earlier story suggests what "Heart of Darkness" might have been like, had it been about Kurtz only and told in a conventional realistic manner. "An Outpost of Progress" is carefully, ploddingly, plausibly constructed to throw a full expository light on its theme. The ominiscient author pauses to deliver brief intelligent essays and moves at will into the minds of all the characters. Thus we generally lack the relationship that Conrad later saw to be so important to his manner of telling: "perfectly devoid of familiarity as between author and reader, aimed essentially at the intimacy of a personal comunication . . ." [6] And if the reader of "An Outpost of Progress" is left cold (i.e., "left out") so too was its author. There are no important signs of subjective involvement; Conrad could look at such a "flabby devil" only with ironic disdain. His story is wholly conscious and intellectual.

As a result, the most personal voice of the early Conrad, with its unpunctuated running rhythms and overloaded syntax, is rarely heard, and never speaks with distinction. "And through the deep and tremendous noise sudden yells that resembled snatches of songs from a madhouse darted shrill and high in discordant jets of sound which seemed to rush far above the earth and drive all peace from under the stars." The sentence, bad as it is, suggests the author has momentarily become excited by his story. But most of "An Outpost of Progress" comes to us in a plain, efficient, and unevocative prose.

"The Lagoon" is a distinctly less coherent story which may well have deserved Max Beerbohm's amusing parody.[7] And yet it has the very originality and personal accent that provoke parody. It is indeed an eccentric dream, and one that touches on several of Conrad's lasting preoccupations. The story opens with an unnamed white man in a canoe with natives; we learn presently that some time in the past he had been, like Lingard and Lord Jim, involved in native intrigue.

He moves through a dream landscape "bewitched into an immobility perfect and final"; enters a narrow creek that is tortuous and "fabulously deep"; reaches a stagnant lagoon where his Malayan friend Arsat lives with his wife in a house perched on high piles. There he discovers that the wife is dying, and — after a sudden and astonishingly adjectival nightfall — listens to Arsat's story of crime and remorse. The Malayan was in love with one of the Ruler's servants and kidnapped her with the help of his brother. The brother would have welcomed a fight — "There is half a man in you now — the other half is in that woman" — but Arsat wants only peace of heart and his love. They are pursued; the brother remains behind to hold off the first warriors; Arsat and the girl get the canoe afloat. "Then I looked at her. Tuan, I pushed the canoe!" The crime of desertion is presented, as in *Lord Jim,* as an involuntary act, to be paid for by years of remorse. As Arsat ends his story, a saving breeze comes up, the sun rises, and inside the house the woman is dead. Arsat is now free to go back to avenge his brother's death. And he stands "lonely in the searching sunshine; and he looked beyond the great light of a cloudless day into the darkness of a world of illusions."

The story of Arsat, like that of Karain, is interesting as part of the misogynous pattern and even more interesting as an early version of the essential Conradian crime. But the unnamed white man, who seems indirectly responsible for the pretentious "Conradese," gives us greater pause. He is nominally present to listen to a story, but really present to occasion the rendering of a highly subjective landscape. A Jungian reading might well find another night journey into the unconscious in his movement from the broad river, through the fabulously deep creek, to the lagoon and its house on pilings — there to confront this Arsat feared by the native crew. But any reading would find the lagoon and jungle strange. At times the landscape is menacing, as darkness oozes "through the tangled maze of the creepers"; at other times the woods "whisper into his ear the wisdom of their immense and lofty indifference." The stars glitter "ceaseless and vain" in a dead universe. In one passage the staring into darkness seems almost paranoid:

The fear and fascination, the inspiration and the wonder of death — of death near, unavoidable, and unseen, soothed the unrest of his race and stirred the most indistinct, the most intimate of his thoughts. The ever-ready suspicion of evil, the gnawing suspicion that lurks in our hearts, flowed out into the stillness round him — into the stillness profound and dumb, and made it appear untrustworthy and infamous, like the placid and impenetrable mask of an unjustifiable violence.[8]

There is no need to argue that this writing (which is certainly bad writing) is markedly subjective, and even compulsive. *And there is nothing in the story itself to occasion it.* It suggests, I think, that Conrad was moving simultaneously, and no doubt unknowingly, toward the narrator as technical device and the involved narrator as intimate author-projection. As yet the white man is only a listener, who can interrupt the adventure narrative (and so lend it suspense) by looking out at the landscape. And as yet he is probably only a half-conscious projection of the author, and only incidentally a "brother" of the criminal. But no very long technical step would need to be taken to a first-person narrator directly responding alike to a soulless universe and to a brother's marginal unintended crime.

The uncertainty of impulse behind "The Lagoon" — at once symbolist prose-poem, story of crime and punishment, and exotic local-color story — makes it the incoherent performance it is. It has no conception of its own complexity. But it is also a very personal story, containing some of Conrad's most idiosyncratic and most uninhibited writing. The obvious idiosyncrasy is the one of which Beerbohm made such capital: the French post-positioning of adjectives. The *sun . . . unclouded and dull, leaves enormous and heavy,* an *immobility perfect and final,* a *cry discordant and feeble* — these appear in the first two long paragraphs alone. The most pretentious passage of all — with its overextended syntax, long periods, adjectival insistence, and contrasts of light and dark — suggests that the true Conradian style was, like certain other great styles, achieved through the disciplining of initial excess:

> The white man came out of the hut in time to see the enormous conflagration of sunset put out by the swift and stealthy shadows that, rising like a black and impalpable vapour above the tree-tops, spread over the heaven, extinguishing the crimson glow of floating clouds and the red brilliance of departing daylight. In a few moments all the stars came out above the intense blackness of the earth and the great lagoon gleaming suddenly with reflected lights resembled an oval patch of night sky flung down into the hopeless and abysmal night of the wilderness.[9]

"An Outpost of Progress" has no such purple patch as this. On the other hand, it would be difficult to infer from it the presence of a major writer. Retrospectively, "The Lagoon" 's confused dream seems much more promising.

Conrad's first two novels and his next-to-last completed one — *Almayer's Folly* (1895), *An Outcast of the Islands* (1896), and *The Rescue* (1920) — form a loose trilogy, connected by the enigmatic figure of Tom Lingard and his romantic illusions. The three books record, in reverse chronological order, the history of his intervention in Malayan affairs, and the ruin of his dreams of benevolent despotism and untold wealth. This is not their main explicit emphasis. But the historian of Sambir who sought some single explanation for the events of twenty years would find it in Lingard's romantic ego, in his grandiloquent dreams and "infernal charity."

The dates of publication are deceptive. *The Rescue* (then "The Rescuer") was begun in 1896, worked on intermittently until 1899, and again from 1916 until its completion by dictation in May 1919. Conrad considered resuming it at various times during the intervening years. He broke away from it, in the 1890's, to write *Tales of Unrest, The Nigger of the "Narcissus,"* "Youth," "Heart of Darkness," and *Lord Jim;* in 1910 debated whether to finish it or *Chance*; in 1917 abandoned it for *The Arrow of Gold*. Significantly, notes for "The Rescuer" appear on the manuscript of the sketch "Tuan

Jim," early draft of the first pages of *Lord Jim*.[10] The notes suggest a continuing attention (even during the writing of what was intended to be a short story) to the real job at hand. There is good reason to believe that Conrad long regarded "The Rescuer" as the major work to be achieved in his early years as a writer. But it would not be achieved. In *Almayer's Folly* and *An Outcast of the Islands* we follow the interesting drama of a novelist searching for an elusive and central theme (the character of the vulnerable romantic idealist) and not wholly finding it. He allows himself to be diverted by foreground figures of lesser importance. Conrad found the subject all right, but found it in *Lord Jim* and *Nostromo*. Historically, "The Rescuer" manuscript is most interesting for its foreshadowings of *Lord Jim*.[11]

Thus our reconstruction of Lingard's life makes an emphasis that Conrad never achieved himself. Yet the clues to deepest preoccupations and convictions often lie in such half-realized conceptions. In *The Rescue* — to attend for the moment only to Lingard — the motives are very mixed. Lingard's intentions are always the best. Hassim, an exiled Malayan prince, had saved his life; in turn he could do no less than rescue the prince and his sister, and help them recover their kingdom. "He worked prosaically, earning money to pay the cost of the romantic necessity that had invaded his life." But men are often unsure of their own motives:

"I took these people off when they were in their last ditch. That means something. I ought not to have meddled and it would have been all over in a few hours. I must have meant something when I interfered, whether I knew it or not. I meant it then — and did not know it. Very well. I mean it now — and do know it. When you save people from death you take a share in their life." [12]

In time the motive of gratitude gives way to a more naked egoism: Lingard will bring peace and justice to the country, for "he alone had the means and the pluck 'to lift up the big end' of such an adventure." His first act of compassion involves him in complicated native intrigue. His second act of compassion — the rescue of Mr. Travers and his party — begins as innocently. But, as with Lord Jim and Gentleman Brown, it results in the ruin of his friends.

In *An Outcast of the Islands* an older Lingard is still in the fullness of his powers: the esteemed "Rajah Laut," King of the Sea. This time he has interfered in the politics of Sambir, bringing peace and prosperity to "his river":

> His deep-seated and immovable conviction that only he — he, Lingard — knew what was good for them was characteristic of him, and, after all, not so very far wrong. He would make them happy whether or no, he said, and he meant it. His trade brought prosperity to the young state, and the fear of his heavy hand secured its internal peace for many years.[13]

But once again his fatal impulse to rescue the downtrodden proves his undoing. He had already brought the weak Almayer to Sambir, to provide a husband for a Malayan child he had "orphaned" in a fight with pirates. Now he brings the criminally irresponsible Willems. In exchange for the savage Aïssa, Willems betrays his benefactor and guides the Arabs up his secret river. With the coming of Abdulla, Lingard's monopoly and exclusive power are destroyed. But he still has power enough to take justice in his own hands and condemn Willems to perpetual exile in the jungle outskirts of the community.

Almayer's Folly is the story of Sambir fifteen or twenty years later, of a squabbling community and enterprise ruined and decayed. The great secret of the aging Lingard was a rumored mountain of gold and treasure of diamonds in the interior. But Lingard himself has vanished to Europe, leaving Almayer to his rotting station and his Bovaryish dreams of European splendor, of prestige for his half-caste daughter. There is an oppressive sense of slowly invading corruption; the Arabs and natives triumph over Almayer, the only remaining embodiment of Lingard's dreams. At the end of the book even Almayer is dead, and Abdulla piously tells his beads over the universal ruin. But long since Almayer had discerned indiscriminate good will, the impulse to meddle, and an "infernal charity" to be Lingard's crucial faults. They are the real corruptors of Sambir.

Such would seem to be (after historical reordering and abstraction) the pessimistic burden of Conrad's Malayan trilogy. What we actually have are three fairly separate novels, and only *The Rescue* is centered in Lingard himself. By 1919, too, Lingard had lost his most interesting attributes. It appears Conrad discerned, but too late, that the ambiguous Lingard should have been a foreground figure all along: a character of greater intrinsic interest than the flabby Almayer and the flabby Willems.

And yet — *Almayer's Folly* is a strange and at times impressive first novel. It plunges us with its first pages into a true Conradian darkness: a river in flood, bordered by tumescent jungle; a solitary dreamer ruined by his own greed and by his benefactor's sentimentalism, married to a snarling native and harboring possibly incestuous feelings for his daughter; entangled in local intrigue. Its early readers (possibly coming to it from one of Stevenson's clear-cut South Sea yarns) had justifiable difficulty in discerning its center of interest. It really has none. *Almayer's Folly* is instead the unconstructed dreaming of a small real world: a world with its richly evoked daily life and its infinitely complicated politics. Politics, surely, provides the greatest obstacle to the reader. Against the distant background of British, Dutch, and Arab struggle for domination of the islands, the local Arabs and Malays compete for trade and political power. But they join forces in seeking gunpowder with which to fight the Dyak tribes of the interior, and jointly hope to oust the white man. Dain Maroola, meanwhile, wants to buy gunpowder for other Malayan wars. And Almayer himself — since this is the only way to finance an expedition to the mountain of gold — is intimately involved in the smuggling. Will Dain Maroola return from a profitable smuggling voyage and help him realize his dreams at last? Instead Dain runs off with his daughter.

This political situation, which may seem obscure even in summary, reaches the reader of the novel in no such summary form. On the contrary we see these matters only dimly, and through the thick screen of individual obsessions. We must wait forty-five pages to learn why the Arabs and Malays are to a degree allied and eighty pages to learn why Almayer seems to be working with his enemy Lakamba, and what both expect from Dain Maroola. Only on pages 81–83 are we offered at last the authorial summary with which most Victorian novelists would have begun. This could be the *escamotage de l'essentiel* of which Claude-Edmonde Magny accuses Faulkner, the perverse deliberate withholding of the few facts we need to know. Or perhaps Conrad himself was struggling to discover his world through parting mists, as he struggled in creating *Nostromo.* It is amusing to learn that the first reader of any part of *Almayer's Folly,* when pressed by Conrad, insisted that the story was "perfectly" clear.[14]

It certainly is not. And it would be difficult to say which of his interlocked subjects engaged Conrad the most: the progress of Almayer's deterioration, the study of the Malayan scene with its intuitions into the savage mind, the struggle of Almayer and his native wife for the mind of their half-caste daughter, or the love affair of Nina and Dain Maroola with Almayer as the jealous rival. In the dim background, occasionally, is the disruptive force of Lingard. But of these various interests and subjects the most peripheral is probably the most successful: the Malayan local color and picture of Sambir, and the insight into native psychology. As omniscient author Conrad now and then frankly pauses to discourse on the "abyss" of barbarism, the torpor and apathy of a mind with "no wish, no hope, no love, no fear except of a blow," knowing nothing of the world in which it moves, "seeking the light, desiring the sunshine, fearing the storm, unconscious of either." His brief somber portraits of Mrs. Almayer's reversion to barbarism and of Nina's delicate wavering between two worlds are surprisingly convincing. But he is certainly at his best when he looks at the squatting, betel-nut-chewing Lakamba and at Babalatchi, "the statesman of Sambir," with the cold amused irony of Flaubert. Here he keeps a congenial distance wholly lost in his attempt to render Almayer's despair, or the jungle-haunted and terrified passion of Dain Maroola for Nina. One of the better pictures of the royal household recalls, in fact, the organ-grinding scene of *Madame Bovary,* that brilliant forestatement of Emma's squalid destiny:

> "Almayer must die," said Lakamba, decisively, "to make our secret safe. He must die quietly, Babalatchi. You must do it."
> Babalatchi assented, and rose wearily to his feet. "To-morrow?" he asked.
> "Yes; before the Dutch come. He drinks much coffee," answered Lakamba, with seeming irrelevancy.
> Babalatchi stretched himself yawning, but Lakamba, in the flattering consciousness of a knotty problem solved by his own unaided intellectual efforts, grew suddenly very wakeful.
> "Babalatchi," he said to the exhausted statesman, "fetch the box of music the white captain gave me. I cannot sleep."
> At this order a deep shade of melancholy settled upon Babalatchi's features. He went reluctantly behind the curtain and soon reappeared carrying in his arms a small hand-organ, which he put down on the table with an air of deep dejection. Lakamba settled himself comfortably in his arm-chair.
> "Turn, Babalatchi, turn," he murmured, with closed eyes.
> Babalatchi's hand grasped the handle with the energy of despair, and as he turned, the deep gloom on his countenance changed into an expression of hopeless resignation. Through the open shutter the notes of Verdi's music floated out on the great silence over the river and forest. Lakamba listened with closed eyes and a delighted smile; Babalatchi turned, at times dozing off and swaying over, then catching himself up in a great fright with a few quick turns of the handle. Nature slept in an exhausted repose after the fierce turmoil, while under the unsteady hand of the statesman of Sambir the Trovatore fitfully wept, wailed, and bade good-bye to his Leonore again and again in a mournful round of tearful and endless iteration.[15]

The method, for this passage at least, was certainly congenial. And in general the struggle for method and style, in *Almayer's Folly,* is of even greater interest than the exotic dream itself. The question begged by the passenger on the *Torrens,* who found the story perfectly clear, leaves unasked the larger question: how much of all this obfuscation and ambiguity was intended only for dramatic suspense; how much of it to create a strain in the reader through manipulation of his feelings; and how much of it was, simply, the product of temperamental evasiveness? There is the further possibility of a sheer inability to make things clear.

The essential technical problem is, as so often, that of point of view or narrating consciousness. The first full sentence of the novel has a characteristic Conradian gait; it is the product of an omniscient irony: "The well-known shrill voice startled Almayer from his dream of splendid future into the unpleasant realities of the present hour." But the next sentences close down to a rough interior monologue, and so anticipate many of the novel's clumsier moments: "An unpleasant voice too. He had heard it for many years, and with every year he liked it less. No matter; there would be an end to all this soon." For two pages the point of view wavers between omniscience and intimacy, as Almayer stares at the river in a present time and *medias res* opening. But then he thinks of Macassar, of the old days there, and his revery is obliged to carry (nominally at least) seven pages of vivid flashback. Conrad stumbled thus soon onto the defective method for which so many beginning writers have an affinity! He must keep us conscious of the man in the present time, remembering, yet re-create with immediacy the past he remembers:

> After those twenty years, standing in the close and stifling heat of a Bornean evening, he recalled with pleasurable regret the image of Hudig's lofty and cool warehouses with their long and straight avenues of gin cases and bales of Manchester goods; the big door swinging noiselessly; the dim light of the place, so delightful after the glare of the streets; the little railed-off spaces amongst piles of merchandise where the Chinese clerks, neat, cool, and sad-eyed, wrote rapidly and in silence amidst the din of the working gangs rolling casks or shifting cases to a muttered song, ending with a desperate yell.[16]

The chapter ends with a few pages in the present, reported by an omniscient author, and with two paragraphs of stormy landscape seen through Nina Almayer's eyes but expressed in the author's language.

The next four chapters present a different kind of flashback, bringing us to the present time; in the eighth chapter we have still another flashback, carried for seven pages by the dim consciousness of the slave-girl Taminah. Thus sixty-seven of the first one hundred and sixteen pages are retrospective; only forty-nine in a dramatic present time. The remainder of the novel (pages 118–208) occurs in a continuing present, rendered through various points of view, nearly all of them uncongenial. And these later chapters are distinctly commonplace. Conrad is doubtless most uncomfortable when he attempts true interior monologue ("Am I awake? — Why do I hear voices?" he argued to himself, hazily. — "I cannot get rid of the horrible nightmare yet. — I have been very drunk. — What is that shaking me? I am dreaming yet. — I must open my eyes and be done with it. I am only half awake, it is evident.") But he is little more comfortable when, a page later, a camera observes Almayer chasing Taminah around a room of overturned furniture. Elsewhere the frank expository analyses of an omniscient author seem machine-made, as such analyses usually do when intruded very suddenly and without novelty of style. But another kind of awkwardness is commoner. This occurs whenever the subjective view of one of the characters (reported in the third person and without irony) is used to convey intense emotion or intense dramatic action: when, for instance, Dain Maroola is sexually excited by the approach of Nina, meditates on his excitement, and strikes at the air with his kris. The method is a conventional one, the whole stock-in-trade of many popular novelists today, but Conrad finds it hard to use consistently or with vigor. Dain feels "a great numbness in all his limbs" and (*author watching*) is immobilized into "chiselled bronze." Is it Dain or the author who comments at length on "a woman's most terrible weapon . . . more dangerous than the thrust of a dagger, because it also whips the soul out of the body . . ."? This is, we learn, "the look of woman's surrender." The author at least is more at his ease, technically speaking, when the lovers *walk away from him* and into a jungle region of death, there to consummate their love. "A sigh as of immense sorrow passed over the land in the last effort of the dying breeze, and in the deep silence which succeeded, the earth and the heavens were suddenly hushed up in the mournful contemplation of human love and human blindness." Thus Conrad's sympathy for his young hero in his moment of romantic fulfillment.

It could well be argued that such a scene demonstrates uncongenial material rather than method. But the fact is that Conrad fumbles all his major dramatic scenes, and defers them as long as possible: Almayer's revelation to the Dutch officers, for instance, of what he thinks is Dain's mutilated body. He cannot dramatize important physical action occurring in the present; and does not want to. And he recovers his normal stylistic energy only when a distancing, whether of time or irony, is possible. Doubtless this accounts in part for the excessive amount of authorial comment and the excessive amount of landscape description. These too, though they may reflect intimate preoccupations, are modes of evasion and withdrawal.

There remains one narrative method to be considered: the long flashback of Chapters 2–5; in these pages we find some of the best writing of the book. The method does not prevent the evocation of scenes — including the first tryst of Dain and Nina in their "two little nutshells," surrounded by the intense corrupting "work of tropical nature" — but for the creating imagination these scenes exist in the past. For that reason, they may be dramatized selectively and closed off whenever the author pleases. Some thirty-five of the fifty-four pages are historical summary, and they offer us the closest approach to Conrad's later impressionism: a panoramic survey covering a large tract of time, but constantly animated by vivid particulars. The flashback comes to us not as the nominal recollection of one of the characters (as in pages 5–11), and not as the orderly reconstruction of an omniscient author (except in pages 62 and 81–83) but, at its best, as the free wandering flow of an unidentified memory speaking in a personalized often ironic voice. This nameless narrator, even when he constructs a meaning, constructs it with the haphazard and abrupt transitions of memory. Since he has no reader (only an implicit listener) he rarely explains the historical events to which he alludes, and he offers no orderly account of the passage of time; leaps forward days or years as with the same breath. Above all, he shares Marlow's impulse to actualize the irrelevant through highly visual detail; and to pass over the absolutely essential in a casual subordinate clause. He has begun to develop, in other words, the vocabulary of that impressionism allegedly taught by Ford Madox Ford: a narrative method of deceptive emphasis and constantly shifting perspective, depending for much of its beauty on swift oscillations between the long view and the close, between the moralizing abstract and the highly visualized particular.

It would be an exaggeration to say that these chapters offer more than a promising glimpse of the later method. But it is interesting to see Conrad approach so soon this congenial manner, then quickly abandon it. The same comment may be made of style. The first pages contain their moderately successful imitations of Flaubert.* But we see surer signs of a future Conrad in certain overextended and even overloaded sentences, whose multiplying modifiers carry the reader without punctuation past the natural resting places: "The crude light of the lamp shone on the gold embroidery of his black silk jacket, broke in a thousand sparkling rays on the jeweled hilt of his kris protruding from under the many folds of the red sarong gathered into a sash round his waist, and played on the precious stones of the many rings on his dark fingers."

* For instance: "The young man himself too was nothing loth to leave the poisonous shores of Java, and the meagre comforts of the parental bungalow, where the father grumbled all day at the stupidity of native gardeners, and the mother from the depths of her long easy-chair bewailed the lost glories of Amsterdam, where she had been brought up, and of her position as the daughter of a cigar dealer there" (p. 5). Conrad's memory, often faulty, may have failed him when he denied reading Flaubert before finishing *Almayer's Folly*. See letter to Hugh Walpole, June 7, 1918, in Jean-Aubry, *Life and Letters,* II, 206.

Doubtless this is the prose of an inexperienced writer refusing to omit any of the single adjectives each noun deserves. But it is also the prose of a voice introducing certain variants on the normal tempo of the language. "While the sun shone with that dazzling light in which her love was born and grew till it possessed her whole being, she was kept firm in her unwavering resolve by the mysterious whisperings of desire which filled her heart with impatient longing for the darkness that would mean the end of danger and strife, the beginning of happiness, the fulfilling of love, the completeness of life." The sentence begins and ends conventionally. But the unbroken period of thirty-three words (beginning with "she was kept firm") is — in its rhythms as in its uninhibited rhetoric — the expression of a temperament.

An Outcast of the Islands is a much longer and more conventional book, generically a more popular one. "The mere scenery got a great hold on me as I went on, perhaps because (I may just as well confess that) the story itself was never very near my heart. It engaged my imagination much more than my affection." [17] No doubt the slightness of the subjective involvement accounts for much. So too must the fact that Conrad was exploiting a fictional world — Lakamba, Babalatchi, and the rest — already discovered and dreamed. But also we must reckon with a professional ease, slickness even, developed in an alarmingly short time. The first third of the novel was written in five and a half months, and shows some willed attention to craft. But the last 75,000 words were written in approximately ten weeks; the final sections are intolerably diffuse. Conrad would seem to have been well on his way to becoming a popular, and mediocre, novelist.

The most striking change is the relative absence of ambiguity, deliberate or undeliberate. An omniscient observer, often an omniscient author, keeps the reader at a clear, even distance from the action. Thus the reader knows where he stands. So too, obviously, did the author, who shows a relatively high degree of intellectual control over much of his material. Hence we have less uncertainty of subject and theme than in *Almayer's Folly*. The interest in the local color of Sambir and its politics remains, and is even amplified, partly because an omniscient observer is free to record certain details of daily life that an Almayer would take for granted. Meanwhile the enigmatic figure of Tom Lingard has been brought into the action, though as a secondary character. This fearless man of good will, of "stupidly guileless heart" — interfering in the lives of individuals and communities for their own good, and for the satisfaction of his ego — is Conrad's first suggestive study of the destructive sentimental idealist. He is an incorrigible rescuer of drifters and castaways, and Almayer (one of the rescued) tells us what to think of him:

> "Yes! Cat, dog, anything that can scratch or bite; as long as it is harmful enough and mangy enough. A sick tiger would make you happy — of all things. A half-dead tiger that you could weep over and palm upon some poor devil in your power, to tend and nurse for you. Never mind the consequences — to the poor devil. Let him be mangled or eaten up, of course! You haven't any pity to spare for the victims of your infernal charity." [18]

This Lingard is interesting. But *An Outcast of the Islands* is unmistakably about the drifting, dishonest Willems and his slow then sudden deterioration. Lingard had rescued him once, and found him a position with Hudig's trading company in Macassar; Hudig in turn had married him off to his illegitimate daughter. When the monstrously vain Willems steals from Hudig and can't face the ensuing humiliation, Lingard rescues him again. He takes him up his secret river to Almayer and Sambir. There Willems is enthralled by the girl Aïssa, and is soon wearing a sarong. He becomes crazed by desire, when the local politicians separate them for a few days, and consents to guide Abdulla's ship up the river. Thus Lingard returns to find his navigational secret and commercial monopoly gone. He recognizes Willems' horror of native life, and horror of the girl; and condemns him to live with her to the end of his days. Here the novel should have ended, as the excellent motion picture does. But a confused and irrelevant fifth part brings Mrs. Willems to the isolated hut, where she naturally cries out, "Who's that woman?" In the ensuing squabble Willems is shot by Aïssa.

Conrad's nominal interest in Willems' deterioration (in the flimsiness of his vanity as a moral support, in his vain white man's horror of descent into savage torpor) is clear enough, though seldom entirely convincing. It engaged him about as much or as little as Stevenson's stories of drifters engaged Stevenson. The novel's one real area of ambiguity, and of obscure author-involvement, concerns Willems' sexual passion— a passion Conrad here explicitly defines as corrupt.* The desire is immediate and allegedly of the greatest intensity, to be dramatized in the twisting of fingers, cracking of joints, and other signs of frustration. It is strong enough to conquer racial pride and any lingering loyalty to Lingard. But the fascination is presently mingled with disgust, and in the end leads to sexual failure. "He took her in his arms and waited for the transport, for the madness, for the sensations remembered and lost; and while she sobbed gently on his breast he held her and felt cold, sick, tired, exasperated with his failure — and ended by cursing himself." But the fiasco was symbolically predicted many pages earlier in the situation that would become a Conradian stereotype: when Aïssa flings her father's unsheathed kris at his feet, and he stoops to pick it up. "Was this the answer to his pleading, to the hot and living words that came from his heart?" And now as we look back to the first meeting of the two lovers, Willems' allegedly uncontrollable passion becomes rather suspect. There is the grass standing high, "unstirring, with drooping heads in the

* "With that look she drew the man's soul away from him through his *immobile* pupils, and from Willems' features the spark of reason vanished under her gaze and was replaced by an appearance of physical well-being, an ecstasy of the senses which had taken possession of his rigid body; an ecstasy that drove out regrets, hesitation and doubt, and proclaimed its *terrible work* by an appalling aspect of idiotic beatitude. He never stirred a limb, hardly breathed, but stood in stiff *immobility*, absorbing the delight of her close contact by every pore" (p. 140, italics mine). And: ". . . that whisper of deadly happiness, so sincere, so spontaneous, coming so straight from the heart — like every corruption. It was the voice of madness, of a delirious peace, of happiness that is infamous, cowardly, and so exquisite that the debased mind refuses to contemplate its termination . . ." (pp. 141–142).

warm and motionless air," and, two pages later, another gratuitous description of menaced trees and of nature at its terrible work. The girl is specifically equated with the tropical life that "works in gloom," that is "only the blossoming of the dead," that "contains nothing but poison and decay." The novel's only area of unconscious or half-conscious creation tells us that Willems is horrified by sex *from the first,* and from the first threatened by impotence. (Though Conrad refers once to his "continence," on page 334.) Thus the axis of the plot, and the direct cause of Abdulla's historical arrival in Sambir, is a passion that has no reality.

And yet through all this Conrad was moving, unknowingly, toward one of his great themes and best books. *Almayer's Folly* is an important first experiment in the impressionist method. But *An Outcast of the Islands* is chiefly interesting for its situational prefigurations of *Lord Jim.* As Lingard hides Willems from his humiliation in Sambir (now ruled by Patalolo), so Marlow and Stein will hide Jim in Patusan. As Aïssa questions Lingard on Willems' status in the outside world, and complains that he won't fight, so Jewel will question Marlow and complain. Lingard must shake his head when asked whether Willems was "great" in the world of white men; Marlow will blurt out that Jim was "not good enough." To this degree Lingard prefigures Marlow. But he anticipates Jim himself in his romantic egoism and his self-deceptions. He too thinks of the river as *his,* and takes pride in his benevolent despotic role. There are certain other foreshadowings: details of the jockeying for power after Abdulla's coming, and Almayer's boat stuck in the mud during his attempt to let Willems (i.e., Gentleman Brown) escape. But the essential combining still to be made was this: Conrad must imagine in Willems' situation (the hiding-away of a humiliated man) not a drifter but a man who commands our sympathy, a man of "good intentions." He must be a man possessing the magnitude — and vulnerability — of Lingard.

Technically, the advance over *Almayer's Folly* is a rather equivocal one, though to most commercial publishers it would seem enormous. Clarity has been gained for an exotic adventure story which certainly has its popular side. But meanwhile we have lost the beauty of changing perspectives, lost too the sense of immersion in an alien world, and all the strain that comes from shifting distances between author, subject, and reader. Hence we remain passive and unengaged, finally indifferent. The author's intellectual control is certainly greater than before; through much of the novel he appears to know exactly how his plot must move. But this surface understanding of everything (except Willems' passion) leads to loss of a more important kind of control. The relaxed imagination permits itself a wearying diffuseness. It is no paradox to say that Conrad's imagination — in the intensities and violences of the book's last seventy-eight pages — is more relaxed than almost anywhere in his early work.

Literal interior monologue is used briefly on at least four occasions, and is always grossly unsuccessful. It even ventures to render from within the last moments of Willems' life!* This method, which implies no distance at all, is by all odds Conrad's most uncongenial. He is rather more successful when, for four paragraphs, he changes into the present tense, and so gives the impression of a fascinated and puzzled *watcher.*† But such immediacy was not Conrad's strength, and never would be. The important lesson he had begun to learn was that he could not long depend on a character's subjective view of experience (reported in the third person without irony) to render that experience. No little of *An Outcast of the Islands* is presented through this point of view, but much more through a point of view truly omniscient. This omniscience is abused more frequently than in *Almayer's Folly* — as in the little essay on passion as corrupt,

* The passage must be given the decent secrecy of footnote: "He tried to cough; spat out . . . Who shrieks: In the name of God, he dies! — he dies! — Who dies? — Must pick up — Night! — What? . . . Night already. . . ." (p. 360). The dots and dashes are Conrad's.

† *The Great Gatsby* similarly breaks into the present tense for the moment of Gatsby's death and has what may be an echo of Conrad: "Through that lurid glare Syed Abdulla, in his long white gown, seems *to glide fantastically,* like a dignified apparition . . ." (p. 135). It is interesting to watch Faulkner, trying out the instrument of the novel, make the same brief experiment in *Soldier's Pay.*

or in the formal comparison of Willems' character and Aïssa's. But often it is simply the conventional novelist's vehicle and "easiest way" of letting the reader know everything there is to be known — the narrator an observing camera when only observation is desired, but moving at will into any and all minds to reveal what they are thinking. The time-honored method invites, of course, a straightforward chronological treatment.

The word "narrator" is used with hesitation, since in the later parts we usually have an author writing rather than a voice speaking; the product is machine-made. But once again (as in *Almayer's Folly*) we do hear a genuine and interesting voice in the early retrospective chapters. This voice offers us an often ironic and highly selective history of Willems' rise and decline, and of the earlier days of Omar and Babalatchi. It reports the self-flattering reveries of Willems in Macassar, yet keeps through phrasing a saving distance of irony. Twice Conrad almost commits himself to a genuinely human narrator, a speaker who is truly a person.[19] But he seldom achieves the effect of free-flowing memory which we have in *Almayer's Folly* at its best. It would perhaps be most accurate to say that we have, in Part I, an omniscient historian-author who has developed a good spoken style. He summarizes exciting events laconically, and combines immediacy and austere detachment. The energized prose yet suggests the coolness and control of "history":

Babalatchi, with the clear perception of the coming end, devoted all his energies to saving if it was but only one of them. He succeeded in time. When the end came in the explosion of the stored powder-barrels, he was ready to look for his chief. He found him half dead and totally blinded, with nobody near him but his daughter Aïssa: — the sons had fallen earlier in the day, as became men of their courage. Helped by the girl with the steadfast heart, Babalatchi carried Omar on board the light prau and succeeded in escaping, but with very few companions only. As they hauled their craft into the network of dark and silent creeks, they could hear the cheering of the man-of-war's boats dashing to the attack of the rover's village.

. . . And then began Omar's second flight. It began arms in hand, for the little band had to fight in the night on the beach for the possession of the small canoes in which those that survived got away at last.[20]

In *An Outcast of the Island* we have — for all the gross syntax of the first sentence above — very little idiosyncratic Conradese. But these sentences do have the extended yet varied rhythm of his later eloquence.

One more fact is of importance, as we watch Conrad's complex temperament demand certain methods and reject certain others. This is a tendency to evade the dramatic scene even more marked than in *Almayer's Folly*. We are not taken into the room where Willems gets his moral lashing from Hudig; we merely see him go into the room, and in the next sentence come out. Two of the most striking scenes in the motion picture — Willems' guiding Abdulla's ship up the river and the "outrage" of Almayer stitched in his hammock — are given no real visualization; they reach us through Almayer's retrospective report. So too Omar's death reaches us through Babalatchi's account. It would be idle to regret these losses. On the contrary, we can welcome Conrad's recognition of his own real limitations. The evasiveness is most manifest, it may be, in the major dramatic meeting of Lingard and Willems, benefactor and traitor. For the actual meeting is unreasonably deferred for over thirteen thousand words.[21] And when it comes, it is bungled very badly. *An Outcast of the Islands* reminds us again that some of Conrad's greatest dramatic scenes will reach us distanced by time and retrospect; or, at least, by irony.

The Rescue, especially after Moser's two studies, need not detain us long. Only the first three parts and a few pages of the fourth reflect work done in the 1890's, and the published text is very different from "The Rescuer" manuscript, involving much later chastening of style and some weakening of conception. Moser makes a very plausible case for "The Rescuer" as an *ur-Lord Jim,* with "King Tom" Lingard foreshadowing the "Tuan Jim" of Patusan, and Edith Travers occupying Gentleman Brown's paralyzing role. Unfortunately the interesting, vulnerable romantic egoist of "The Rescuer" becomes by 1919, an impeccable hero and innocent victim of circumstance. Furthermore, certain important passages — notably a mysterious Mr. Wyndham's urgent advice to Lingard not to become involved with natives — have disappeared.* "The Rescuer" came to a halt in 1899, Moser argues, because Conrad's imagination could not cope with the intruders on the stranded yacht or with the sexual situation that had begun to develop. The increasingly chaotic state of the manuscript lends visual support to such reasoning.

The Rescue of 1920 is certainly one of Conrad's lesser novels. But even "The Rescuer" represented a serious backward step and a deliberate courting of popularity. "If the virtues of Lingard please most of the critics, they shall have more of them. The theme of it shall be the rescue of a yacht from some Malay vagabonds and there will be a gentleman and a lady cut out according to the regulation pattern." [22] The first part, written in 1896, shows Conrad dramatizing a captain at sea for the first time. He handles nautical detail with assurance and offers several elaborate seascapes, much reduced in the published text. And the retrospective second part has some of the vividness of the historical flashbacks in *Almayer's Folly* and *An Outcast of the Islands.* The disorganized presentation of evidence from many sides anticipates the first part of *Nostromo.* But elsewhere the narrative method has become distinctly more conventional. A standard Victorian omniscient author locates the reader carefully in the exotic scene, explains unfamiliar customs, offers static and minute descriptions (not impressions) of faces; and, of course, moves at will into the minds of many characters. Yet he does not always avail himself of the omniscient point of view's privileges. He even uses dialogue to convey geographical information to the reader.[23] The method is, briefly, so haphazard as to be no method at all.

* "First you fight with them — then you fight for them — no closer tie than spilt blood — then you begin to think they are human beings." The next step is to love them, and this is "Damnation." Wyndham knows he cannot follow his own advice; he knows he will return to his native community (British Museum, Ashley 4787, pp. 141, 142).

These crudities are present in manuscript and published text alike. The cool prose style of *The Rescue*'s first three parts also seems, at a glance, more conventional than that of *An Outcast of the Islands,* and doubtless more efficient so far as mere narrative is concerned; there is very little Conradese. But here we must take into account substantial and often indiscriminate later cutting. In the final version two pages of controlled historical proem replace a long meditative evocation of the sea; elsewhere a thousand words of ornate visual writing have been reduced to a few hundred. It is even dangerous to draw inferences from the relative absence of the characteristic Conradian sentence and its unpunctuated running rhythms. No small number of commas have been inserted by the late Conrad or by his editor. A sentence on the first page of Part II has a modest but genuine Conradian gait: "In the long season of unclouded days it presents to view only *a strip of sombre green,* a narrow band of earth crushed flat upon the vast level of waters by the weight of the *over-arching* sky whose immense dome rests on it in a line as fine and true as that of the sea horizon itself." But the published version — by inserting "that appears" after "earth," by omitting the italicized words, by adding two commas — is much less original.

It is interesting to observe Conrad (if we may judge by the neatness of this page of the manuscript) commit without forethought one of his rare audacities, and at the same time achieve a certain eloquence. Near the end of Chapter 4 of Part II he suddenly addresses the "shades of forgotten adventurers" in his own voice:

> Did you follow with your ghostly eyes the quest of this obscure adventurer of yesterday you shades of forgotten adventurers who in leather jerkins and sweating under steel helmets attacked with long rapiers the palisades of the strange heathen, or musket on shoulder and match in cock guarded lonely forts built upon the banks of rivers that command good trade? [24]

We are reminded of Faulkner's abrupt violation of point of view, in *Sartoris,* to deliver his eloquent apostrophe to the mule — a very long passage carrying for almost the first time the uninhibited rhythms and exaggerations of true Faulknerese; a long-strangled voice has burst into song. And even the chastened later Conrad must have liked the phrasing of this isolated flight, since there is only one verbal change from the manuscript — "timber blockhouses" for "lonely forts." But somebody has added to the sentence no less than five commas, and so destroyed its movement. Doubtless the same person, Conrad or an editor, was acutely embarrassed, retrospectively, by the break in point of view. He inserts three dots before the sentence to indicate such a break will occur.

This then is the curious history of the divided Conrad and his three Malayan novels: that in them he was slowly moving toward *Lord Jim* and Patusan, progressing as it were up a dark undercurrent of theme, yet all the while floating down a progressively debased surface. Superficially, he was moving from an original and visionary concern with moral deterioration, in the direction of ordinary popular romance and its artificial conflicts. So too for method. In the three novels Conrad intermittently came very close to the manner of Marlow; also he went through the useful experience of trying to do what he could do only very badly. He learned to depend less on interior monologue, less on a single character's subjective view of dramatic action. But the process of elimination threatened (for the moment) to eliminate everything of value. The general movement was thus from a groping original experiment in ambiguity to the most conventional form of Victorian looseness and banality.

We can see, sixty years after the event, the great lesson to be learned. We can see, in all three novels, that Conrad wrote most impressively when he allowed himself ironic or retrospective distance and exploited his temperamental evasiveness; when he adopted an austere meditative stance. It would appear, however, that Conrad himself did not yet see this clearly, and perhaps thought he was mastering certain gross faults. Or did he, discouraged by commercial failure and seeking popularity, deliberately conventionalize his art? It would be impossible, now, to draw the right fine line. We can say that, luckily, the debasement of this emerging Malayan material and method (which would have made him at best another Stevenson) did not continue.

(A glance at the South Sea Yarns of Stevenson, which immediately preceded *Almayer's Folly,* indicates in what sense Conrad "brought seriousness" to the exotic novel of adventure. It also reminds us of what Conrad's early readers must have expected and not found. Admittedly, Stevenson could handle violent action with a directness and brutality beyond Conrad's grasp. Some of his striking scenes — a secret pearl-fishing station ruled by a religious fanatic, a schooner abandoned on a lonely atoll — have an impressive material reality. Futhermore, the middle portion of *The Wrecker* of 1892 and the final chapters of *The Ebb-Tide* of 1894 are brilliantly conceived; the melodramatic plots profess to demand intense moral choices. But only profess to demand. The difference from *Lord Jim* and even *Almayer's Folly* is largely one of subjective involvement. Where Conrad exhibits a conflict between judgment and sympathy, between moral repudiation of the rebel or outlaw and strong identification with him, Stevenson shows neither the judgment nor the sympathy. His beachcombers are completed moral ruins, not men on the edge of ruin; they are too distant from their creator. So too the careful descriptions of sea and jungle are never charged descriptions, projections of the author's anxieties. The art is wholly impersonal.

Perhaps we should not quarrel with novels so entertaining and so unpretentious. But in technique too what divides Conrad at his best from Stevenson is, simply, seriousness and sincerity. The indirections and involutions of *The Wrecker* anticipate Conrad's impressionism in certain respects: the oblique approach, the circlings and evasions, the narratives within narratives. But where the Conrad of *Lord Jim* tried to involve his readers in the ambiguities faced by his characters, and made every digression bear on the central situation, Stevenson deferred his main plot through some hundred and fifty pages of trivial satire for the sake of giving greater reality to his "police tale." *The Wrecker*'s comment on its own technique, in the Epilogue, is nevertheless interesting. How many modern experiments in structure — even those of Faulkner — owe something to the "police tale," and to the later Dickens?

> But the question of treatment was as usual more obscure. We [Stevenson and his collaborator Lloyd Osbourne] had long been at once attracted and repelled by that very modern form of the police novel or mystery story, which consists in beginning your yarn anywhere but at the beginning, and finishing it anywhere but at the end; attracted by its peculiar interest when done, and the peculiar difficulties that attend its execution; repelled by that appearance of insincerity and shallowness of tone, which seems its inevitable drawback. For the mind of the reader, always bent to pick up clues, receives no impression of reality or life, rather of an airless, elaborate mechanism; and the book remains enthralling but insignificant, like a game of chess, not a work of human art. It seemed the cause might lie partly in the abrupt attack; and that if the tale were gradually approached, some of the characters introduced (as it were) beforehand, and the book started in the tone of a novel of manners and experience briefly treated, this defect might be lessened and our mystery seem to inhere in life . . . After we had invented at some expense of time this method of approaching and fortifying our police novel, it occurred to us it had been invented previously by some one else, and was in fact — however painfully different the results may seem — the method of Charles Dickens in his later work.

The resemblances of Conrad to his most obvious contemporary rival are relatively superficial. The uneasy bogus survivors of the *Flying Scud* in *The Wrecker* distantly remind us of the officers of the *Patna;* the invasion of Attwater's secret atoll, in *The Ebb-Tide,* as distantly of Heyst's island invaded.)[25]

One further Malayan story, "Karain," was very important to Conrad's ultimate discovery of congenial theme and method. It was written in the spring of 1897, immediately after *The Nigger of the "Narcissus"* and simultaneously with the wretched "The Return." In his author's Note to *Tales of*

Unrest Conrad remarks on its resemblance to "The Lagoon" in motif, but today it seems striking as a further step toward *Lord Jim*. Conrad had discovered an "I" in *The Nigger of the "Narcissus"* — a first-person narrator who is a member of the ship's crew — but this "I" becomes a fairly direct projection of the author, and his vocabulary and manner are not Marlow's. To discover an engaged "I" at all was certainly the one great stride to be taken. But the narrator of "Karain" is much closer to Marlow the communicant and evasive reporter of lost souls.

The narrator, recalling the old adventurous days in the East, devotes three chapters and almost half the story to creating a visual impression of Karain and his land: ". . . the master of an insignificant foothold on the earth — of a conquered foothold that, shaped like a young moon, lay ignored between the hills and the sea." Karain has great prestige and a splendid appearance. "To no man had been given the shelter of so much respect, confidence, and awe." But he is, the narrator suggests, vulnerable. He cannot bear to be alone, and is always accompanied by his sword-bearer. And he will never go back to his native country on the Celebes. Precisely like Marlow, the narrator withholds later knowledge, reconstructs his own original bewilderment, yet puts us on guard with pertinent asides. "He was ornate and disturbing, for one could not imagine what depth of horrible void such an elaborate front could be worthy to hide." On a return voyage the narrator is surprised not to be welcomed by Karain; the sword-bearer has died and the ruler is in seclusion. But on their last night before sailing Karain appears on board, dripping, and begs to be taken away. "Of course it had been a long swim off to the schooner; but his face showed another kind of fatigue, the tormented weariness, the anger and the fear of a struggle against a thought, an idea — against something that cannot be grappled, that never rests — a shadow, a nothing, unconquerable and immortal, that preys upon life." Hitherto the old sword-bearer (to whom he had confessed) had held off the ghost of Pata Matara, the friend he had killed. But now (Conrad's first narrator within a narrator) he must thrust his confession on the white men, and beg for their help.

Karain's confession, which occupies less than a third of the story, is itself an evasive impressionistic narrative. He had sworn to help his friend Pata Matara find and kill his dishonored sister and the Dutch trader who had taken her away. But during the long period of wandering and pursuit, Karain becomes obsessed with an image of the girl and falls in love with it; at the moment of crisis he *involuntarily* shoots Pata Matara instead. And here the first narrator breaks in briefly, as Marlow will break in on Lord Jim. "And I looked on, surprised and moved; I looked at that man, loyal to a vision, betrayed by his dream, spurned by his illusion, and coming to us unbelievers for help — against a thought." Karain goes on to tell of Pata Matara's ghostly apparition, and again appeals for help. "He had given himself up to us; he had thrust into our hands his errors and his torment, his life and his peace; and we did not know what to do with that problem from the outer darkness." The story ends in trivial anecdote; one of the white men gives Karain a Jubilee sixpence, and convinces him the Queen's image will be an effective propitiatory charm. It is as though Conrad did not yet want to admit that Lord Jim with his crime was "one of us." As Willems was only an outcast drifter, so Karain is only a superstitious native. Yet one of the listeners anticipates Marlow's recurring and key phrase: " 'Every one of us,' he said, with pauses that somehow were more offensive than his words — 'every one of us, you'll admit, has been haunted by some woman . . . And . . . as to friends . . . dropped by the way . . . Well! . . . ask yourselves.' "

The man of good intentions and his impulsive crime and long remorse; his need to communicate guilt and so acquire further witnesses; the desperate attempt to leave in space what always travels with him in time; the sympathetic yet detached listener — these foreshadowings of *Lord Jim* are obvious. The technical anticipations are almost as clear. The narrator, like Marlow, pauses occasionally to comment on his own story. Chronologically he is straightforward enough, apart from the fact that he withholds revelation of the crime for thirty-three of fifty-three pages. But his evocations and transitions are those of a free wandering memory. His style is rich, at times epigrammatic, and builds certain scenic effects rather formally; "Karain" contains some of the most controlled writing of the early period. But also the style, thanks to occasional colloquial incursions and to much variation of sentence structure, conveys a speaking voice. And that voice, like Marlow's, rejoices in swift movements from the abstract to the particular and back; from long moralizing sentences to very brief and concrete ones; or, to sum up, rejoices in controlled variations of the distance from which we view the "case exposed." The following passage would not be out of place in *Lord Jim*. The rhythms building toward "darkness" are certainly those of Marlow.

> He looked round the little cabin, at the painted beams, at the tarnished varnish of bulkheads; he looked round as if appealing to all of its shabby strangeness, to the disorderly jumble of unfamiliar things that belong to an inconceivable life of stress, of power, of endeavour, of unbelief—to the strong life of white men, which rolls on irresistible and hard on the edge of outer darkness. He stretched out his arms as if to embrace it and us. We waited. The wind and rain had ceased, and the stillness of the night round the schooner was as dumb and complete as if a dead world had been laid to rest in a grave of clouds. We expected him to speak.[26]

Such were the occasional striking successes and the interesting failures of the 1894–1897 period, as Conrad's imagination worked on his Malayan recollections: a series of intricately connected dreams of moral deterioration in exotic settings, variously looking ahead to *Lord Jim*. The great success of the period was, of course, *The Nigger of the "Narcissus"* (1897), the first important transposition of life at sea and first major symbolist experiment. But during the same years Conrad also tried to dramatize entirely different materials and settings, and to use more conventional methods. Here the three failures may be regarded as total. They demonstrate how completely a creative temperament can refuse materials and methods uncongenial to it.

The Sisters is the 10,000 word fragment of a novel begun after *An Outcast of the Islands,* given up in March 1896. Ford Madox Ford much regretted the abandonment. He asserts that Conrad wanted to be "a straight writer, treating of usual human activities in cities and countryside" — especially the relationship of the sexes — and blames Garnett and Henley for urging a return to the sea: to "the simple psychology, the naïve approach to moral problems and the relative optimism of such Britons as follow the sea." [27] Ford's appalling misvaluation requires no comment, though his description of Conrad's conscious ambition is plausible enough. But Moser's analysis is even more plausible: that *The Sisters* is a first adumbration of *The Arrow of Gold,* exploiting memories of the Marseilles romance, and that it foundered on precisely the same rock that stopped "The Rescuer" in 1899. A sexual relationship was about to take place. I think it is well to add that Conrad was unable to dramatize a projection of his artist-intellectual self (as opposed to the adventurous-seaman self), and that he could not look at Paris from a sufficient psychic distance. His brief satirical view of an artistic Bohemia and of artistic aspirations is as implausible as that of Stevenson's *The Wrecker.* Every reader must notice how Stevenson's imagination and style intensify, once this triviality is dropped and the Pacific adventure begins.

So too any reader of stories by college freshmen should recognize, in *The Sisters,* the woolly rhetoric and oblique embarrassed self-justifications of autobiography imperfectly transposed:

> He was not a man to leave a mark on the minds of his contemporaries; for he, strange monster, had not been provided with that touch of commonplace which makes us all brothers — and some of us illustrious. His work lay yet in the future, his lips were mute — and he pushed his aimless way through youthful crowds leaving no trail: unless a faint sense of hostility, awakened in some well ordered minds, may be put down to his account for a memorable distinction.[28]

The Sisters offers the classic components of the autobiographical first novel: the betrayal of home and parents, the frustrations of the misunderstood artist, and (still implicitly here) the sufferings of guilt and sexual malaise. These matters had been important to Conrad as they are important to innumerable young men. But he had enough critical sense, conscious or unconscious, to give up a hopeless job. He was writing with his own rhythms and overextended syntax, especially in the retrospective passages, but with the monotony of a man blowing up many balloons of the same size. "The vagaries of Dolores she met with a rigidity of demeanour which caused that worthy woman to foam at the mouth in the imperfect privacy of a big glass cage where she sat from morning to night with her yellow profile of a bilious parrot hovering over the pages of account books." The sentence, as *The Sisters* goes, is interesting; at least it could hardly have been written by anybody else. But all the passages devoted to an omniscient author's sympathetic rendering of Stephen's subjective experience are bad. One astonishing paragraph converts grass in a Passy courtyard into a corrupt, devouring jungle.[29] Otherwise, the most striking passage in the fragment converts a Slavic plain into a limitless sea: "Far off on the line of horizon, another village showed above the monotony of yellow corn, the green path of its few trees, and lay lone, minute and brilliant, like an emerald negligently dropped on the sands of a limitless and deserted shore." The rhythms are familiar. And they warn us that the superficial characteristics of an author's style may (very occasionally) survive uncongenial material and method.

A short story, "The Idiots" (written May 1896), is an experiment of a quite different kind: a somber naturalistic anecdote of inherited idiocy in a family of Breton peasants. The story was written in Brittany, during Conrad's honeymoon there, and presumably as the first of many truancies from "The Rescuer." It was suggested by the sight of the "actual idiots," [30] and thus is almost unique in Conrad's work as an attempt to dramatize fictional material immediately after observing it. And "fictional material" it is, in the crudest sense — the local tragedy of Jean-Pierre Bacadou marrying to acquire sons for his farm, fathering four idiots, and stabbed to death by his wife Susan. After the murder, she rushes distraught near the edge of a cliff, mistakes a rescuer for the ghost of her husband, and falls to her death. An extreme psychiatric approach might take satisfaction in the fact that Conrad's first work, after his own marriage, was this story of a disastrous marriage. But the writing itself suggests that no story could have involved Conrad less, so far as the true creative imagination is concerned. It seems rather the product of an amateur's desperate search for a "subject" after a dismal experience of "writer's block."

The Author's Note to *Tales of Unrest* dismisses "The Idiots" in four lines, as an "obviously derivative piece of work." A brief account of the wedding procession and feast immediately recalls *Madame Bovary,* and any useful derivation was from Flaubert. The story opens, as does *Madame Bovary,* with a first person narrator — the very first in Conrad's fiction — but this "I" vanishes after three introductory pages. There follow ten retrospective pages of omniscient narrative: a moderately successful imitation of Flaubert's cold and ironic understatement.

He would sacrifice his convictions. One day he told his wife —
"See what your God will do for us. Pay for some masses."

Susan embraced her man. He stood unbending, then turned on his heels and went out. But afterwards, when a black *soutane* darkened his doorway, he did not object; even offered some cider himself to the priest. He listened to the talk meekly; went to mass between the two women; accomplished what the priest called "his religious duties" at Easter. That morning he felt like a man who had sold his soul.[31]

The lesson in holding pathetic or humble material at a fixed ironic distance, and in reporting the arrival of another idiot in six words, could well have been a useful one. But with the crisis Conrad abandons all such control, and tries to convey the total experience of hysteria and shock. In the last sixteen pages the point of view wanders distractedly: records the wife's fear and her illusion of seeing a ghost, the bewilderment of her mother, the emotions of her would-be rescuer. We even attend, but from at least two points of view, the final moments of Susan's life. Thus Conrad had yet to learn (and to the end of his career occasionally forgot) that he had no talent at all for the immediate dramatic treatment of a violent scene. The material of "The Idiots" was essentially too remote. To compensate for this remoteness, Conrad tried to come too close to it; tried to beat an inert story into life.

"The Return," written in 1897, was by no means remote enough. It seems, rather, the most troubled expression of Conrad's confused misogyny and the extreme example of his creative bewilderment in the presence of a sexual situation. Ford reports that Conrad looked upon "The Return" (as upon *The Sisters*) as something "obscene." [32] In the Author's Note Conrad describes it as "a left-handed production" that cost him much "in sheer toil, in temper, and in disillusion." His reserves are justified. "The Return" is certainly Conrad's worst story of any length, and one of the worst ever written by a great novelist. The first three thousand words offer a crude but fairly controlled satirical portrait of a typical respectable and conceited man of moderate wealth. Alvan Hervey returns to his home through the sordid and inhuman gloom of London, and finds a note saying that his wife has run off with another man. The remaining twenty-two thousand words — as Hervey ponders the note, as he gives his returned wife an upbraiding, as he discovers that he has wanted love and also discovers that morality is not happiness, as he feels a flickering of desire — attempt to convey without relief an incoherent and violent distraction. Hervey's emotions are compared to explosions, meteors, volcanoes, and creation-shattering tumults.

The nominal theme is stated on an early page. Husband and wife are incapable of "real intimacy." The wife, we shall learn, was almost capable of passionate life, but lacked the courage of her convictions, and returned to her home after only a few hours of revolt; the husband had exhausted his small fund of longing after five months of marriage. "They skimmed over the surface of life hand in hand, in a pure and frosty atmosphere — like two skilful skaters cutting figures on thick ice for the admiration of the beholders, and disdainfully ignoring the hidden stream, the stream restless and dark; the stream of life, profound and unfrozen." When the wife returns he feels, beyond humiliation, a horror of her apparent capacity for passion: passion, "the unpardonable and secret infamy of our hearts, a thing to curse, to hide and to deny . . . It had laid its unclean hand upon the spotless draperies of his existence, and he had to face it alone with all the world looking on." The treatment of Hervey's ensuing moralizings, his cruel and pompous lectures on self-restraint, could hardly be more satirical. Reduced to outline, "The Return" would appear to be a story of Gidean subtlety embodying a Gidean affirmation of life. For the secret clue to Hervey's conventionality is impotence. He may be regarded as a mildly intellectual London counterpart of the *Outcast*'s Willems.

Such a theme would hardly have been congenial to Conrad, even had he fully understood it. But the total intellectual rejection of Hervey and the occasionally sympathetic treatment of his wife are contradicted by several curious passages, suggesting the underlying misogyny. The analytic voice is Conrad's not Hervey's:

> She stopped for an almost imperceptible moment to give him an indignant glance, and then moved on. That feminine penetration — so clever and so tainted by the eternal instinct of self-defence, so ready to see an obvious evil in everything it cannot understand — filled her with bitter resentment against both the men who could offer to the spiritual and tragic strife of her feelings nothing but the coarseness of their abominable materialism.[33]

The sentence is double-edged, and typical in its confusion. But another one, two pages later, goes straight to its point: "She panted, showing her teeth, and the hate of strength, the disdain of weakness, the eternal preoccupation of sex came out like a toy demon out of a box." Thus a story proposing the values of the passionate life dramatizes, at some of its most intense moments, exactly the opposite.

There can be little doubt that Conrad was deeply and even neurotically involved in this wretched story; the confused involvement is betrayed by gross crudities of method. The minute-by-minute torment of Alvan Hervey seemed important, and had to be given justice through intimate subjective recording of his feelings. But so too it must have seemed important to detach oneself from this squirming and contemptible sufferer. The record of feeling is therefore constantly interlarded by the omniscient author's satirical comments and pretentious psychological analyses. Some of Conrad's greatest novels benefit from ambivalence, from the subtle oscillations of condemning judgment and identifying creative sympathy. But the contradictions of "The Return" never come under artistic control. The test is in the prose, some of the worst Conrad ever wrote. A very little will suffice:

> No escape! He felt something akin to despair. Everybody must know. The servants must know to-night. He ground his teeth . . . And he had never noticed, never guessed anything. Every one will know. He thought: "The woman's a monster, but everybody will think me a fool"; and standing still in the midst of severe walnut-wood furniture, he felt such a tempest of anguish within him that he seemed to see himself rolling on the carpet, beating his head against the wall. He was disgusted with himself, with the loathsome rush of emotion breaking through all the reserves that guarded his manhood.[34]

Could there be a better demonstration than this story of the obscure all-important relationship of temperament to material and method? In "The Return" everything was uncongenial, and not least the London setting: the lives of mediocre sophisticates and the theme of their sexual difficulties, the nominal ethic of unrestraint not really meant, the unacceptable author-identification, the attempt to report emotional crisis subjectively and in a fictional present yet maintain an omniscient-author's detachment. The man who wrote this rubbish had just finished "Karain"; a few months later, would begin *Lord Jim* and write "Youth." He had also completed, three months before beginning "The Return," *The Nigger of the "Narcissus."* It exploits neither Malayan intrigue nor marriage in Western Europe, and is his first great work of art.

Chapter Three

THE NIGGER OF THE "NARCISSUS"

THE complexities of *Almayer's Folly* are those of a man learning — and with what a perverse instinct for the hardest way! — the language of the novelist. *The Nigger of the "Narcissus"* is the first of the books to carry deliberately and with care the burden of several major interests and various minor ones. The one interest which existed for most readers in 1897 remains a real one today: the faithful document of life and adventure at sea. The story is indeed the tribute to the "children of the sea" that Conrad wanted it to be: a memorial to a masculine society and the successful seizing of a "passing phase of life from the remorseless rush of time." [1] It is certainly a tribute to this particular ship on which (for her beauty) Conrad chose to sail in 1884. But it is also a study in collective psychology; and also, frankly, a symbolic comment on man's nature and destiny; and also, less openly, a prose-poem carrying overtones of myth. No small burden, and one which Conrad carried with more care than usual: one passage exists in as many as seven versions.[2] "It is the book by which, not as a novelist perhaps, but as an artist striving for the utmost sincerity of expression, I am willing to stand or fall." [3]

A rich personal novel can hardly be overinterpreted, but it can be misinterpreted easily enough. The dangers of imbalance are suggested by three other masculine narratives which similarly combine faithful reporting and large symbolic suggestion. *The Red Badge of Courage* may well present a sacramental vision and still another of the ubiquitous Christ figures which bemuse criticism; the patterns of imagery are challenging. But it is also, importantly, a record of military life. So too I would allow that "The Bear" contains primtive pageant-rites, initiation ritual, the Jungian descent into the unconscious, perhaps even the Jungian mandala. These matters put the critic on his mettle. But he should acknowledge that some of the story's best pages concern hunting in the big woods and the vanishing of these woods before commercial encroachment. The dangers of imbalance are even more serious when provoked by a slighter work, such as *The Old Man and the Sea.* To say that the novel is about growing old, or about the aging artist's need to substitute skill for strength, is plausible. But can a critic be satisfied with so little? One has gone so far as to find a parable of the decline of the British Empire. This, I submit, takes us too far from the boat and the marlin attached to its side; from the small greatness of a story whose first strength lies in its faithful recording of sensations, of fishing and the sea.

The Nigger of the "Narcissus" (sixty years after the event) is peculiarly beset with dangers for the critic. For Conrad has become fashionable rather suddenly, and comment on this story has passed almost without pause from naïve recapitulation to highly sophisticated analysis of "cabalistic intent." The older innocence is suggested by Arthur Symons' complaint that the story had no idea behind it, or by a journeyman reviewer's remark that James Wait had no place in this record of life at sea.[4] An example of recent sophistication is Vernon Young's important essay "Trial by Water," in the Spring 1952 issue of *Accent.* A single sentence will suggest its bias: "Fearful of overstressing the subaqueous world of the underconsciousness, the symbol-producing level of the psyche which, in fact, was the most dependable source of his inspiration, Conrad overloaded his mundane treatment of the crew." The comment is provocative; it leads us to wonder whether the crew isn't, for this fiction, too numerous. Yet we must rejoin that the crew is very important, and that many of the book's greatest pages have little to do with this subaqueous world. There remains the vulgar charge yet real menace that the critic may oversimplify a novel by oversubtilizing and overintellectualizing it — not merely by intruding beyond the author's conscious intention (which he is fully privileged to do) but by suggesting patterns of unconscious combination which do not *and cannot operate* for the reasonably alert common reader. Much of any serious story works on the fringes of the reader's consciousness: a darkness to be illumined by the critic's insight. But that insight remains irrelevant which can never become aesthetic enjoyment, or which takes a story too far out of its own area of discourse. I say this with the uneasy conviction that criticism should expose itself to as many as possible of a novel's suasions, and that it is only too easy (above all with a Conrad or a Faulkner) to stress the abstract and symbolic at the expense of everything else. One might begin by saying that *The Nigger of the "Narcissus"* recasts the story of Jonah and anticipates "The Secret Sharer"'s drama of identification. This is a truth but a partial truth. And how many partial truths would be needed to render or even evoke such a mobile as this one. Touch one wire, merely breathe on the lovely thing and it wavers to a new form! In the pursuit of structured meaning — of obvious purpose and overtone of conviction and "cabalistic intent" and unconscious content; of stark symbol and subtle cluster of metaphor — one is tempted to ignore the obvious essentials of technique and style. One may even never get around to mentioning what are, irrespective of structure or concealed meaning, the best-written pages in the book. They are these: the arrival of James Wait on board, the onset of the storm, the overturning of the ship, the righting of the ship, old Singleton at the wheel, the quelling of the mutiny, the death of Wait and his burial, the docking of the ship, the dispersal of the crew.

It seems proper for once to begin with the end: with that large personal impression which an embarrassed criticism often omits altogether. *The Nigger of the "Narcissus"* is the most generalized of Conrad's novels in its cutting of a cross-section, though one of the least comprehensive. It is a version of our dark human pilgrimage, a vision of disaster illumined by grace. The microcosmic ship is defined early in the second chapter with an almost Victorian obviousness: "On her lived truth and audacious lies; and, like the earth, she was unconscious, fair to see — and condemned by men to an ignoble fate. The august loneliness of her path lent dignity to the sordid inspiration of her pilgrimage. She drove foaming to the south as if guided by the courage of a high endeavour." Or we can narrow the vision to a single sentence near the end: "The dark knot of seamen drifted in sunshine." The interplay of light and dark images throughout conveys the sense of a destiny both good and evil, heroic and foolish, blundered out under a soulless sky. If I were further to reduce the novel to a single key-word, as some critics like to do, I should choose the word *grace.* In thematic terms not the sea but life at sea is pure and life on earth sordid. Yet the pessimism of *The Nigger of the "Narcissus"* is (unlike that of *The Secret Agent*) a modified pessimism, and the gift of grace can circumvent thematic terms. Thus England herself is once imaged as a great ship. The convention of the novel is that the gift of grace may fall anywhere, or anywhere except on the Donkins. The story really ends with the men clinging for a last moment to their solidarity and standing near the Mint, that most representative object of the sordid earth:

> The sunshine of heaven fell like a gift of grace on the mud of the earth, on the remembering and mute stones, on greed, selfishness; on the anxious faces of forgetful men. And to the right of the dark group the stained front of the Mint, cleansed by the flood of light, stood out for a moment dazzling and white like a marble palace in a fairy tale. The crew of the *Narcissus* drifted out of sight.[5]

So the novel's vision is one of man's dignity but also of his "irremediable littleness" — a conclusion reached, to be sure, by most great works in the Christian tradition. In "Heart of Darkness," *Lord Jim,* and "The Secret Sharer" we have the initiatory or expiatory descents within the self of individual and almost lost souls; in *Nostromo* we shall see the vast proliferation of good and evil in history and political institution. But *The Nigger of the "Narcissus"* presents the classic human contradiction (and the archetypal descent into self) in collective terms, reduced to the simplicities of shipboard life. The storm tests and brings out the solidarity, courage, and endurance of men banded together in a desperate cause. And the Negro James Wait tests and brings out their egoism, solitude, laziness, anarchy, fear. The structural obligation of the story is to see to it that the two tests do not, for the reader, cancel out.

Presented so schematically, Conrad's vision may seem truly Christian. But this is indeed a soulless sky. In the restless life of symbols sunlight is converted, at one point, to that inhuman Nature which Man must oppose. The Norwegian sailor who chatters at the sun has lost his saving separateness from Nature, and when the sun sets his voice goes out "together with the light." The "completed wisdom" of old Singleton (one of the first Conrad extroverts to achieve some of his own skepticism) sees "an immensity tormented and blind, moaning and furious . . ." And in one of the novel's central intellectual statements (the first paragraph of the fourth chapter) the indifferent sea is metaphorically equated with God, and the gift of grace is defined as labor, which prevents man from meditating "at ease upon the complicated and acrid savour of existence." The dignity of man lies in his vast silence and endurance: a dignity tainted by those who clamor for the reward of another life. The message is rather like Faulkner's, and these good seamen are like "good Negroes." But here too, as in other novels of Conrad, man's works and institutions must prepare him to profit from even such grace as this. From our human weakness and from the eternal indifference of things we may yet be saved . . . by authority, tradition, obedience. Thus the only true grace is purely human and even traditional. There are certain men (specifically Donkin) who remain untouched. But such men exist outside: outside our moral universe which is both dark and light but not inextricably both. And James Wait, as sailor and person rather than symbol? I am not sure. He seems to suffer from that "emptiness" which would be Kurtz's ruin: "only a cold black skin loosely stuffed with soft cotton wool . . . a doll that had lost half its sawdust."

This, speaking neither in terms of gross obvious intentions and themes nor of unconscious symbolic content but of generalized human meaning and ethical bias, is what *The Nigger of the "Narcissus"* says. This is its reading of life.

"My task which I am trying to achieve is, by the power of the written word to make you hear, to make you feel — it is, before all, to make you *see*." [6] The sea story is beyond praise; there is no need to defend the amount of space and emphasis Conrad gives it. The long third chapter on the storm is one of the summits of Conrad, and the pages on the righting of the ship one of the summits of English prose. This is, as few others, a real ship. At the start the solidarity of the forecastle is built up gradually, presumably as on any ship, then disrupted by the foul Donkin and the lazy, narcissistic Wait. A sham fellowship first occurs when the seamen give clothing to Donkin, and is increased by their lazy sympathy for the malingering Negro. The true solidarity is created by the exigencies of the storm, and during the worst hours of crisis the good seamen are significantly separated from Wait, who is trapped in his cabin, buried. With the storm over the individuals again become Individuals, and by the same token capable of mutiny. In the Conrad universe we often have this sense of a few men banded together in desperate opposition to a cosmic indifference and to human nature itself. For this voyage ordinary men have come together, been isolated by their weaknesses, and have come together again. On land they separate once more; for one last poignant moment they are the dark knot of seamen drifting in sunshine. "Good-bye brothers! You were a good crowd. As good a crowd as ever fisted with wild cries the beating canvas of a heavy foresail; or tossing aloft, invisible in the night, gave back yell for yell to a westerly gale." The novel is also about that solidarity Conrad admired but rarely dramatized.

In these last sentences of the novel Conrad himself is speaking, rather than the anonymous narrator. And this is perhaps the best place to consider the often-noted waywardness in point of view. The novel opens with objective reporting, and the first narrative voice we hear is stiff, impersonal, detached, a voice reading stage directions. But Conrad's natural impulse is to write in the first person, if possible retrospectively; to suggest action and summarize large segments of time. His natural impulse is to meditative and often ironic withdrawal. (It is author not narrator who pauses to comment on the popularity of Bulwer-Lytton among seamen: an extreme withdrawal.) On the seventh page the narrator momentarily becomes a member of the crew, but we must wait until the second chapter for this identification to be made frankly. Meanwhile we may detect in Conrad a restless impatience with the nominal objectivity adopted — a coolness of manner sharply broken through as he speaks out his admiration for Singleton, his contempt for Donkin. Passionate conviction energized Conrad's visualizing power as nothing else in the chapter did; and we have immortally the Donkin of white eyelashes and red eyelids, with "rare hairs" about the jaws, and shoulders "peaked and drooped like the broken wings of a bird . . ."

With the second chapter, and the sailing of the ship, the prose takes on poetic qualities. A meditative observer outside and above the *Narcissus* sees her as "a high and lonely pyramid, gliding, all shining and white, through the sunlit mist." We return briefly to the deck for a paragraph of flat reporting, then have the developed and Victorian analogy of the ship and the earth with its human freight. The paragraph has the kind of obviousness an intentionalist would welcome, but I suspect its real purpose was tactical. By generalizing his ship in this gross fashion, Conrad freed himself from the present moment and from the obligation to report consecutively. "The days raced after one another, brilliant and quick like the flashes of a lighthouse, and the nights, eventful and short, resembled fleeting dreams." And now he can pursue his natural mode: to hover selectively over a large segment of time, dipping down for a closer view only when he chooses. On the next page (as though to achieve still further retrospective freedom) the narrator identifies himself as a member of the crew. Suddenly we are told that Mr. Baker "kept all our noses to the grindstone."

The subsequent waverings of point of view are the ones that have disturbed logicians. Vernon Young puts their case clearly: "Presumably an unspecified member of the deck crew has carried the narration; in this case the contents of the thoughts of Mr. Creighton and of the cook, and many of the conversations, between Allistoun and his officer or between Donkin and Wait, for example, are impossibly come by." [7] The classic answer to such logic is that all eggs come from the same basket. It may be given more lucidly thus: the best narrative technique is the one which, however imperfect logically, enlists the author's creative energies and fully explores his subject. We need only demand that the changes in point of view not violate the reader's larger sustained vision of the dramatized experience. Creighton's thoughts (since he is no more nor less than a deck officer) can violate nothing except logic. But serious violation does occur twice: when we are given Wait's broken interior monologues (pages 113, 149). For we are approaching the mysterious Negro's death, and it has been the very convention of the novel that Wait must remain shadowy, vast, provocative of large speculation; in a word, symbolic. The very fact that he comes in some sense to represent our human "blackness" should exempt him from the banalities of everyday interior monologue. It would be as shocking to overhear such interior monologue of Melville's Babo or of Leggatt in "The Secret Sharer."

For the rest, the changes in point of view are made unobtrusively and with pleasing insouciance. What is more deadly than the ratiocinations of a narrator trying to explain his "authority," as the Marlow of *Chance* does? The movement of point of view through this novel admirably reflects the general movement from isolation to solidarity to poignant separation. So the detached observer of the first pages becomes an anonymous member of the crew using the word "we." He works with the others during the storm and joins them in the rescue of Wait; and he too, both actor and moralizing spectator, becomes prey to sentimentalism, laziness, fear. Then in the final pages the "we" become an "I," still a nameless member of the crew but about to become the historical Joseph Conrad who speaks in the last paragraph. "I disengaged myself gently." The act of meditative withdrawal at last becomes complete. Approach and withdrawal, the ebb and flow of a generalizing imagination which cannot leave mere primary experience alone — these are, in any event, the incorrigible necessities of the early Conrad, and they account for some of his loveliest effects.

So we have first of all, reported and meditated, the sea story and memorial realism suggested by the early American title, *The Children of the Sea.* But there is also (and almost from the beginning) the insufferable Negro James Wait. In his own right he is mildly interesting: as a lonely and proud man who is about to die, as an habitual malingerer whose canny deception becomes at last desperate self-deception. But his role in the novel is to provide the second test; or, as Conrad puts it in his American preface, "he is merely the centre of the ship's collective psychology and the pivot of the action." Merely! His role is to provoke that sympathetic identification which is the central chapter of Conrad's psychology, and through it to demonstrate Conrad's conviction that sentimental pity is a form of egoism. In their hidden laziness the members of the crew sympathize with Wait's malingering; later, seeing him die before their eyes, they identify their own chances of survival with his. The process of identification (dramatized with little explanation in *Lord Jim*) is defined explicitly here:

Falsehood triumphed. It triumphed through doubt, through stupidity, through pity, through sentimentalism . . . *The latent egoism of tenderness to suffering appeared in the developing anxiety not to see him die* . . . He was demoralising. Through him we were becoming highly humanised, tender, complex, excessively decadent: we understood the subtlety of his fear, sympathized with all his repulsions, shrinkings, evasions, delusions — as though we had been over-civilised, and rotten, and without any knowledge of the meaning of life.[8]

It could be argued that Conrad recapitulates too obviously, and reiterates rather too often, Wait's demoralizing influence. But the process of irrational identification was little understood by readers in 1897, or in fact by many readers since. It required explication. Thus the sentence I have italicized, almost the central statement of the novel, was omitted in Robert d'Humières' translation.[9] The "egoism of tenderness to suffering" must have struck him as meaningless.

Such, on the "mundane" or naturalistic level of psychology, is the function of Wait; and even the captain is finally corrupted by pity. He pretends to share in Wait's self-deception: "Sorry for him — like you would be for a sick brute . . . I thought I would let him go out in his own way. Kind of impulse." And this moment of pity causes the incipient mutiny. As for the crew, they cared nothing for Wait as a human being, hated him in fact, but had accepted him as a precious token. "We wanted to keep him alive till home — to the end of the voyage." But this is, of course, impossible. James Wait must die in sight of land, as Singleton said, and the *Narcissus* cannot finish her voyage until the body of Wait (like the living bodies of Leggatt and of Jonah) has been deposited into the sea. Then but only then the "ship rolled as if relieved of an unfair burden; the sails flapped." And the ship rushes north before a freshening gale. To the personal and psychological-naturalistic burden of Wait is added — almost "unfairly" for a story of little more than 50,000 words — the burden of an audacious symbolic pattern. In certain early pages Wait is A Death, and a test of responses to death. But ultimately he is written in larger terms: *as something the ship and the men must be rid of before they can complete their voyage.* What this something is — more specific than a "blackness" — is likely to vary with each new reader. But its presence as part of the wavering mobile, as a force the story must allow for, raises crucial questions of technique.

Conrad's task, briefly, was to respect both flesh ("A negro in a British forecastle is a lonely being")[10] and symbol; to convey a vivid black human presence which could yet take on the largest meanings; which could become, as in Melville, "the Negro." Conrad faces the double challenge with the moment Wait steps on board, calling out that name which is mistaken for an impertinent command, "Wait!" Whether or not Vernon Young is right in detecting a play on the word (Wait: weight, burden), symbolic potentialities exist from the start. As we shall first see of Leggatt only a headless corpse floating in the water, so here we see only a body. "His head was away up in the shadows." And — cool, towering, superb — the Nigger speaks the words which, in a true morality, a symbolic force might speak: "I belong to the ship." But what saves the scene (what prevents the reader from detecting larger meanings too soon) is its concrete reality. The ambiguous arrival at once provokes action and talk, a dramatic interchange. And when it is over the magnitude of the Nigger is firmly established. We are able to accept that first "cough metallic, hollow, and tremendously loud," resounding "like two explosions in a vault."

I would insist, in other words, that Old Ben is also a real bear, and Babo a fleshly slave, and Moby Dick a real whale, and James Wait (though his name was "all a smudge" on the ship's list) a proud consumptive Negro. It is truly the critic's function to suggest potentialities and even whole areas of discourse that a hasty reading might overlook. But the natural impulse to find single meanings, and so convert symbolism into allegory, must be resisted. James's classic comment on "The Turn of the Screw" is relevant here: "Only make the reader's general vision of evil intense enough, I said to myself — and that already is a charming job — and his own experience, his own imagination, his own sympathy (with the children) and horror (of their false friends) will supply him quite sufficiently with all the particulars. Make him *think* the evil, make him think it for himself, and you are released from weak specifications." [11] Or, as Robert Penn Warren remarks, every man has shot his own special albatross.

I am willing with Vernon Young to accept that Wait suggests the subconscious, the instinctual, the regressive; or, with Morton D. Zabel, to see him as the secret sharer and "man all men must finally know"; or, with Belfast more curtly, to know that Satan is abroad. This is neither evasion nor a defense of solipsism, I trust, but mere insistence that no rich work of art and no complex human experience has a single meaning. Wait is, let us say, a force; an *X*. But it is his role to elicit certain responses from the crew, and, through them, from the reader.

Thus our task is not to discover what Wait precisely "means" but to observe a human relationship. And the clue to any larger meanings must be found, I think, in the pattern of Wait's presences and absences. He is virtually forgotten (after that first dramatic appearance) while the men get to know each other and the voyage begins; he is something they are too busy to be concerned with. We return to him only when they have little work to do; when "the cleared decks had a reposeful aspect, resembling the autumn of the earth" and the soft breeze is "like an indulgent caress." And he is literally forgotten (by crew as well as reader) during the worst of the storm. After he is rescued, he is again neglected for some thirty pages, and returns only with the sinister calm of a hot night and beshrouded ocean. In the two major instances, the lazy Donkin is the agent who takes us back to him, the Mephistopheles for this Satan. The menace of Wait is greatest when men have time to meditate. Thus Conrad's practical ethic of a master-mariner (seamen must be kept busy) may not be so very different from the ethic of the stoic pessimist who wrote psychological novels. The soul left to its own devices scarcely bears examination, though examine it we must.

The pages of Wait's rescue (63–73) are central, and manage brilliantly their double allegiance to the real and to the symbolic. Here more than anywhere else, even on a quite naturalistic level, the two sides of the seamen coexist, the heroic and the loathsome. "Indignation and doubt grappled within us in a scuffle that trampled upon our finest feelings."

They risk their lives unquestioningly to rescue a trapped "chum." Yet these men scrambling in the carpenter's shop, tearing at the planks of the bulkhead "with the eagerness of men trying to get at a mortal enemy," are compulsive, crazed, and full of hatred for the man they are trying to save. "A rage to fling things overboard possessed us." The entire scene is written with vividness and intensity: the hazardous progress over the half-submerged deck, the descent into the shop with its layer of nails "more inabordable than a hedgehog," the smashing of the bulkhead and tearing out of Wait, the slow return to a relative safety. Everything is as real and as substantial as that sharp adze sticking up with a shining edge from the clutter of saws, chisels, wire rods, axes, crowbars. At a first experiencing the scene may seem merely to dramatize the novel's stated psychology: these men have irrationally identified their own survival with Wait's and are therefore compelled to rescue him. Ironically, they risk their lives to save a man who has already damaged their fellowship, and who will damage it again.

But the exciting real scene seems to say more than this. And in fact it is doing an important preparatory work, in those fringes of the reader's consciousness, for Wait's burial and for the immediate responding wind which at last defines him as "symbol." On later readings (and we must never forget that every complex novel becomes a different one on later readings) the resonance of these pages is deeper, more puzzling, more sinister. We observe that the men remember the trapped Wait only when the gale is ending, and they are free at last to return to their normal desires. Thereupon they rush to extricate what has been locked away. The actual rescue is presented as a difficult childbirth: the exploratory tappings and faint response; Wait crouched behind the bulkhead and beating with his fists; the head thrust at a tiny hole, then stuck between splitting planks; the "blooming short wool" that eludes Belfast's grasp, and at last the stuffed black doll emerging, "mute as a fish" before emitting its first reproach. At least we can say, roughly, that the men have assisted at the rebirth of evil on the ship.

It may well be that Conrad intended only this (and conceivably less), or to insist again that men are accomplices in their own ruin. But the larger terms and very geography of the scene suggest rather a compulsive effort to descend beneath full consciousness to something "lower." The men let themselves fall heavily and sprawl in a corridor where all doors have become trap doors; they look down into the carpenter's shop devastated as by an earthquake. And beyond its chaos (beneath all the tools, nails, and other instruments of human reason they *must* fling overboard) lies the solid bulkhead dividing them from Wait.* The imagery of this solid barrier between the conscious and the unconscious may seem rather Victorian. But the Jungians too tell us that the unconscious is not easily accessible. In such terms the carpenter's shop would suggest the messy preconscious, with Wait trapped in the deeper lying unconcious.

This is plausible enough, but does not account for the curious primitive figure of Wamibo glaring above them: "all shining eyes, gleaming fangs, tumbled hair; resembling an amazed and half-witted fiend gloating over the extraordinary agitation of the damned." Wamibo could, if we wished, take his obvious place in the Freudian triad (as savage super ego) — which would convert Wait into the id and the whole area (carpenter's shop and cabin) into all that lies below full consciousness. But such literalism of reading, of psychic geography, is not very rewarding. It could as usefully be argued that Wamibo is the primitive figure who must be present and involved in any attempt to reach a figure still more primitive, as the half-savage Sam Fathers and half-savage Lion must be present at the death of Old Ben. Is it not more profitable to say, very generally, that the scene powerfully

* "Then the mariners were afraid, and cried every man unto his god, and cast forth the wares that were in the ship into the sea, to lighten it of them. But Jonah was gone down into the sides of the ship; and he lay, and was fast asleep" (Jonah 1:5). It is Jonah who must be cast out. But he has *already* had an experience of descent: "The waters compassed me about, even to the soul: the depth closed me round about, the weeds were wrapped about my head. I went down to the bottom of the mountains; the earth was about me for ever: yet hast thou brought my life from corruption, O Lord my God" (2:5, 6).

dramatizes the compulsive psychic descent of "Heart of Darkness" and "The Secret Sharer"? In any event the men emerge as from such an experience. "The return on the poop was like the return of wanderers after many years amongst people marked by the desolation of time." (As for the rescued Wait, he presents the same contradictions as the rescued Kurtz. Wait locked in his cabin and the Kurtz of unspeakable lusts and rites suggest evil as savage energy. But the rescued Wait and the rescued Kurtz are "hollow men," closer to the Thomist conception of evil as vacancy.)*

So the night journey into self is, I think, one of the experiences this scene is likely to evoke, even for readers who do not recognize it conceptually as such. But it may evoke further and different responses. It is so with any true rendering of any large human situation, be it outward or inward; life never means one thing. What I want to emphasize is not the scene's structuring of abstract or psychic meaning only, but its masterful interpenetration of the realistic and symbolist modes. Its strangeness and audacity (together with its actuality) prepare us for the symbolic burial which is the climax of the novel.

"We fastened up James Wait in a safe place." It is time to return to technical matters, and specifically to the art of modulation that was one of Conrad's strengths.

The ambiguous episode of a suspect heroism is over, Wait is again forgotten, and the chapter returns to its record of a genuine not specious courage. The impression left by the

* One is reminded of the surrealist disorder of the cuddy on the *San Domenick,* where Babo shaves Don Benito: the room an effective image of the unconscious, whatever Melville intended. And, more distantly, of Isaac McCaslin's discarding of gun, watch, compass (comparable to the tools thrown overboard) as he moves toward his archetypal confrontation of the unconscious and primitive. To the few intentionalists who may have consented to read this far: a great intuitive novelist is by definition capable of dramatizing the descent into the unconscious with some "geographical" accuracy, and even without realizing precisely what he is doing. If he is capable of dreaming powerfully he will dream what exists (the "furniture" of the mind) as he will dream archetypal stories. The more he realizes what he is doing, in fact, the greater becomes the temptation to mechanical explanation and rigid consistency to received theory.

storm test must finally be affirmative, and we move toward that impression at once. Podmore madly offers to make hot coffee; and succeeds. "As long as she swims I will cook." And already the *Narcissus* herself has shown a tendency to stand up a little more. In the final pages of the third chapter the white virginal ship with her one known weakness is the human protagonist exerting a puny stubborn will; old Singleton is the indestructible machine. But the ship's heroism rubs off on the men. Captain Allistoun gives the command to "wear ship," the men do their work, but their eyes and ours are fixed on the wounded, still-living *Narcissus*. "Suddenly a small white piece of canvas fluttered amongst them, grew larger, beating." The ship makes several distinct attempts to stand up, goes off as though "weary and disheartened," but at last with an unexpected jerk and violent swing to windward throws off her immense load of water. And now she runs "disheveled" and "as if fleeing for her life," spouting streams of water through her wounds, her torn canvas and broken gear streaming "like wisps of hair." The chapter ends with old Singleton still at the wheel after thirty hours, his white beard tucked under his coat. "In front of his erect figure only the two arms moved crosswise with a swift and sudden readiness, to check or urge again the rapid stir of circling spokes. He steered with care."

This is the end of the first great test. But this is also and only, and almost exactly, the middle of the novel. These men united by crisis must return again to the egoism of their several lives, and hence face again that other test of their selfish allegiance to Wait. The return to Wait (i.e., to the Wait theme) posed one of the sharpest of the novel's many tactical problems: how to modulate downward from the heroic to the everyday, then upward again to the symbolic death and burial. Such "modulations" (for they are much more than transitions) take us close to Conrad's technical art at its best; they show an exceptional sense of how language can manipulate the reader's sensibility.

The end of the storm was grand enough to break such a novel in two. What sentence, to be precise, what particular level of language could succeed such a stroke as "He steered with care"? In *Typhoon* Conrad solves, with one laconic sentence, the whole problem of transition: "He was spared that annoyance." In *Lord Jim* we are told, a little more evasively, "These sleeping pilgrims were destined to accomplish their whole pilgrimage to the bitterness of some other end." The one fact to be communicated is that the ships did not sink; that these men were reprieved. But in *The Nigger of the "Narcissus"* the reader's feelings and beyond them his attitude toward the crew must be handled with extreme care.

Here is the way it is done. I submit the paragraph not as an example of supreme prose but rather to suggest that Conrad's evasiveness and difficulty, his grandiloquence even, may serve at times a dramatic end and solve a tactical problem:

> On men reprieved by its disdainful mercy, the immortal sea confers in its justice the full privilege of desired unrest. Through the perfect wisdom of its grace they are not permitted to meditate at ease upon the complicated and acrid savour of existence, *lest they should remember and, perchance, regret the reward of a cup of inspiriting bitterness, tasted so often, and so often withdrawn from before their stiffening but reluctant lips.* They must without pause justify their life to the eternal pity that commands toil to be hard and unceasing, from sunrise to sunset, from sunset to sunrise; till the weary succession of nights and days tainted by the obstinate clamour of sages, demanding bliss and an empty heaven, is redeemed at last by the vast silence of pain and labour, by the dumb fear and dumb courage of men obscure, forgetful, and enduring.[12]

The paragraph does tell us something: these men were reprieved, and had no chance to rest from their labors. Everything else might seem to belong to that rhythmed and global moralizing that enrages certain lovers of the plain style. And in fact the lines I have italicized do border on double talk. Is the "cup of inspiriting bitterness" life itself? And if so, how can it be withdrawn "so often"? We seem to have a passage as suspect, logically, as the famous one on the "destructive element." And even Conrad must have come to wonder what these lines meant, for he removed them from the definitive edition.

The rest of the paragraph offers, most obviously, its dignity of tone. We move from the elevation of Singleton steering with care to the austere elevation of a narrator's statement on man and destiny, before returning to the drenched decks and exhausted swearing crew. But the language is more highly charged than it might seem at a first glance. The double metaphor (*sea–indifferent justice–God*) is obvious enough, underlined as it is by so much irony: *reprieved, disdainful mercy, immortal, in its justice, the perfect wisdom, grace, justify, the eternal pity, commands toil to be hard, redeemed.* The paragraph expresses an ultimate skepticism; or, a conviction that man's dignity lies in his courage, labor and endurance. But the particular Conradian difficulty (or "tension") comes from the suddenness of the narrator's subversive intrusions. Thus the men desire life; it is the narrator who reminds us that life is unrest. And the sages who tarnish man's dignity by their references to an afterlife demand only the bliss of heaven. It is the narrator who remarks (a parenthesis within a parenthesis) that this heaven is empty. There is much more to say about the passage, and it would be interesting to know whether such flowing rhythms do not carry most readers, unnoticing, past these ironies. In general, however: not merely the austerity of tone and dignity of rhythm but the very difficulty of the language help to manipulate the reader's feelings, chill them even, in a way quite necessary at this point in the story.

This fine management of the reader through tone, style, and structure is the largest achievement, in 1897, of Conrad's technique. It would require a comment as long as Conrad's fourth chapter to describe and analyze the tact with which it leads us through the hard work of the storm's aftermath, through the desolation of the forecastle, through Singleton's physical collapse and also his collapse into skepticism, through Donkin's mutinous talk — back to Wait's cabin as the source of contagion. "The little place, repainted white, had, in the night, the brilliance of a silver shrine where a black idol, reclining stiffly under a blanket, blinked its weary eyes and received our homage. Donkin officiated." Only through many careful modulations (the gray human mixture a little darker after each) can we be made to accept the fact that such a brave crew would be capable of mutiny. The chapter is certainly more flawed than any of the others. But the transitional task it had to accomplish, and modulative task, was much the most difficult.

"A heavy atmosphere of oppressive quietude pervaded the ship." Thus begins the fifth and last chapter. The threat of mutiny has been broken; we are nearing the end of the voyage; ultimate meanings must be achieved now or not at all; and James Wait must die. Like Melville in *Benito Cereno* Conrad has prepared us early in the story for the themes of ambiguity and death by mortuary images:

> Over the white rims of berths stuck out heads with blinking eyes; but the bodies were lost in the gloom of those places, that resembled narrow niches for coffins in a whitewashed and lighted mortuary.

> The double row of berths yawned black, like graves tenanted by uneasy corpses.

> And alone in the dim emptiness of the sleeping forecastle he appeared bigger, colossal, very old; old as Father Time himself, who should have come there into this place as quiet as a sepulchre to contemplate with patient eyes the short victory of sleep, the consoler.[13]

Beyond this Conrad has more than once asked us to regard the ship as a microcosm, and (in the rescue scene) has appealed darkly to the fringes of consciousness. But the hardest task remains, and this is to bring the symbolic possibilities of the ship and of Wait into full awareness. To put matters crudely: we must be directly prepared for the occult circumstance of a wind rising the moment Wait's body reaches the sea.

Singleton's prediction — his Ancient Mariner's knowledge that "Jimmy was the cause of the head winds" and must die in the first sight of land — accomplishes something. But the somber rhythms and Coleridgean distracted movement of the ship accomplish more. And there is at last the critical moment itself, a moment requiring audacity. How convince the reader that *anything* can happen on this more than ordinary ship? One way would be to use such words as "illusive," or frankly to say that nothing in the ship is "real." But more than flat statement is required to make us accept Coleridge's phantom ship. One could further suggest death through allusions to the moon, or *evoke a magic ship and transnatural night by imposing images of snow and cold and ice upon a hot night.* One could, indeed, appeal to the reader's recollection of *The Ancient Mariner.* And all this occurs, is done, in the last modulative paragraph:

> On clear evenings the silent ship, under the cold sheen of the dead moon, took on a false aspect of passionless repose resembling the winter of the earth. Under her a long band of gold barred the black disc of the sea. Footsteps echoed on her quiet decks. The moonlight clung to her like a frosted mist, and the white sails stood out in dazzling cones as of stainless snow. In the magnificence of the phantom rays the ship appeared pure like a vision of ideal beauty, illusive like a tender dream of serene peace. And nothing in her was real, nothing was distinct and solid but the heavy shadows that filled her decks with their unceasing and noiseless stir: the shadows darker than the night and more restless than the thoughts of men.
>
> Donkin prowled spiteful and alone amongst the shadows, thinking that Jimmy too long delayed to die. That evening land had been reported from aloft . . .[14]

These are matters of style: style as temperament, style as meaning, style as suasion and manipulation of the reader. And in *The Nigger of the "Narcissus"* we are watching the formation of a great style in which meditation becomes dramatic. We are dealing with a temperament chronically addicted to approach and withdrawal, and which can make the very ebb and flow of generalizing intellect an element of suspense. Thus a scene of action may be suddenly broken off and the reader alienated, *removed,* by the act of meditative withdrawal. And this removal intensifies the drama:

He shrieked in the deepening gloom, he blubbered and sobbed, screaming: " 'It 'im! 'It 'im!" *The rage and fear of his disregarded right to live tried the steadfastness of hearts more than the menacing shadows of the night that advanced through the unceasing clamour of the gale.* From aft Mr. Baker was heard: — "Is one of you men going to stop him — must I come along?" "Shut up!" . . . "Keep quiet!" cried various voices, exasperated, trembling with cold.[15]

This sudden deliberate distancing of narrator and reader will give *Lord Jim* and *Nostromo* some of their richest effects.

The writing of *The Nigger of the "Narcissus"* remains uneven, though vastly superior to that of the earlier stories. But the Conradian richness, it must be admitted again, is built out of initial excess. "The Lagoon" and its parody have shown us what Conradese could be, with its pervasive melodrama of language and landscape and its monotonies of sentence structure. The most monotonous paragraph in *The Nigger of the "Narcissus"* occurs in the first chapter, before the narrator has begun to speak in his own right and voice. We have instead a writer methodically blocking out and methodically enriching a static scene and mood. The passage suggests some of the indulgences which could, chastened, become strengths:

Outside the glare of the steaming forecastle the serene purity of the night enveloped the seamen with its soothing breath, with its tepid breath flowing under the stars that hung countless above the mastheads in a thin cloud of luminous dust. On the town side the blackness of the water was streaked with trails of light which undulated gently on slight ripples, *similar to* filaments that float rooted to the shore. Rows of other lights stood away in straight lines *as if* drawn up on parade between towering buildings; but on the other side of the harbour sombre hills arched high their black spines, on which, here and there, the point of a star *resembled* a spark fallen from the sky. Far off, Byculla way, the electric lamps at the dock gates shone on the end of lofty standards with a glow blinding and frigid *like* captive ghosts of some evil moons. Scattered all over the dark polish of the roadstead, the ships at anchor floated in perfect stillness under the feeble gleam of their riding-lights, looming up, opaque and bulky, *like* strange and monumental structures abandoned by men to an everlasting repose.[16]

The paragraph is unmistakably Conradian, and has its genuine felicities; the rhythm of any one of the overextended periods is lovely. But the passage fails by attempting too many felicities; analogy becomes a weary obligation, to be met once or twice each sentence. And yet, the captive ghosts and monumental abandoned structures operate in a characteristic manner: taking the reader on far meditative journeys from their banal tenors, to "evil moons" and "everlasting repose." We are invited to dream and are being imposed upon by a temperament. A doubtful procedure, if the object is to clarify the tenor. But that is not Conrad's object, which is to create a tone and bemusing impression. Far more conducive to monotony are certain repetitions: the regular assignment of one adjective and one only to approximately half the nouns (the French "glow blinding and frigid" comes as a relief); the almost identical length of the first three flowing periods and of the second, fourth, and fifth sentences; and the predictable positioning of the subject in four sentences out of the five. This is, one detects, the prose of a writer even more devoted to cadence than to evil moons; who must (for the moment) externalize rhythms rather than visions; who enjoys expending to its fullest each long drawn-in breath. The first sentence is in fact the most Conradian of all, since it pushes past no less than five natural stopping-places. The style (as in certain other novels the plot and over-all structure) refuses the reader's reasonable expectations, and hence — if it does not merely lull — excites a certain strain. This impulse to frustrate the reader's ear will presently, and even in this novel, produce great prose.

Another reader, less conscious of rhythms, would be irritated by the fact that the night's purity is "serene" and repose "everlasting." Let us acknowledge at once that Conrad, early or late, could stock a sizable dictionary of bromidic clichés. Another way to put it is that some of his best pages are built with exceedingly obvious blocks. Most readers would agree (unless they are compiling dictionaries) that the first five pages of the second chapter, the sailing of the *Narcissus* and its first days at sea, are successful. But if one is compiling a dictionary! The water sparkles *like* a floor of jewels, and is as empty *as* the sky; the upper canvas *resembles* small white clouds; the tug *resembles* a black beetle (this analogy extended for twelve lines), a ship on the horizon lingers and hovers *like* an illusion; stars people the emptiness of the sky, are *as if* alive, are *more intense than* the eyes of a staring crowd, and *as inscrutable as* the souls of men; the ship is a microcosm of the earth (extended for a full paragraph) and is a high and lonely pyramid; the days are *like* flashes of a lighthouse and the nights *resemble* fleeting dreams; the Captain is "such *as* a phantom above a grave," his nightshirt flutters *like* a flag; and his gray eyes are still and cold *like* the loom of ice. He seldom descends from the Olympian heights of his poop.

How does Conrad get away with so much obviousness, as by and large he does? For one thing, the elaborate rhythms are both more varied and more "spoken" than in the first chapter, and this emerging meditative voice gives us, along the way, a good deal of authenticating nautical detail. Further, some of these analogies work visually and morally at the same time. The high and lonely pyramid is also lovely: "gliding, all shining and white, through the sunlit mist." But the tug, stained by land and steam, leaves a memorable round black patch of soot on the water, "an unclean mark of the creature's rest." The analogies taken together have begun to establish two of the novel's secondary meanings: its contrast between life at sea and life on land, its contrast between sail and steam. And even the captain as a phantom above a grave has its place in a novel depending upon much mortuary imagery to prepare us for the occult death of Wait. As for the studied and Victorian analogy of the ship and the earth, it can well be argued that Conrad should have permitted the reader so to generalize his ship. But we would be the poorer if we censored all Conrad's deeply meant skeptic's comments on our human lot. "The august loneliness of her path lent dignity to the sordid inspiration of her pilgrimage." We would be the poorer without that sentence and its several considered judgments.

In the best pages of *The Nigger of the "Narcissus,"* the storm action in Chapter III, the elaborate prose conveys action, motion, as well as a trembling and menaced beauty of sound.* But some of the striking Conradian effects are based on insistences which turn out to be obvious, and on a certain lack of inhibition. In context the docking of the *Narcissus* is very moving. It sums up the differences of sea and land, high endeavor and commerce, the beautiful and the sordid; it is the violation of the virgin by the soiled and practical; it brings the great adventure to an end. Only by underlining our text do we discover how obvious the insistences have been, in this devaluation of the land: "the steaming brows of millions of men," "drifts of smoky vapours," "an immense and lamentable murmur," "the anxious earth," "the shadows deepened," "barges drifted stealthily on the murky stream," "begrimed walls," "a vision of disaster," "a mysterious and unholy spell," and — horror of horrors in this story of masculine integrity and weakness — "two bareheaded women." "The *Narcissus* came gently into her berth; the shadows of soulless walls fell upon her, the dust of all the continents leaped upon her deck, and a swarm of strange men, clambering up her sides, took possession of her in the name of the sordid earth. She had ceased to live."

"My Lord in his discourse discovered a great deal of love to this ship." Conrad began with the ship, and it is with the *Narcissus* that the critic is well advised to end. And not only because the sea story as sea story is one of the greatest

* Consider the imitative rhythms of these lines, and the dramatic change of the sentence from passive to active force, ending in a dying close: "The hard gust of wind came brutal like the blow of a fist. The ship relieved of her canvas in time received it pluckily: she yielded reluctantly to the violent onset; then, coming up with a stately and irresistible motion, brought her spars to windward in the teeth of a screeching squall. Out of the abysmal darkness of the black cloud overhead white hail streamed on her, rattled on the rigging, leaped in handfuls off the yards, rebounded on the deck — round and gleaming in the murky turmoil like a shower of pearls. It passed away" (p. 53).

in English fiction. For the ship reminds us of the novel's overall structural problem, which I have neglected to discuss. This structural problem, and even Conrad's solution of it, can be simply stated. It is only in the doing, only in the demands for sensitive modulation made by every paragraph, that such matters become truly difficult! The problem was simply to avoid writing two distinct short novels, one optimistic and the other pessimistic. The two tests and two impressions of human nature must not be allowed to cancel out; we must forget neither the men's sentimentality and egoism nor their heroic endurance; at the last, the dark knot of seamen must drift in sunshine.

Conrad's tact becomes evident once we conceive any other structure than the one he actually presents. Had the near-mutiny and Wait's death occurred before the storm, we would have had the two short novels, and been left with a more affirmative statement than Conrad wanted to make. Had Wait's demoralizing effect begun only after the storm, we would have been left with no affirmation at all. The first necessity, then, was to introduce the Wait-story (tentatively, on the whole realistically) before the storm, return to it briefly during the storm, but give it major symbolic import only afterward. We are introduced to dim potentialities of anarchy and fear before knowing, through much of the third chapter, a magnificent courage and endurance. So much is simple indeed, in the describing. But having the near-mutiny and symbolic death occur after the storm still threatened, of course, to leave an impression essentially negative and, it may be, excessively symbolic. What is to remind us, after Wait's burial, that these men were also, had also been, true extrovert children of the sea? How could the story redress its balance? The obvious answer would be to show them reacting heroically to another great storm. But this too would have left an imbalance, and invited further circular movements.

What Conrad does, instead, is to give up any close view of the men; to focus attention on the ship rather than on them; to make *her* swift homeward progress heroic; to distance the reader from human perils either outward or inward and so confer on the crew, by association, some of the ship's glamour. The individuals on board give way to the ship as microcosm and finally to the ship as ship. Thus the object that unifies the two stories is not really an object at all, but the white female ship, which had left the stained land and now returns to it. What connects nearly every page is the *Narcissus* herself. At the very end the seamen are revalued by our distaste for the children of commerce, who can dismiss Singleton as a disgusting old brute; and the *Narcissus* is consecrated by the land that stains her. Crew and ship become part of history:

The dark knot of seamen drifted in sunshine. To the left of them the trees in Tower Gardens sighed, the stones of the Tower gleaming, seemed to stir in the play of light, as if remembering suddenly all the great joys and sorrows of the past, the fighting prototypes of these men; press-gangs; mutinous cries; the wailing of women by the riverside, and the shouts of men welcoming victories. The sunshine of heaven fell like a gift of grace on the mud of the earth, on the remembering and mute stones, on greed, selfishness; on the anxious faces of forgetful men. And to the right of the dark group the stained front of the Mint, cleansed by the flood of light, stood out for a moment dazzling and white like a marble palace in a fairy tale. The crew of the *Narcissus* drifted out of sight.[17]

"I disengaged myself gently." And by the same token the reader disengages himself from an adventure both extraordinary and intimate. There are novels whose endings suggest a continuation of the lives we have watched. But *The Nigger of the "Narcissus"* is a completed experience, recorded of a dead time; the voyage becomes at last the book we have just read.

In mere outline the matter is as simple as that. But there are novelists who in all their calculating careers never achieve such a triumphant simplicity and rightness of structure.

Chapter Four

LORD JIM (I)

LORD JIM is a more ambitious and more vulnerable book: Conrad's first great impressionist novel. We may recognize various anticipations: the involutions of *Our Mutual Friend* and *The Possessed,* the narrator-witnesses and atmospheres of *Wuthering Heights* and *Bleak House,* the minute control of the reader's responses to ambiguity in *Benito Cereno,* even (after all) *Madame Bovary*'s ambivalence. Yet *Lord Jim* is not really like any of these novels, though it is most like *Benito Cereno.* It appears at the turn of the century as the first novel in a new form: a form bent on involving and implicating the reader in a psycho-moral drama which has no easy solution, and bent on engaging his sensibilities more strenuously and even more uncomfortably than ever before. An essential novelty, though borrowed perhaps from the mystery or "police" tale, is to force upon the reader an active, exploratory, organizing role; compel him, almost, to collaborate in the writing of the novel. Ford Madox Ford liked to define the impressionist aim as a higher realism: to come closer to actual life by presenting experience as a sensitive witness would receive it—casually, digressively, without logical order. But the game is a more sinister one than that. We certainly do not receive the facts of Lord Jim's life in the order that a citizen and observer of 1880, say Marlow himself, would have received them. The digressive method does indeed convey the "feel" of life. But the impressionist aim is to achieve a fuller truth than realism can, if necessary by "cheating"; and to create in the reader an intricate play of emotion and a rich conflict of sympathy and judgment, a provisional bafflement in the face of experience which turns out to be more complicated than we ever would have dreamed. This aim is present even in the spare and unintellectual *The Great Gatsby,* certainly in the endless *Remembrance of Things Past,* even (since everything is present there) in *Ulysses.* But the culminating triumph of Conradian impressionism is *Absalom, Absalom!* This austere masterpiece, by complicating each of Conrad's complications, helps us define the earlier experiment. We see the novel developing a musical form. But the main instruments are the reader's mind, feelings, nerves.

"If he keeps on writing the same sort," an early reviewer of *Lord Jim* remarked, "[Conrad] may arrive at the unique distinction of having few readers in his own generation, and a fair chance of several in the next." [1] The impressionist novel, obscuring story, requires a certain magnitude and universality if it is to survive its own difficulty; requires these as a novel say by Trollope does not. *Absalom, Absalom!* is strengthened by its myths of a doomed family and land under a curse, and by the violence of Thomas Sutpen's destructive "innocence." Also: who has not been turned away from a door? And who has not, briefly at least, harbored an obsessive design? The universality of *Lord Jim* is even more obvious, since nearly everyone has jumped off some *Patna* and most of us have been compelled to live on, desperately or quietly engaged in reconciling what we are with what we would like to be. It may be that Jim should have required no more than that thickness of paper between the right and wrong of the affair. Yet he faces "boundary-situations" both on board the *Patna* and in Patusan, and these necessarily involve us. Dorothy Van Ghent argues that the derelict which strikes the *Patna* is an epiphany and manifestation of " 'dark power' . . . coincident with and symbolically identifiable with the impulse that makes Jim jump, an impulse submerged like the wreck, riding in wait, striking from under." [2]

Even more persuasively, she compares Jim with Oedipus, that other man of good intentions. The impulse to discriminate between what we are and what we do, or to dissociate our*selves* from what exists in our unconscious, is a form ancient enough of making excuses. And the experience in Patusan, which to some critics seems irrelevant, corresponds to the fairly common dream of a second chance and total break with the guilty past. "A clean slate, did he say? As if the initial word of each our destiny were not graven in imperishable characters upon the face of a rock." Jim can only go to meet that destiny or await it, since it exists in his temperament; his failure is tragically certain. But he is one of those great fictional characters whose crime, like Michael Henchard's, makes as well as breaks him. A Henchard who did not sell his wife would have been a haytrusser to the end of his days; would have had neither the strength to become mayor of Casterbridge nor the strength to destroy himself so completely. So too Jim, had the *Patna* not struck a derelict, would presumably have drifted through life seeking ever softer and more suspect berths. The first four chapters show him clearly headed down that path, and content to substitute revery for action. It is discomforting but true to say that involuntary crime brings him into the moral universe. At least this: a reader cannot fail to care about a man of good intentions who deserts a supposedly sinking ship, leaving eight hundred persons to die.

A further obvious remark on the humanity of great fictions is worth making, since critics rarely pause to make it: that the Lord Jims and Thomas Sutpens are more interesting and more attractive to us than they would have been had we met them in "real life." In real life (unaware of Sutpen's childhood or of his grand design) we might have shared all Miss Rosa's distaste for the "demon." Certainly we would have been disgusted by the surface personality of this somber and rude man. And in real life we might have felt toward Jim what Marlow professes to feel only once so strongly: "I perceived myself unexpectedly to be thoroughly sick of him. Why these vapourings?" We might dismiss as intolerable this aggressive yet overly sensitive man in his vanity and his clean white shoes, perpetually thrusting on us his introspections and excuses. We would probably not accept him as "one of us." And would we not, in real life, also turn away from the gross vulgarity of Jay Gatsby and his mass of silk shirts, or from the rugged brutality of Michael Henchard, or from the violent tirades of Ahab, or from the posturings of Emma Bovary, or from the lank ugliness and mad loquacity of Don Quixote? Or from Lear, Macbeth, perhaps even Hamlet? Art induces greater sympathies (but also sterner judgments) than most of us are capable of in the daily conduct of our lives; it compels us to live less indifferently, and frees us from the irrelevant. This does not mean that art, cheating us, is untrue to life, but that it asks for an intensified response to something "like life." In fiction we may, for one thing, be more than once spectators of the same event! The spectator in real life of Jim's death would indeed be inhuman who blamed him for his last "proud and unflinching glance," sent right and left after Doramin's shot. But the novel, especially on a rereading, legitimately asks us to decide whether Jim, still "at the call of his exalted egoism," is really in the clear at this moment; whether he is truly redeemed.

Lord Jim rests, then, on the bedrock of a great story and an important human situation;* it has some appeal even for the casual reader who moves through a novel as clumsily as

* A summary is offered for the reader who does not want, still another time, to disentangle the story of *Lord Jim:* The pilgrim-ship *Patna* strikes a derelict or other floating object at night, and her officers (believing she will sink quickly, and knowing there are not lifeboats enough) abandon her, leaving the pilgrims to drown in their sleep. Jim hesitates; and then, in spite of his romantic egoism and pride, impulsively jumps after the others. But the *Patna* does not sink. Marlow meets Jim at the court of inquiry: at this first of Jim's many efforts to rehabilitate himself in his own eyes and in the eyes of the world. He would like it believed that it was not he, the conscious man, who had jumped, yet can endure no reference to the incident. He wanders over the earth, generally eastward, pursued by guilt and shame. Marlow, sympathizing with Jim for various reasons, consults the entomologist and trader Stein, who sends Jim to Patusan—where he will be protected by isolation from the accusing world of white men. There Jim is a successful benevolent despot, and enjoys almost godlike power and prestige. His reign is ended, however, when he refuses to destroy the first intruding whites: "Gentleman" Brown and his villainous pirate crew. The intruders massacre Jim's friends, including the son of the chief, and thereupon he surrenders his own life to the natives in atonement. He goes away from his native mistress Jewel for his pitiless wedding with a shadowy ideal of conduct.

he moves through life. And yet it is, of course, an art novel, a novelist's novel, a critic's novel — perhaps the first important one in England after *Tristram Shandy*. This means that it becomes a different novel if read very attentively; or, becomes a different novel when read a second or third time. The usual Victorian novel surrenders most of its drama and meaning at a first rapid reading and thereafter becomes inert. If we return to *David Copperfield* after a year or twenty years and find it a different book from the one we remembered, this is not because the book has changed. It is we who have changed. But certain novels — *Benito Cereno* as a mild example, *Absalom, Absalom!* as an extreme one, *Lord Jim* somewhere between the two — do change. They do become different novels at a second attentive reading. The mere factual mysteries are solved, and no longer preoccupy us. We now know that Don Benito is not a villain, that Thomas Sutpen is the father of Charles Bon, that the *Patna* did not sink; we cannot twice be made dupes of deceptive appearance to the same degree. But now by the same token we can watch the drama of moral ambiguity as such, and the mechanisms of deception; and can watch the observers or narrators of the action, their mistakes, their withheld or grudging commitments. The human situation becomes more rather than less complex. Yet we are at the same time somewhat freer to observe art as art: the game of management and grouping and perspective. And matters that merely baffled or exasperated at first, notably the "irrelevant" digressions, assume an ironic or clarifying force. Only at a second reading — only, specifically, when we have come to share most of Marlow's knowledge — can we begin fully to share or imagine his feelings: the horror he would have felt, for instance, during his interview with the dying Gentleman Brown. For we know now, as Marlow knew then, that Brown was responsible for the death of Jim, this "younger brother."

The difference is important and even generic: between the complex art novel and the novel that is, rather, a clear orderly imitation of life; between *Lord Jim* and *Middlemarch* or *Barchester Towers*. A great deal of confusion may be traced to the critic's refusal to recognize this difference as generic, and to his tacit assumption that all novels ought to accomplish whatever they are going to accomplish on a first reading. Normally, I should think, the critic ought to be concerned with the impression *Middlemarch* or *Barchester Towers* might make on an ideally alert first reading; neither novel intends a subtle or deceptive relationship with the reader. But the critic of *Lord Jim* and of most impressionist novels ought to be concerned, and ought to admit this frankly, with both first and subsequent readings, and especially with the latter. For the novel of psycho-moral ambiguity can never, reread, be quite the same book.

No amount of casual rereading, to be sure, will discover *Lord Jim*'s full complexity. Isn't this one secret purpose or at least value of Conrad's difficulty, as of Joyce's and Faulkner's: that it makes casual reading less likely? Anyone who truly cares for fiction cares for story, experiences sympathies and repulsions, is interested in places and lives different from his own. We may define a casual reader (and many professional critics are casual readers) as one who cares for little else. And who, above all, identifies very quickly with one of the characters on the basis of the most obvious appeal and thereafter refuses all other appeals. In a word, the reader becomes one of the characters himself; climbs into the book, and, having done so, turns all complex situations into simple ones. It is easy enough to separate the critical from the casual reader of *Lord Jim,* and not merely from that casual reader for the New York Tribune who remarked that "on a night of tropic calm the rotten craft goes to the bottom like a shot, with all hands save a few members of the crew." [3] For the casual reader usually ignores or minimizes the important evidence *against* Lord Jim, is insensitive to ironic overtone and illustrative digression, assumes that Conrad wholly approved of his hero, and is quite certain that Jim "redeemed himself" in Patusan. Thus this casual reader, identifying with Jim so completely, is incapable of responding to the novel's suspended judgments and withheld sympathies; he has committed himself, simply and unequivocally, to a highly equivocal personage. (Very rarely a casual reader is found who goes to the opposite extreme, and develops no sympathy for Jim at all.) So too, since his whole concern is with Jim, the casual reader regards Marlow as no more than an irritating technical device. And he responds not at all to structure and style, to the beauty and meaning inherent in the elaborate ironic play of recurrence and reflexive reference.

But even for a more alert reader, that first reading of *Lord Jim* is very different from a second. Can we remember a genuine first impression, unaffected by our later knowledge of what happened to the *Patna*? The conflict of judgment and sympathy would already exist, but in much simpler terms. Through four chapters we would listen to an omniscient narrator, who gives us a distinctly ironic portrait of Jim: a man of "exquisite sensibility" who has "elected to conceal" some "deplorable faculty"; who as a boy in training dreamed of rescues but did not act when action was demanded, who could yet return at once to his self-deceptive dreams. And presently we see him on board the *Patna,* the chief mate of a steamer, still dreaming of heroic rescues. We then move to the court of inquiry: see Jim's shame and assume there is some reason for this shame. The officers must have deserted a sinking ship. At what point does our hypothetical first reader realize that the ship didn't sink? On page 51 the crazed chief engineer's remark that he saw her go down is referred to as a "stupid lie"; on page 82 Marlow speaks of an "unforseen conclusion of the tale" and on the next page interjects, casually: "So that bulkhead held out after all." On page 97: "These sleeping pilgrims were destined to accomplish their whole pilgrimage to the bitterness of some other end." Conceivably our reader might not know what happened until page 134 ("towed successfully to Aden") or even until the French lieutenant refers very specifically to his own role in the salvage. But meanwhile he has come to sympathize with Jim as a conscientious man on a rack, who stayed to face the inquiry. He is hardly prepared to recognize how damaging it is — the evidence of this French lieutenant who stayed on board the *Patna* thirty hours and who recalls that the unloading of the pilgrims at Aden was accomplished in twenty-five minutes. The sympathetic reader is not likely to remember that Jim stayed on board twenty-seven minutes before jumping. These figures (rather deceptive, since the situations were not comparable and lifeboats were lacking) may have a sharply devaluing effect on later readings.

As with large conceptions, so with fine details of texture: a first valid and interesting effect may, on rereading, be replaced by a very different one. Consider, for instance, the elaborate description of the pilgrims streaming onto the *Patna*:

> They streamed aboard over three gangways, they streamed in urged by faith and the hope of paradise, they streamed in with a continuous tramp and shuffle of bare feet, without a word, a murmur, or a look back; and when clear of confining rails spread on all sides over the deck, flowed forward and aft, overflowed down the yawning hatchways, filled the inner recesses of the ship — like water filling a cistern, like water flowing into crevices and crannies, like water rising silently even with the rim.[4]

At a first reading we watch these ghostly pilgrims with some detachment, though they and the rising water are secretly preparing us for disaster at sea; the tenor is "drowned" by the vehicle. In any event this seems to be a matter concerning only the reader and the narrator, who strikes us as rather literary. We are not particularly conscious of Jim as a possible watcher of the scene. But on a second reading we may see these flowing silent pilgrims and this drowning ship only through his eyes. And now the scene reminds us of something we have come to know fairly well: Jim's faculty of "swift and forestalling vision." It prepares us to accept more fully than before the fact that he will be immobilized by his power to imagine these same pilgrims in panic. Thus what had seemed a rather literary comment by a detached narrator is now, intimately, in character with Jim. He, not the author or narrator, is the dangerously "imaginative beggar."

One further example of reflexive reference will indicate how a second reading differs from a first. In Chapter 26, after a brief introduction of the chief Doramin and his son Dain Waris, Marlow summarizes Jim's account of his already legendary exploit: the capture of Sherif Ali's camp. "He has made himself responsible for success on his own head." Not a very disturbing remark, since we know that he was successful. And the portrait of Doramin may seem merely amusing. He is carried up the hill in his armchair, then sits with a pair of flintlock pistols on his knees. "Magnificent things, ebony, silver-mounted, with beautiful locks and a calibre like an old blunderbuss." They were, Jim adds, a present from Stein, in exchange for the talisman ring. All this may seem unimportant and digressive, no more than the small vivid details that confirm a novel's authority and actualize its scenes. But in fact the passage is dropping its associations — "Upon my head" . . . flintlock pistols . . . talisman ring — into the fringes of our consciousness; it is preparing us to respond to the full significance, a hundred and fifty pages later, of Jim's words, "Upon my head." And above all preparing us to recognize and believe the Doramin of the last pages and those pistols on his knees: the deliberateness of the shooting, and the ironic closing of a circle as the ring rolls against Jim's foot. Thus the first reading. On a second reading of Chapter 26 those pistols reflect a light thrown backward; we respond very strongly to the scene itself and its tragic irony. For it reminds us — at the very moment that we hear about the greatest active success of Jim's life, in fact almost his only active success to reach us dramatically — of how the story will end: with Jim immobilized once more by a dream, and then immobile in death.

The differences between first and second readings are more striking as we look at whole chapters. For with *Lord Jim,* and specifically with the beginning of Marlow's narrative in Chapter 5, Conrad gives truly free play to his temperamental evasiveness, and to his delight in digression and distorted perspective. And now we are exposed to Marlow at his most exasperatingly roundabout: refusing to tell us the few facts we need to know, refusing to stay put in place or time, and offering a complex flow of thought and feeling over a situation of which we know next to nothing. The tactics of this chapter (since it offers the first rich sample of Conradian impressionism) are perhaps worth recording in rough summary form. What happens to the reader, both on first and subsequent readings?

The first three chapters had introduced us to a vulnerable Jim (egoist, dreamer, drifter) and to the vulnerably ancient *Patna* on its errand of faith. The fourth chapter, also conducted by an omniscient author or narrator, takes us to the official inquiry in the police court, and brilliantly evokes the scene, and Jim's "burning cheeks in a cool lofty room." Still, we do not know why he is there. We do not know what they are, these "facts that had surged up all about him to cut him off from the rest of his kind." And this is one reason why Marlow must appear, and why we must have the fiction of after-dinner listeners: the first narrator could not have justified much longer such a refusal to explain. But Marlow has a good reason not to tell his listeners that the *Patna* didn't sink. They would already know this much of the story, though perhaps little more. This is the basic convention of Conradian and Faulknerian impressionism: that the reader (who is merely "listening in") knows as much as the narrator's nominal listeners. But of course he doesn't.

Present time and action, through the main part of Chapter 5, are actually very limited. Marlow sees the four officers of the *Patna* (who still do not know the ship survived, though everyone else in town does) arrive, at the harbor office; he watches the captain of the *Patna* go inside to make his report, while Jim and the others remain outside. Through a window Marlow hears some of the row as Captain Elliot chews up the offender "very small, and—ah! ejected him again." Meanwhile Marlow is distressed to find Jim, whom he is seeing for the first time, look so unconcerned. The enraged captain of the *Patna* talks briefly with Marlow, is about to tell his officers the astounding news, then jumps into a gharry and drives off. He is never seen again. A half-caste clerk appears to take the officers into a kind of custody. That is about all there is to the sequence. But neither the extremely limited amount of action nor the gross improbability (that the *Patna* officers shouldn't have heard) is likely to disturb anyone at a first reading. For this hypothetical reader would be largely unaware of what, physically, is happening, and be totally unaware of the *Patna* circumstance. All the real drama of the chapter is withheld, together with the essential facts. These must be discovered, presumably on a later reading.

But here is the chapter, paragraph by paragraph:

Paragraph 1 (page 34). Marlow introduces himself evasively: an insecure and moralizing person who is subjected to the confidences of men with soft and plague spots. (Carraway's introduction in *The Great Gatsby* derives directly from this.) Marlow refers to a "mangy, native tyke" tripping people up — a tripping which does not occur until page 70 and which leads to a misunderstanding (did Marlow call Jim a "wretched cur"?) not clarified until page 73. At a second reading we pay more attention to Marlow's "confidential information about myself."

Paragraph 2 (page 35). At a first reading, this chiefly serves to establish the setting of Marlow and his listeners: "after a good spread, two hundred feet above the sea-level, with a box of decent cigars handy, on a blessed evening of freshness and starlight . . ." But the scene, especially as we return to it, creates some early sympathy for "Master Jim," who did not enjoy such untempted security.

Paragraph 3 (page 35). The narrative begins, as Marlow refers back (to page 32) and forward (to page 69) to the moment when his eyes and Jim's met in the courtroom. Five or six of the paragraph's thirty-five lines actually give us some information. A "mysterious cable message" from Aden had aroused much attention; it contained an ugly "naked fact." And Marlow sees four men walking toward him along the quay near the harbor office.

Paragraph 4 (page 36). They are, we learn, the officers of the *Patna*. Marlow recollects a meeting with the captain nine months before; and, with diverting vividness, the disgust of the ship chandler De Jongh.

Paragraph 5 (page 37). A striking picture of the fat captain in his soiled sleeping-suit, walking toward the harbor office. At the end of the paragraph a disarmingly subordinate phrase (which I have italicized) gives the reader his only clue to the centrally important fact: the captain does not yet know that the ship he abandoned survived. "On he came in hot haste, without a look right or left, passed within three feet of me, and in *the innocence of his heart* went on pelting upstairs in the harbour office to make his deposition, or report, or whatever you like to call it." Theoretically, we have no chance to understand this phrase on a first reading. Yet it radically affects our ultimate imagining of the whole chapter, and greatly intensifies its drama.

Paragraph 6 (page 37). A digression on Archie Ruthvel's Portuguese half-caste clerk, and his love of perquisites. This is the same clerk who a few minutes (but 95 pages) later will be quoted: informing Jim, and thus the reader, that the *Patna* was towed successfully to Aden.

Paragraph 7 (page 38). At a first reading the paragraph seems to be trivially and gratuitously humorous: as the enormous up-ended captain slides into Ruthvel's office, as we are introduced to old Captain Elliot's bluntness and even to his daughters. There is a row; the captain of the *Patna* is ejected. But the great dramatic moment of the paragraph can be apprehended only if we are fully aware both of the truth and of the captain's ignorance. Startled by Ruthvel's manner, he guesses at the last moment that something is amiss; hangs back and snorts "like a frightened bullock." The outraged confrontation of the two captains is left entirely to the reader. (In the actual *Jeddah* incident, the captain who had salved her "entered the Consulate to report the salving, just as the master of the *Jeddah* was leaving after reporting his vessel lost with all hands.") [5]

Paragraph 8 (page 40). We return to Marlow as witness for a long and important paragraph, but one which is (again) much richer on second or subsequent readings. The captain and his "monstrous bulk" emerge from the harbor office. He does not yet join the three other officers, but instead speaks to Marlow; complains because Captain Elliot had called him a "hound." And Marlow for the first time notices Jim — "as unconcerned and unapproachable as only the young can look" and with "no business to look so sound."

Paragraph 9 (page 42). At a later reading we may discover the dramatic center of the paragraph: that Marlow was waiting "to see the effect of a full information" upon Jim. But this is fairly certain to be lost at first. For the paragraph begins with a vivid report of the captain's fulminations, and ends with a major intellectual and moral utterance: on the menace that lies in wait for all of us, on Jim as "one of us," on courage and "an unthinking and blessed stiffness," on the corroding effect of ideas. We have, in other words, an important and presumably retrospective response to a man just seen for the first time.

Paragraph 10 (page 43). A long digression (deriving from Marlow's feeling that Jim was "one of us") takes us far from the present scene and involves no less than four shifts in time. Marlow speaks of his paternal affection for the young seamen he has turned out, the pleasure of seeing them in later years, and recollects vividly such a youngster going to sea for the first time.

Paragraph 11 (page 45). The digression continues briefly. Then Marlow makes an important comment on Jim: "I would have trusted the deck to that youngster on the strength of a single glance, and gone to sleep with both eyes — and, by Jove! it wouldn't have been safe." Again he is disturbed by Jim's "standing there with his don't-care-hang air."

Paragraph 12 (page 46). The dramatic character of the paragraph is at first concealed by our continuing ignorance of the facts, and later is obscured by the vividness of the captain's grotesque departure. He is on the point of telling his officers that the *Patna* did not sink, then realizes that if he is to escape an inquiry he must do so at once and alone. But none of this is told. We are simply given his appalling act, and "the size of those straining thighs, the immense heaving of that dingy, striped green-and-orange back, the whole burrowing effort of that gaudy and sordid mass." Marlow tells us the captain was never seen again; then returns to record the astonishment of one of the officers left behind.

Paragraph 13 (page 48). An extreme understatement: "All this happened in much less time than it takes to tell." Marlow goes away without waiting to see the end, or to record what might have been the scene's dramatic climax: Jim's first reaction to the news — which, *nota bene,* the reader still cannot, on a first reading, share.

Paragraph 14 (page 48). A long wandering three-page paragraph, which moves from an account of the *Patna's* chief engineer who drank himself into delirium tremens to another major moral utterance by Marlow: on society's dependence on fidelity; on his own longing to overcome his doubt "of the sovereign power enthroned in a fixed standard of conduct"; on the "secret motive" of his prying into Jim's case (that he hoped, for his own sake, "to find some shadow of an excuse for that young fellow I had never seen before"). Then, with our minds entirely diverted onto this moralizing track, we are given, most casually, our first chance to discover the truth about the *Patna.* Marlow refers to the crazed engineer's report that he had seen the ship go down as a "stupid lie."

Paragraph 15 (page 51). A vivid account of the engineer further diverts us from our momentary suspicion.

Paragraph 16 (page 52). Through the engineer's wild tale, now of pink toads, an extraordinarily alert reader might detect certain important fragments of truth. "The ship was full of them, you know, and we had to clear out on the strict Q.T." And, "Bash in the head of the first that stirs. There's too many of them, and she won't swim more than ten minutes."

The chapter, with the very short seventeenth and eighteenth paragraphs, concludes with a resident surgeon of the local hospital commenting briefly on the engineer's case and on his inability to attend the inquiry.

Such, roughly, is the perverse and wandering movement of a chapter that, at a generous estimate, advances our knowledge in less than one line out of ten and that actively deceives us in far more than one out of ten. We can experience its full drama and irony only if we are aware of the difference between reality and the illusion under which the *Patna* officers still live; however, we are bound, through a first reading, to share that illusion almost completely. The experience, through that first reading, must rather be one of exploring and groping in a dense mist, with only the gravity of a guiding voice to sustain us. Through the strange chapter Marlow is creating an impression — and first of all an impression of himself as a man of intense curiosity and intensely conservative ethic, who is in some respect insecure and who likes to speak of "secret motives." At the expense of dramatic obfuscation he is establishing a serious atmosphere. He is also, through the vividness and ease of his digressions, thoroughly etablishing his authority as someone who knows very well this Eastern world.

Yet the critic hostile to Marlow might point to this chapter as a useful exhibit of an alleged pervasive fault: that Marlow and hence Conrad make a great deal out of nothing. For the Jim who immediately provoked such a strong emotional and moral response in Marlow has done nothing, through Chapter 5, except stand in the street looking unconcerned. For the moment he is nothing, or nothing but his plight. The common impression received on a first reading of the whole novel (that Jim is an exceedingly complicated person) has in fact much excuse but little solid foundation. Conrad is closer to the truth in his Author's Note when he refers to Jim as "a simple and sensitive character." So too is Marlow when he says that Jim "complicated matters by being so simple." Simple he is, in the strength and pertinacity of his several urgent longings — as simple, or almost so, as Henchard, as Gatsby, as Sutpen. In fact not very much may seem left of Jim, after we have discounted Marlow's partialities and distortions. He is a rather adolescent dreamer and "romantic" with a strong ego-ideal, who prefers solitary reveries of heroism to the shock and bustle of active life. Hence he is lazy and a poor seaman. (The sea's only reward, perfect love of the work, "eluded him"; he chose the easier way of service with Eastern owners and native crews.) He has a strong visual imagination and vividly foresees the worst; this faculty, combined with other temperamental traits, tends to immobilize him in crisis. He seems radically incapable of acting properly at the important junctures of his life. Sometimes he cannot act at all. He differs from other introverted dreamers chiefly in the degree of his Bovaryism; he can literally confuse reality and dream at times, and so can hardly believe his own disreputable acts. But, precisely because the jump from the *Patna* so offends his dream of self, he enters into active if self-destructive life. He tries to live his dream. So too, though living in the dreamer's natural isolation, he wants the confirmation of other men's admiration and love and at the least needs one man (Marlow) who will believe in him. Shock, shame, or guilt, the loyalty of Marlow, the challenging opportunity of Patusan — these very nearly carry him out of his dreaming solitude and mist of self-deception. Yet in Patusan, as the dream gets some encouragement from life, revery and reality interfuse more than ever. Thus Jim can come to half-believe in the supernatural power with which local legend has endowed him.

There is a little more to Jim than this unsympathetic outline suggests. But there is nothing radically abnormal or obscure in his "acute consciousness" of lost honor, nor even in the durability of his romantic egoism and the magnitude of his self-deceptions. Our sense of depth comes rather from the complexity of Marlow's spiraling response to this not abnormal man, who is "one of us." It comes partly too from Marlow's long deceptive insistence on Jim's "truth" and "constancy": deceptive, since they turn out to be a truth and constancy to the exalted egoism rather than to Marlow's own strong sense of community obligation. And our sense of depth comes also from the paradoxical nature of Marlow's psychologizing. For Marlow insists on the "mysterious" or "inscrutable" side of Jim only when speaking of matters that are familiar enough to all of us (though they may indeed be "mysteries"): the selfish potentialities of idealism or the saving potentialities of egoism, the human capacity for evasion and self-deception, and so forth. (Unquestionably too he interjects these comments on the mysterious and the inscrutable for the dramatic purpose of disengaging the reader from present action or scene, of controlling distance and perspective.) But Marlow does not comment, or comments very little, on the occasions when Jim's actions are truly complex or truly enigmatic. Here the healthy novelistic impulse — to dramatize rather than explain important psychological insights — nearly always prevails.

Not all of Marlow's moralizing and psychologizing interruptions can be defended. There are too many of them. And the ambiguous presentation of Stein (himself so ambiguous as to be very commonly misunderstood) probably points to a major and sentimental uncertainty in the author. With these reservations, we may defend Marlow's rhetoric by pointing out that he talks more often about moral than about psychological problems, and more about our relationship to Jim and his problems than about a fixed state of soul or fixed state of mind. *Lord Jim* is a novel of intellectual and moral suspense, and the mystery to be solved, or conclusion to be reached, lies not in Jim but in ourselves. Can we, faced by the ambiguities and deceptions of life itself (and more!), apprehend the whole experience humanly? Can we come to recognize the full complexity of any simple case, and respond both sympathetically and morally to Jim and his version of "how to be"? The reader, in a sense — and how true this will be of *Absalom, Absalom!* — turns out to be the hero of the novel, either succeeding or failing in his human task of achieving a balanced view.

The "simple" Jim provokes then, within the largest question of whether he is "in the clear," certain basic questions of moral response:

1. *Guilt and disgrace: the moral character of the psychomachia.* "I don't mean to say that I regret my action," Marlow remarks, "nor will I pretend that I can't sleep o'nights in consequence; still the idea obtrudes itself that he made so much of his disgrace while it is the guilt alone that matters." To what extent does Jim see his jump from the *Patna* as a

crime to be atoned for, to what extent as an "opportunity missed"? To what extent is "facing the music" (and the inquiry) a moral act, and to what extent an act of pride? And how pejorative or favorable a construction are we to give to the word *romantic* in "the reproach of his romantic conscience"?

2. *Is self-destructive behavior moral, and courageous?* Marlow raises these questions in connection with Jim's sudden departures from his jobs when reminded of the *Patna*. "Obviously Jim was not of the winking sort; but what I could never make up my mind about was whether his line of conduct amounted to shirking his ghost or to facing him out . . . It might have been flight and it might have been a mode of combat." Does Jim achieve the stature of a Henchard, who feels morally obligated to punish himself yet also obligated to resist merely compulsive self-punishment? Or, as the question is put by "The Secret Sharer" — how shall we weigh and distinguish between the moral act of self-repudiation and the manly act of wanting redemption through action?: "No! the proper thing was to face it out — alone for myself — wait for another chance — find out . . ." Thus Jim, who like any human being in crisis can contradict himself from moment to moment. He can move without pause from honest recognition to self-deception and back. He debates the moral value of suicide. He had considered it, when in the narrow company of the other deserters:

"I am — I am not afraid to tell. And I wasn't afraid to think either. I looked it in the face. I wasn't going to run away. At first — at night, if it hadn't been for these fellows I might have . . . No! by heavens! I was not going to give them that satisfaction. They had done enough. They made up a story, and believed it for all I know. But I knew the truth, and I would live it down — alone, with myself. I wasn't going to give in to such a beastly unfair thing. What did it prove after all? I was confoundedly cut up. Sick of life — to tell you the truth; but what would have been the good to shirk it — in — in — that way? That was not the way. I believe — I believe it would have — it would have ended — nothing." [6]

3. *Does Jim redeem himself in Patusan?* He wins the confidence and love of the natives, and (temporarily) brings them order and justice. But Marlow realizes he has not escaped the egoism and pride which menaced him from the start:

"He had to give in to my arguments, because all his conquests, the trust, the fame, the friendships, the love — all these things that made him master had made him a captive, too. He looked with an owner's eye at the peace of the evening, at the river, at the houses, at the everlasting life of the forests, at the life of the old mankind, at the secrets of the land, at the pride of his own heart: but it was they that possessed him and made him their own to the innermost thought, to the slightest stir of blood, to his last breath." [7]

The central ambiguities and the two sides of honor — guilt or disgrace? act of ritual atonement or act of pride? — follow him to the last moments of his life. When Jim says "There is nothing to fight for" and "I should not be worth having" he seems to achieve Henchard's excommunication of self. But moments later — "in a last flicker of superb egoism" — he says, "Nothing can touch me." He moves toward Doramin and the fatal destiny itself, to make the only psychologically complete payment for crime and criminal failure. After the shot he sends "right and left at all those faces a proud and unflinching glance":

"And that's the end. He passes away under a cloud, inscrutable at heart, forgotten, unforgiven, and excessively romantic. Not in the wildest days of his boyish visions could he have seen the alluring shape of such an extraordinary success! For it may very well be that in the short moment of his last proud and unflinching glance, he had beheld the face of that opportunity which, like an Eastern bride, had come veiled to his side." [8]

(Our evaluation of the Patusan episode will be partly determined, we shall see, by our response to *veiled,* and by associated images of fog, cloud, mist, and moonlight.)

4. *How to be?* We are thus asked to evaluate a romantic pride, a romantic conscience, an exalted egoism as solutions

to the essential problem of "how to be." We must locate on a moral spectrum "a sort of sublimated, idealised selfishness." What we as readers are likely to think of such attitudes, or of Jim as a person, will depend partly on the persons we are, and not merely on the novel's success or failure. But *Lord Jim*'s impressionistic structure prevents us from bringing to bear too easily our preconceptions. Its shattering complexity compels us to set out anew. And asks us to compare Jim and his way of life with several others: with the meditative idealist who is also capable of action (Marlow, Stein); with the cynic who, unlike Jim, sees things "exactly as they are" (the captain of the *Patna,* Chester, Gentleman Brown, Cornelius); with the simple and unreflective men who almost effortlessly do the right thing (the French lieutenant, Stanton, the helmsman). The first and the third types may be among Aristotle's "truly fortunate" richly endowed by nature. Jim was not so richly endowed. Part of his appeal lies in his stubborn refusal to recognize that he is not by nature "good enough."

Lord Jim, then, is an intricate novel about possible emotional and moral responses to a relatively simple man, even to a "type" of man. However, it would be a mistake to dwell too much on Jim's simplicity, or to say that there's "nothing there." For this man repeatedly taken "unawares," and who is possessed by what he thinks he possesses, offers a major dramatic image of the will and the personality in conflict, of the conscious mind betrayed by the unconscious, of the intent rendered absurd by the deed. The conscious mind discovers, belatedly, what the betraying dark powers have accomplished: "I had jumped, it seems . . ." Just so Jim makes his more successful jump over the palisade in Patusan: "at once, without any mental process as it were, without any stir of emotion, he set about his escape as if executing a plan matured for a month." A little more addicted than most men to deliberate revery, Jim is a little more than most subject to the undeliberate unconscious mind and its sympathetic or hostile acts. This is best dramatized in the major scene of crippling identification with Gentleman Brown. But it also appears very interestingly in his compulsion to make others reënact his sudden jump from the *Patna*. This may be too elaborate a construction to put on Jim's act of throwing the crosseyed Dane, now of the Royal Siamese Navy, into the Menam river. But it does seem to account for his curious behavior in making the would-be assassins jump into the river in Patusan. There is a link with the *Patna* incident, in Conrad's imagination if not in Jim's unconscious, between the torch flung in the river and the *Patna*'s masthead light, which had seemed to drop "like a lighted match you throw down."

" 'Jump!' he thundered. The three splashes made one splash, a shower flew up, black heads bobbed convulsively, and disappeared . . . His heart seemed suddenly to grow too big for his breast and choke him in the hollow of his throat. This probably made him speechless for so long, and after returning his gaze she flung the burning torch with a wide sweep of the arm into the river. The ruddy fiery glare, taking a long flight through the night, sank with a vicious hiss, and the calm soft starlight descended upon them, unchecked." [9]

A novelistic portrait may show psychological intuition through its accurate dramatization of mental processes and significant notation of behavior. But it may also show it through the efficiency of its often unconscious symbolizing imagination. Significantly enough, if a hat does truly symbolize the personality, Jim turns up on board Marlow's ship without a hat, after throwing the Dane into the river. He has been stripped once again of his disguise, or stripped of his illusion of self. So it is at his most critical hours. He lost his cap, jumping from the *Patna,* and the next day the "sun crept all the way from east to west over my bare head." And when the time comes, at the end, to meet the fatal destiny, he is "fully dressed as for every day, but without a hat." Is it or is it not the *real* Jim who, hatless, takes the disaster "upon his own head" in pride and/or atonement?

Simple Jim may be. But there is nothing simple about Conrad's own understanding of him. We must, as always, except Dostoevsky: the first Freudian novelist and still the greatest dramatist of half-conscious and unconscious processes. And we have seen how *The Nigger of the "Narcissus,"* a symbolist study of identification, prepared the way. Otherwise, *Lord Jim* is perhaps the first major novel solidly built on a true intuitive understanding of sympathetic identification as a psychic process, and as a process which may operate both consciously and less than consciously. The fact that *Lord Jim* takes this process as its center long eluded its readers. But this does not mean that the subject and interest were not unequivocally "there," or that Conrad left matters unreasonably obscure. The fault was ours not his. We may put the case as we must often put it for Dostoevsky: that Conrad dramatized relationships which we could recognize as interesting and perhaps feel to be true, but which we could not accept or explain conceptually.

Dramatically as well as theoretically, *Lord Jim* is a story of sympathies, projections, empathies . . . and loyalties. The central relationship is that of Marlow and Jim. We can see why Jim needs Marlow, as an "ally, a helper, an accomplice." He cannot believe in himself unless he has found another to do so. And he needs a judge, witness, and advocate in the solitude of his battle with himself. All this is evident. But why does Marlow go so far out of his way, very far really, to help Jim? Why does Marlow need Jim? He speaks of the fellowship of the craft, of being his very young brother's keeper, of loyalty to "one of us," of mere curiosity, of a moral need to explore and test a standard of conduct. And we may say with much truth that this is a novel of a moving and enduring friendship between an older and a younger man. But Marlow — in several passages recalling *The Nigger of the "Narcissus"* 's central comment on identification — acknowledges a more intimate or more selfish alliance. He is loyal to Jim as one must be to another or potential self, to the criminally weak self that may still exist:

"Was it for my own sake that I wished to find some shadow of an excuse for that young fellow whom I had never seen before, but whose appearance alone added a touch of personal concern to the thoughts suggested by the knowledge of his weakness—made it a thing of mystery and terror—like a hint of a destructive fate ready for us all whose youth—in its day—had resembled his youth? I fear that such was the secret motive of my prying." [10]

"He appealed to all sides at once—to the side turned perpetually to the light of day, and to that side of us which, like the other hemisphere of the moon, exists stealthily in perpetual darkness, with only a fearful ashy light falling at times on the edge." [11]

"If he had not enlisted my sympathies he had done better for himself—he had gone to the very fount and origin of that sentiment, he had reached the secret sensibility of my egoism." [12]

Marlow is not fatally paralyzed or immobilized by this young "double." But Big Brierly is. Brierly is successful, and seems to know nothing of indecision and self-mistrust:

"The sting of life could do no more to his complacent soul than the scratch of a pin to the smooth face of a rock. This was enviable. As I looked at him flanking on one side the unassuming pale-faced magistrate who presided at the inquiry, his self-satisfaction presented to me and to the world a surface as hard as granite. He committed suicide very soon after.

"No wonder Jim's case bored him, and while I thought with something akin to fear of the immensity of his contempt for the young man under examination, he was probably holding silent inquiry into his own case. The verdict must have been of unmitigated guilt, and he took the secret of the evidence with him in that leap into the sea." [13]

Insofar as Brierly can explain matters to himself (or to Marlow) he feels humiliated, a white man and seaman, by Jim's evidence given in the presence of natives — "enough to burn a man to ashes with shame." He wants Jim to run away, and offers two hundred rupees to finance the evasion. But professional and racial pride are scarcely sufficient motives for suicide. Marlow sees, in retrospect, that "at bottom poor Brierly must have been thinking of himself" when he wanted Jim to clear out. He had recognized in Jim an unsuspected potential self; he had looked into himself for the first time. "If I understand anything of men, the matter was no doubt of the gravest import, one of those trifles that awaken ideas — start into life some thought with which a man unused to such a companionship finds it impossible to live."

Doubtless Conrad was interested in the case of Brierly (presumably based on the suicide of Captain Wallace of the *Cutty Sark*) in its own right. And for some readers it may exist as one of the many sources of a light thrown obliquely on Jim: possibly (by the very fact of the suicide) to magnify him and give his case importance; possibly (by the integrity of Brierly's last moments as a seaman) to devalue Jim the poor officer. But the episode's chief function is to prepare us to understand (or at least accept) Jim's paralyzed identification with Gentleman Brown and suicidal refusal to fight him; and to prepare us, also, for the deliberateness of Jim's march up to Doramin. The aesthetic principle may be obvious, but the execution of it is seldom easy — to prepare the reader to accept a "strangeness" of major importance and concern by first dramatizing that strangeness in a setting seemingly minor, anecdotal, neutral. And we will need to believe, dramatically if not conceptually, that interview with Gentleman Brown, since it is the direct cause of Jim's death.

The immediate preparation for the interview (Chapters 37–40) shows Conrad's impressionism at its most successful, dramatically speaking. We have an inkling from Brown, on his unclean deathbed, that Jim himself may be dead; we learn from the benumbed Tamb' Itam that Jim "would not fight," and from Jewel that "he had been driven away from her by a dream." Thus in Brown and his cutthroat crew, but also in what we know and recall of Jim's character, we see his destiny approach. It became probable from the moment Brown heard of Jim's power, and started upriver to seek his share of the loot. And thus we are conditioned, during Jim's absence, to see the chief menace of Brown as ruthless and cynical intelligence at the service of pure love of destruction; we expect a combat of wills. And such it turns out to be.

"They faced each other across the creek, and with steady eyes tried to understand each other before they opened their lips. Their antagonism must have been expressed in their glances," Marlow suggests. "I know that Brown hated Jim at first sight."

The crafty Brown capitalizes at once on Jim's obvious reluctance to answer questions. He finds a way "as broad as a turnpike, to get in and shake his two penny soul around and inside out and upside down — by God!" He asks Jim what had made him come to Patusan, what had scared him into this infernal hole, and even says something that would inevitably remind Jim of the *Patna.* It is one of the great dramatic scenes in Conrad: the cynical Brown's unerring discovery of his antagonist's weakness. "And there ran through the rough talk a vein of subtle reference to their common blood, an assumption of common experience; a sickening suggestion of common guilt, of secret knowledge that was like a bond of their minds and of their hearts." It is a paralyzing, an immobilizing bond; and Jim refuses to fight. According to Morf, Jim immediately identifies himself with Brown, and identification "is characterized always by an extraordinary indulgence for the second self, an indulgence which must of necessity remain incomprehensible to any other person . . . Jim's indulgence for Brown is typical. He simply cannot resist the evil *because the evil is within himself.*" And his "unconscious wish is to see Brown (i.e., himself) go off free and powerful . . ." [14]

It could be argued that Morf's phrasing is too blunt; it leaves little room for exceptions. And identification may lead to hostility rather than sympathy, as in a condemnation of self by proxy. Still Morf's analysis (which in 1947 struck me as largely mistaken) now seems more accurate than my own rationalist explanation: that Jim's hard-won assurance was destroyed by the fact that the first visitor from the outside world brought a reminder of the *Patna,* and that Jim was unwilling to shed white men's blood. These are indeed possible related or additional motives for Jim's refusal to fight.

But the emphasis Morf gives to half-conscious and unconscious identification is, I am now persuaded, correct. It is at the center of Conrad's psychology — as it was, almost contemporaneously, at the center of André Gide's.

Chapter Five

LORD JIM (II)

NOT only the characters of a fiction experience such sympathies. The related central preoccupation of Conrad's technique, the heart of the impressionist aim, is to invite and control the reader's identifications and so subject him to an intense rather than passive experience. Marlow's human task is also the reader's: to achieve a right human relationship with this questionable younger brother. Marlow must resist an excessive identification (which would mean abandoning his traditional ethic); he must maintain a satisfactory balance of sympathy and judgment. No easy task, since Jim demands total sympathy. "He wanted an ally, a helper, an accomplice. I felt the risk I ran of being circumvented, blinded, decoyed, bullied, perhaps, into taking part in a dispute impossible of decision if one had to be fair to all the phantoms in possession — to the reputable that had its claims and to the disreputable that had its exigencies." And this is, far more than in most novels, the reader's moral drama and situation: to be subjected to all the phantoms in possession, to be exposed to a continuous subtle and flowing interplay of intellectual appeals to his judgment and poignant appeals to his sympathy.

The reader must survive this experience and go through this labyrinth of evidence without the usual guide of an omniscient author or trustworthy author-surrogate. The reader (looking incorrigibly for the author's convictions and final decision) is likely to put his trust in Marlow, including the Marlow who speaks of Jim's "greatness," "truth," and "constancy." But he does so at his peril. Or he may put his trust, even more dangerously, in Stein, Jim's fellow-romantic. Stein's wise and assured tones and his central position in the novel, geographically speaking, have led many readers to assume that he conveys the author's judgment. It would be much more accurate to say that Conrad's moral judgment is isolated, if anywhere, in the austere nameless "privileged man" of Chapter 36, and that his uncorrected sympathy is isolated in Stein. (The "privileged man" would not admit that Jim had mastered his fate, and maintained "that we must fight in the ranks or our lives don't count.") Then to whom and to what should the reader attend, if not to his professed guides? The answer of course is that he should attend, eagerly yet skeptically, to everything: to the moralizing of the guides, yes, but even more to every scrap of evidence they offer by way of anecdote, digression, example. The reading of this novel is a combat: within the reader, between reader and narrators, between reader and that watching and controlling mind ultimately responsible for the distortions.

Doubtless the common impression left by a first reading is that the formal rational evidence is preponderantly favorable to Jim, and that the novel finally reaches a lenient verdict, even a judgment of "approval." Jim emerges as, simply, a hero and a redeemed man. But the evidence (as we discover on rereading) is by no means preponderantly favorable; and *Lord Jim* is as much a novel about a man who makes excuses as a novel that makes excuses. Our first impression that the novel "approves" Jim turns out to derive not from the area of rational evidence and judgment but from the area of novelistic sympathy; we discover, as we look a little more closely, that Marlow has repeatedly taken us in. He is a considerably more lenient witness than his austere moralizing tone suggests. On various occasions he brings in the damaging evidence (he is, after all, obliged to bring it in) very casually and digressively, as though inviting us to overlook it. So too, when we are inclined to judge harshly, Marlow diverts our attention from the suffering, "burning" Jim to those who merely rot in the background, or who live safely in a world of untested rectitude. "You've been tried." Jim has, at least, been tested and tried. Therefore he exists. Marlow evokes both sympathy and a more lenient judgment whenever he reminds us of those who are safe: Marlow's listeners, or Jim's father sending his four-page letter of "easy morality and family news," or the tourists in the Malabar Hotel where Jim begins his story. Their irrelevance colors our response to Jim's very questionable denial that he was afraid of death: "They were exchanging jocular reminiscences of the donkeys in Cairo. A pale anxious youth stepping softly on long legs was being chaffed by a strutting and rubicund globe-trotter about his purchases in the bazaar. 'No, really — do you think I've been done to that extent?' he inquired very earnest and deliberate." When we return to Jim a moment later, we listen to him more attentively: " 'Some of the crew were sleeping on the number one hatch within reach of my arm,' began Jim again."

Such sudden corrective juxtaposition is at once the novel's characteristic way of redressing a balance of meaning and its chief way of moving us emotionally. It may operate in both directions, of course: correcting an excessive austerity of judgment or correcting an excessive sympathy. The matter is not easy to sum up, and my conclusion is perhaps debatable. But here is it: that on a first reading we are inclined to think Marlow's own judgment of Jim too harsh (since we have missed some of the evidence that led him to that judgment); that on a second reading (because we are discovering that evidence with a force of delayed impact) we may think Marlow's judgment too lenient. In other words, the unfavorable evidence that Marlow had half-concealed through deceptive casualness of manner grows upon us at a second or third reading, and becomes more difficult to discount. But meanwhile our natural sympathy for Jim — the center of attention, the man on the rack, the conscientious sinner, the man who has been "tried" — has correspondingly diminished. We have, in other words, the very reverse of the situation that pertains in *Absalom, Absalom!*, where the favorable evidence has been more than half-concealed. Hence, at a second reading, we think more not less of Thomas Sutpen. But the aesthetic principle, and the implicit assumption that a serious novel like a serious poem is meant to be read more than once, is the same.

The delicate interplay of sympathy and judgment, managed with such ease in the novel itself, is difficult to describe. We may take, as an example of crucial evidence within deceptively unemphasized digression, the testimony of the Malay helmsman in Chapter 8. For some pages we have listened to Jim's own vivid account of his emotions after looking at the bulging bulkhead, and to Marlow's slightly more distant and meditative retelling; together they have taken us as close as we ever come to the original experience of quite understandable fear. We are *there* as Jim, thinking the ship may go at any moment, struggles with the pilgrim importuning him for water to drink; as back on the bridge he finds the officers trying to get one of the boats off the chocks. And at the moment of Jim's most urgent appeal for both sympathy and understanding — "Where was the kindness in making crazy with fright all those people I could not save single-handed — that nothing could save?" — Marlow characteristically withdraws to comment on Jim's longing for ally, helper, accomplice.

In the next paragraphs Marlow holds a very fine balance: reminding us of Jim's self-deceptions and weakness but also of his conscientious shame, magnifying the struggle through allusion and analogy, admitting his own allegiance. The effect at a first reading is to transfer our attention from Jim's dubious acts on board the *Patna* to the magnitude of his present "dispute with an invisible personality." When at last we get back to the *Patna,* Marlow not Jim does the telling, and we can see Jim, a not wholly ignoble figure, standing apart from the other officers and the boat. "The two Malays had meantime remained holding to the wheel" — only thoughtless, immobile figures, not even part of our moral universe. We are quickly diverted from them by the stunning retrospective information that the ship didn't sink. "And still she floated! These sleeping pilgrims were destined to accomplish their whole pilgrimage to the bitterness of some other end." Marlow remarks, casually, that the behavior of the two helmsmen was not "the least wonder of these twenty minutes."

We then move away from the *Patna* to the inquiry, where the two helmsmen were questioned, as for relief from dramatic and moral intensity. It is a moment for attention to flag. The first helmsman, when asked what he thought of matters at the time, says he thought nothing. The second "explained that he had a knowledge of some evil thing befalling the ship, but there had been no order; he could not remember an order; why should he leave the helm?" And the evidence he gives — if we attend to it, as we do on later readings — pricks Jim's balloon. Not the man on the rack and tortured sinner but the old Malayan helmsman devoted to and formed by the honest traditions of the sea is heroic. He defines himself when he pours out the names of skippers and ships. We are reminded of Conrad's pride in "these few bits of paper, headed by the names of a few Scots and English shipmasters."

"To some further questions he jerked back his spare shoulders, and declared it never came into his mind then that the white men were about to leave the ship through fear of death. He did not believe it now. There might have been secret reasons. He wagged his old chin knowingly. Aha! secret reasons. He was a man of great experience, and he wanted *that* white Tuan to know —he turned toward Brierly, who didn't raise his head—that he had acquired a knowledge of many things by serving white men on the sea for a great number of years—and, suddenly, with shaky excitement he poured upon our spell-bound attention a lot of queer-sounding names, names of dead-and-gone skippers, names of forgotten country ships, names of familiar and distorted sound, as if the hand of dumb time had been at work on them for ages. They stopped him at last." [1]

Marlow refers to the helmsman rightly as an "extraordinary and damning witness." But he is silenced, in the novel, very quickly indeed. And we are taken back to the ship. There follow thirty-five pages of a detailed and tormented account of Jim's last minutes on board, of his jump "into an everlasting deep hole," of his harrowing time in the lifeboat with the "three dirty owls" and his day spent apart from them under a burning sun, deliberating whether to die. The reader cannot fail to take Jim's part against theirs, and is more and more tempted to take seriously his assertion that it was not *he* who had jumped. "I told you I jumped; but I tell you they were too much for any man. It was their doing as plainly as if they had reached up with a boathook and pulled me over." By the end of Chapter 11, recollecting his debates on suicide, Jim has again threatened to convert the *Patna* episode into an entirely interior affair.

Hence it is high time we return to material matters, to physical things and acts: to what might and might not have been done. And Marlow sweeps us ahead more than three years to his meeting with the French lieutenant of Chapters 12 and 13, who is perhaps the most damning witness and reflector of all. He too appears very casually, within a nominal digression, and I understand he is discounted by some readers as a stuffy and uninteresting figure. Marlow, who in these chapters clearly diverges from Conrad, would have liked so to dismiss him. But his role in the novel may be as crucial as Stein's; the scenes are in a way pendant. For Stein, the intellectual and dreamer who is also a successful man of action, Jim is "romantic" — which is very bad and "also very good." His dream and his anguish are what make him exist. But the French lieutenant, a moving figure of professional competence and integrity, and a man certainly capable of sympathy, at once calls attention to something else: Jim "ran away along with the others." Marlow the observer professes to be irritated by his stolid assurance. But Conrad obviously finds him both likable and admirable, and he has (like a Hemingway figure) the esoteric wound betokening virtue:

"This was absolutely the first gesture I saw him make. It gave me the opportunity to 'note' a starred scar on the back of his hand—effect of a gunshot clearly; and, as if my sight had been made more acute by this discovery, I perceived also the seam of an old wound, beginning a little below the temple and going out of sight under the short grey hair at the side of the head—the graze of a spear or the cut of a sabre. He clasped his hands on his stomach again. 'I remained on board that—that—my memory is going (*s'en va*). *Ah! Patt-nà. C'est bien ça. Patt-nà. Merci.* It is droll how one forgets. I stayed on board that ship thirty hours.' " [2]

Time "had left him hopelessly behind with a few poor gifts . . ." But, unlike Jim, he had done what had to be done. And of the thirty hours during which he remained on board the *Patna,* with two quartermasters stationed with axes to cut her clear of the tow if she sank, he chiefly remembers with irritation having had no wine to go with his food. He too was aware of the chief sources of danger, panic among the pilgrims and the "villainous" bulkhead. But he saw them as matters to be taken care of. The way to behave in crisis is to act efficiently. His words are distantly echoed, from one language to another, by Stein's account of an ambush:

". . . this manoeuvre eased the strain on the bulkhead, whose state, he expounded with stolid glibness, demanded the greatest care (*éxigeait les plus grands ménagements*) ." [3]

"It was a little intrigue, you understand. They got my poor Mohammed to send for me and then laid that ambush. I see it all in a minute, and I think— This wants a little management. My pony snort, jump, and stand, and I fall slowly forward with my head on his mane." [4]

At the end of the interview with the French lieutenant, Marlow is "discouraged about Jim's case." Earlier — noting the lieutenant's admission that everyone experiences fear, and his acknowledgment that Jim "might have had the best dispositions" — Marlow was glad to see him take "a lenient view." A suspicious reader might even suppose the lieutenant had begun to confess, on the preceding page, to an act of cowardice similar to Jim's. But the lieutenant means to do no such thing, and he does not take a lenient view. For he has "no opinion" as to what life is like when honor is gone.

Hence he has not *acted* in cowardice. "I was confronted," Marlow says,

"by two narrow grey circlets, like two tiny steel rings around the profound blackness of the pupils. The sharp glance, coming from that massive body, gave a notion of extreme efficiency, like a razor-edge on a battle-axe. 'Pardon,' he said, punctiliously. His right hand went up, and he swayed forward. 'Allow me . . . I contended that one may get on knowing very well that one's courage does not come of itself (*ne vient pas tout seul*). There's nothing much in that to get upset about. One truth the more ought not to make life impossible . . . But the honour—the honour, monsieur! . . .' "[5]

We do not, even after this second damning witness has spoken, get back to the Malabar House and Jim's narrative at once. Another reflector and witness appears, by way of a digressive development of a modifying clause: Bob Stanton. Marlow has been speaking of Jim's unglamorous mode of life as a water-clerk for De Jongh. Or is the business of an insurance canvasser, which "Little Bob Stanton" had been, even less glamorous? As with the French lieutenant, the introduction is casual and faintly ironic. And then we are told, as though it had no bearing on Jim's case, the story of Stanton's drowning while trying to save a lady's maid in the *Sephora* disaster. He too had done what had to be done. As chief mate he would leave no one on board a sinking ship; Jim had left eight hundred. Stanton reminds us of what the officer is expected to do, irrespective of temptation or mitigating circumstance. And at this point (after seventeen pages of damaging evidence in the guise of digression) we return to Jim and his heroic introspections. "Clear out! Couldn't think of it," he replies, when Marlow offers Brierly's plan of escape. But we are less impressed than we would have been before listening to the French lieutenant and before hearing of Stanton's death.

The natural unreflective heroism of the French lieutenant and Stanton thus help to put Jim's reveries of heroism, and his actual failures and excuses, into a clearer perspective. We must remember that in every chapter and on every page the double appeal to sympathy and judgment is made, though one or the other may dominate; we are not being subjected to the blunt regular swings of a pendulum. Still, this is perhaps the point in the first part of the novel where our view of Jim is most severe. The following chapter sets in a strong returning flow of sympathy. We see Jim's formal punishment delivered in a "chill and mean atmosphere. The real significance of crime is in its being a breach of faith with the community of mankind, and from that point of view he was no mean traitor, but his execution was a hole-and-corner affair." In a sense a proper judgment has been passed on Jim's romantic ego and his vulnerable idealism: *certificate canceled.* Then, and almost at once, we see Jim's version of "how to be" in the very different perspective of Chester's gross cynicism: Chester who wants someone "no good" for his guano island, and who regards Jim as "no good" because he takes his downfall to heart. "You must see things exactly as they are" — as Chester's partner Robinson did, who ate his comrades rather than starve, and afterward showed no remorse.* Marlow does not accept Chester's proposal. But he vivifies it sufficiently to make us more sympathetic with Jim's plight. And again, though in Marlow's imagination only, we have the "secret sharer" image of the guilty man alone under a burning sun:

* *Lord Jim* explores the fine distinctions between guilt and sense of disgrace yet remains ambivalent toward the character who — accepting what he has done as done — lives without remorse. Stein is such a man. But so too is Robinson, who three weeks after his rescue "was as well as ever. He didn't allow any fuss that was made on shore to upset him; he just shut his lips tight, and let people screech. It was bad enough to have lost his ship, and all he was worth besides, without paying attention to the hard names they called him" (p. 163).

In this connection, and though it may reflect only one of several moods, an 1891 letter from Conrad to Marguerite Poradowska is of interest: "Each act of life is final and inevitably produces its consequences in spite of all the weeping and gnashing of teeth and the sorrow of weak souls who suffer as fright grips them when confronted with the results of their own actions. As for myself, I shall never need to be consoled for any act of my life, and this because I am strong enough to judge my conscience rather than be its slave, as the orthodox would like to persuade us to be" (*Letters of Joseph Conrad to Marguerite Poradowska, 1890–1920,* translated and edited by John A. Gee and Paul J. Sturm [New Haven, 1940], p. 36).

"I had a rapid vision of Jim perched on a shadowless rock, up to his knees in guano, with the screams of sea-birds in his ears, the incandescent ball of the sun above his head; the empty sky and the empty ocean all a-quiver, shimmering together in the heat as far as the eye could reach." The classic Promethean image of unending punishment magnifies Jim's suffering; it reminds us too of the moral isolation into which he will now enter more deeply than before. And the section ends (Chapters 15, 16, 17) with the not unsympathetic picture of Jim's long silent struggle with himself, while Marlow writes letter after letter. "He was rooted to the spot, but convulsive shudders ran down his back; his shoulders would heave suddenly. He was fighting, he was fighting — mostly for his breath, as it seemed." The "idea obtrudes itself that he made so much of his disgrace while it is the guilt alone that matters." Nevertheless the impression left, at the end of this part, is of a kind of stubborn courage.

This then is *Lord Jim*'s chief way of provoking in its readers a strong human response and meaningful conflict: to interweave or suddenly juxtapose (rather than group logically and chronologically) the appeals to judgment and sympathy, to criticism and compassion. A man is what he does, which in Jim's case is very little that is not equivocal. But also he "exists" for us by the quality of his feeling and the poignant intensity of his dream. He is not "good enough" (as Marlow tells Jewel, as the Malay helmsman and other witnesses verify) yet his childish romanticism may be preferable to a cynical realism. In any event, as Marlow goes on to say, "nobody is good enough." This is not a relativistic conclusion. It reminds us rather how strong Marlow's moral and community engagement was, against which his brotherly and outlaw sympathy contended.

These peculiar groupings — of incident and witness and evidence, of intellectual and emotional appeal — distinguish *Lord Jim* from most earlier fiction. But imagery also leaves us in provisional and perhaps lasting uncertainty. Is Jim "in the clear"? The novel's chief recurrent image is of substance and reality obscured, often attractively so, by mist or by deceptive light. *Fog, mist, cloud,* and *veil* form a cluster with *moonlight,* and with *dream,* to dramatize certain essential distinctions: between the conscious mind and the unconscious, illusion and reality, the "ego-ideal" and the self's destiny as revealed by its acts. Imagery is supposed to reveal an author's ultimate and perhaps unconscious bias. But much of the imagery here is grouped fairly consciously as part of a multiple appeal to the reader. These images — if they do form a cluster, if we do properly take them together — should help determine the delicate relationship of idealism and self-deception. And hence they should help us to evaluate Stein's advice ("follow the dream") and Jim's ultimate conduct in Patusan, when opportunity comes to his side, veiled like an Eastern bride.

At a first reading all this imagery of nebulosity may magnify and glamorize Jim (as fog magnifies Wordsworth's sheep), and also may be partly responsible for our first impression that Jim is an exceedingly mysterious person. But its later effect may be to persuade us that Stein is not, unequivocally, a spokesman for the author, and to throw still further doubt on Jim's "redemption" in Patusan. "I ask myself whether his rush had really carried him out of that mist in which he loomed interesting if not very big, with floating outlines — a straggler yearning inconsolably for his humble place in the ranks."

The meaning of *mist,* as we look at its various appearances, is clearer than we might have expected. It can refer generally to ambiguity but more centrally refers to the aura of deception and self-deception that surrounds Jim's reality. Now and then Marlow has a "glimpse through a rent in the mist in which he moved and had his being," as Jim says something truly revealing: as he tells of his impulse to go back to the spot of the *Patna*'s abandonment, or as he recognizes the good Marlow does him by listening. But the mists close again at once when Jim refers to his plight as "unfair." Thus we may call the mist his illusion of self or ego-ideal, which is in turn responsible for the deceptions; it may impose the "mask" of a "usual expression." Reality can then appear in an "unconscious grimace," or through rifts caused by the inward struggles. He stumblingly reveals the truth; or, we stumble upon it. "The muscles round his lips contracted into an unconscious grimace that tore through the mask of his usual expression — something violent, short-lived, and illuminating like a twist of lightning that admits the eye for an instant into the secret convolutions of a cloud." The provocative reality in this instance was a fact normally evaded: that he was in the lifeboat with the others. Or, "The mist of his feelings shifted between us, as if disturbed by his struggles, and in the rifts of the immaterial veil he would appear to my staring eyes distinct of form and pregnant with vague appeal like a symbolic figure in a picture." This questionable sentence would suggest that the "real" Jim behind the apparent one has the vague symbolic appeal. Very possibly this dubious phrasing simply came to Conrad, who refused to examine it closely.

Still, we can say that mist, fog, and veil conceal or blur reality. So too does moonlight, whose "occult power" can rob things of their reality: "It is to our sunshine, which — say what you like — is all we have to live by, what the echo is to the sound: misleading and confusing whether the note be mocking or sad. It robs all forms of matter — which, after all, is our domain — of their substance, and gives a sinister reality to shadows alone." Dorothy Van Ghent advances an interesting argument: that the split conical hill on Patusan suggests Jim's spiritual cleavage, and the moon rising between the two halves suggests a "figure of the ego-ideal" with its "illusionariness, and the solitude implied by illusion." [6] The moonlight of Patusan is certainly associated with immobility and isolation, and with times when Jim is seriously entranced by his pride and illusions of success. This moonlight comments on the unreality of his aspirations. So too (when Jim still confuses guilt and disgrace, and thus comes "no nearer to the root of the matter") Marlow notes the "irresistible slow work of the night settling silently on all the visible forms, effacing the outlines . . ." But if the light of the moon is associated with illusion and a blurring of reality, the dark of the moon can be a very important reality, and one largely responsible for our acts: the unconscious itself. "He appealed to all sides at once — to the side turned perpetually to the light of day, and to that side of us which, like the other hemisphere of the moon, exists stealthily in perpetual darkness, with only a fearful ashy light falling at times on the edge." Whatever their sympathies in the matter, Marlow and Conrad clearly believe that we shall be saved by the sunlight of action and that deceptive half-lights are menacing.

All this (if we are to trust Marlow at all) has an important bearing on Stein's ambiguous advice: to submit yourself to the "destructive element" of the ego-ideal; to attempt through action to realize (or live with?) that illusion of self; to "follow the dream." Jewel remarks, very accurately, that Jim "had been driven away from her by a dream." Marlow's introduction ("one of the most trustworthy men I had ever known") together with Stein's grave tones and the memorably cryptic quality of his utterance create an initial confidence. At a first reading we naturally identify Stein's judgment and Conrad's. But the imagery which occurs to Marlow, immediately after Stein gives his advice, seems to say something very different. It associates Stein and his "conviction" with the half-lights of deception and menacing illusion; it brings Stein down to Jim's level rather than raises Jim to his. We cannot be sure what Conrad thought about Stein. Neither, possibly, could Conrad himself. This is Marlow's comment:

"The whisper of his conviction seemed to open before me a vast and uncertain expanse, as of a crepuscular horizon on a plain at dawn—or was it, perchance, at the coming of the night? One had not the courage to decide; but it was a charming and deceptive light, throwing the impalpable poesy of its dimness over pitfalls—over graves. His life had begun in sacrifice, in enthusiasm for generous ideas; he had travelled very far, on various ways, on strange paths, and whatever he followed it had been without faltering, and therefore without shame and without regret. In so far he was right. That was the way, no doubt. Yet for all that the great plain on which men wander amongst graves and pitfalls remained very desolate under the impalpable poesy of its crepuscular light, overshadowed in the center, circled with a bright edge as if surrounded by an abyss full of flames. When at last I broke the silence it was to express the opinion that no one could be more romantic than himself." [7]

"One had not the courage to decide . . ." The passage, which sounds perilously close to deliberate double talk, probably owes some of its ambiguity to Conrad's inner conflicts discussed in the first chapter. For here the idealist, the skeptic, and the outlaw ("strange paths . . . without regret") all have their say. The ambiguity of Stein's remarks on the "destructive element" (which have regrettably come to mean anything any casual reader wants them to mean) may derive from the same conflicts. Conrad wants both the dreamer and the man who acts to survive: ". . . with the exertions of your hands and feet in the water make the deep, deep sea keep you up." But there is also a rhetorical ambiguity in the famous passage, which derives from our habit of thinking of the ideal or the illusory as "higher," and of air as higher than water. This is no doubt one reason why readers are tempted to equate the "destructive element" with life, action, and so on, and the air with ideal illusion. But the passage, which is prefaced by a reference to the "dream" as the dream of what we would like to be, doesn't say that. The dream is equated with the ideal of self or ego-ideal *and* with the sea *and* with the destructive element:

"A man that is born falls into a dream like a man who falls into the sea. If he tries to climb out into the air as inexperienced people endeavour to do, he drowns—*nicht wahr?* . . . No! I tell you! The way is to the destructive element submit yourself, and with the exertions of your hands and feet in the water make the deep, deep sea keep you up." [8]

Or: *A man is born ready to create an idealized conception of self, an ego-ideal. If he tries to escape or transcend this conception of self, he collapses. He should accept this ideal and try through action to make it "viable."* (Which is very far from the frequent reading: *man must learn to live with his unideal limitations.*)

But this has become a very dark saying — not only because we think of the ideal as something that transcends, of the ideal as higher, of air as more illusory than water, but also because we think of those who submit to the ego-ideal as "inexperienced" and of those who try to correct it as "experienced." The passage turns out to say something very different from what it appeared to say. There are several possibilities here, including one seldom considered in discussions of famous passages: that Conrad produced without much effort a logically imperfect multiple metaphor, liked the sound of it, and let matters go at that. There is also the possibility that Conrad wanted to show Stein giving confused advice. And there is the very real possibility that Conrad made less distinction between "ego" and "ego-ideal" than we are now accustomed to make. (If the "dream" is equated with "ego" we have less trouble with the climbing into air.) But whether we begin with the ego or with the ideal which, having originated in the ego, carries its own destruction within it, we can probably ascribe to Conrad the pessimism he ascribes to Anatole France:

> He knows that our best hopes are irrealisable; that it is the almost incredible misfortune of mankind, but also its highest privilege, to aspire towards the impossible; that men have never failed to defeat their highest aims by the very strength of their humanity which can conceive the most gigantic tasks but leaves them disarmed before their irremediable littleness.[9]

Lord Jim has its great structural innovations and successes. What shall we say of its alleged formal weakness: its apparent break into two separate novels, with the second one inferior to the first? A division into two parts certainly exists: the first concerned with Jim's introspective response to the *Patna* incident, the second with his adventurous "second chance" in Patusan. "You've put your finger on the plague spot,"[10] Conrad wrote to Garnett concerning this division. A story of continuing distress or slow deterioration might have been more symmetrical. But the very echoing of the crucial names — *Patna, Patusan* — suggests why we must have that second part. The most remote place and unrelated circumstance discovers, in us, the character with which we set out. "A clean slate, did he say? As if the initial word of each our destiny were not graven in imperishable characters upon the face of a rock." There is an aesthetic reason for the Patusan chapters fully as compelling: that by Chapter 17 a story of passive suffering (though the subject was by no means exhausted) threatened to exhaust the reader. Some outlet in action, or at least the illusion of such an outlet, had become necessary. And it is in fact astonishing to see, as we look back, how little has happened in those seventeen chapters in a fictional present time. We have had Jim's gestures as he talks; Marlow and Jim have had their misunderstanding over "cur"; Marlow has had his conversations with Chester and Brierly and Jim has refused Brierly's offer; Marlow has pressed upon him a letter of recommendation. And that is about all.

At the end of Chapter 17 Jim sets out with renewed confidence; his last words are "clean slate." Chapters 18–20 may be regarded as transitional: the first two on Jim's retreat "in good order towards the rising sun," as he throws up various jobs; the third on the famous interview with Stein, who sends Jim to Patusan. The second part of the novel would then begin with Chapter 21, or at the latest with Chapter 22 and Marlow's forestatement of Jim's initial success in Patusan. And its surface material is that of military and political adventure in a remote exotic setting. We may further divide this "second part" in two. Chapters 22–35 deal with the period of Jim's success and carry us to the end of Marlow's original narrative. Chapters 36–45 deal with the Gentleman Brown incident and Jim's ruin.

It would be pedantic to attach much importance to the fact that *Lord Jim* divides into parts (most novels of its length do) or to be seriously concerned about the shocks of transition. For these shocks are slight, and are not to be blamed on Patusan. The major break comes not with the introduction of the Patusan material (Chapters 21, 22) but with the end of Marlow's oral narrative (Chapter 35). The important question is whether the novel and its reader are violated in a serious way: either because the material of the second half contradicts the material of the first and devalues it, or because Conrad imagined this material less well, or because it is intrinsically less interesting, or because it demands from us an entirely different kind of attention. Is there, that is, any damaging change in the delicate relationship of author-material-reader?

These questions must be asked, more specifically, of Chapters 22–35. For this section of the novel, exciting enough at a first reading, does not bear much rereading. The later chapters (36–45), though "adventurous" and "romantic," are very moving; they recover the *authenticity in depth* of the first part. There, once again we are watching character in action; not luck but destiny. And I think this points to the serious weakness of Chapters 22–35: that the adventures — the wearisome matter of getting the guns up the hill, for instance — have nothing to do with the essential Jim. Hence Conrad (who is less interested in or less convinced by this other Jim) gives a disproportionate attention to the Patusan background. Or can we say — following upon Gordan's demonstration that this successful Jim was based to some degree on James Brooke of Sarawak — that Conrad was here too bemused by his sources? For a while the appalling success of the historic Brooke must have made Jim's introspections seem unimportant; the physical perils are emphasized, not the perils of soul. Marlow now and then steps in to remind us that all this fed Jim's romantic egoism, these successes and physical dangers overcome. But for pages on end the reader is allowed to forget this moral problem and theme. We may add that a characteristic mediocrity sets in with the introduction of Jewel in Chapter 28: with women and their frightening "extra-terrestrial touch," the second standard ingredient of exotic romance. But Chapters 25–27 (on the defeat of Sherif Ali) seem the weakest of all on later readings.

The technical problem for Conrad, at this point in the

novel, was a grave one. Only a continuation of the impressionistic method, he must have reasoned, could bridge the gap between the two parts: cover not only the separation of Marlow from Jim and the passage of time, but also the sharp change from passive suffering to adventurous action. Perhaps the reader, caught in the old familiar web and involuted structure, would not try to escape? The reasoning was sound enough, so far as it went. Yet the impressionistic method is one real source of our irritation with Chapters 25–27, since it has no intrinsic justification. For the method is designed to evoke complex, wavering, suspended responses to infinitely debatable psycho-moral questions; the intricacies and evasions are justified by the fullness of human involvement. But there is little in the three chapters to warrant such reader involvement. They deal with nothing more ambiguous than practical maneuvers: a military action that did or did not succeed.

But this must not be exaggerated. In a novel of great and subtle artistry this structural flaw is one of the few aesthetic facts easy to detect and isolate, hence easy to overemphasize. There is, for instance, no collapse in style as we move into the Patusan material, only a very slight change to suggest that Conrad's creative relationship to the story has changed. With Chapter 37 Marlow begins to *write,* though nominally for only one reader: the "privileged man." But a slight significant change to a more written style had already occurred in Chapters 21 and 22. It suggests that (as Marlow loses his intimate touch with *listeners*) Conrad's own attitude becomes more detached. The style in Chapter 21 now and then approaches that of *The Mirror of the Sea:* "We wander in our thousands over the face of the earth, the illustrious and the obscure, earning beyond the seas our fame, our money, or only a crust of bread; but it seems to me that for each of us going home must be like going to render an account." The distinction between one style and another is a rather delicate one, especially since the speaking Marlow possesses the richness and variety of a written style and the writing Marlow preserves the best qualities of voice. The first of the following passages, though elaborate, keeps the illusion of a man speaking aloud to men; the second, though it has a quality of voice, is essentially "written." The difference comes, among other things, from a higher degree of abstraction in the second passage. There is more of a "novelistic" impulse in the first, no doubt, but both are well done:

"But she turned her back on them as if in disdain of their fate: she had swung round, burdened, to glare stubbornly at the new danger of the open sea which she so strangely survived to end her days in a breaking-up yard, as if it had been her recorded fate to die obscurely under the blows of many hammers. What were the various ends their destiny provided for the pilgrims I am unable to say; but the immediate future brought, at about nine o'clock next morning, a French gunboat homeward bound from Réunion." [11]

"It seems impossible to believe that mere greed could hold men to such a steadfastness of purpose, to such a blind persistence in endeavour and sacrifice. And indeed those who adventured their persons and lives risked all they had for a slender reward. They left their bones to lie bleaching on distant shores, so that wealth might flow to the living at home. To us, their less tried successors, they appear magnified, not as agents of trade but as instruments of a recorded destiny, pushing out into the unknown in obedience to an inward voice, to an impulse beating in the blood, to a dream of the future." [12]

The second passage, frankly expository and transitional, is not of course typical of the later chapters. But it does suggest the greater distance or at least altered angle from which Conrad now looked at his story. The solitary white man adventuring into the interior, there to traffic with the natives and become their virtual ruler, and who is presently possessed by what he possesses — such a figure had fascinated Conrad from the first. At the two extremes of fortune might be the Georges Antoine Klein, or Kurtz, who died on board the *Roi des Belges* and the James Brooke who became Rajah of Sarawak, founding a dynasty which lasted until very recently, and one of the world's great fortunes. Both — together with an officer of the *Jeddah* who was not fast enough to get away with the others and so stumbled into undeserved heroism, and together with the braggart Jim Lingard whom Conrad had met — may have gone into the dreaming of *Lord Jim*.[13] But Conrad could dream failure more easily than he could dream success. He could imagine magnificently the failure of Kurtz (when he broke away from *Lord Jim* to write "Heart of Darkness"). And he could imagine magnificently Jim's failure and death. What he could not imagine, at the same level of intensity and belief, was Jim's period of success.

Discussions of *Lord Jim*, concerned as they are with interpretative and structural problems, regularly neglect the purely novelistic side of vivid particular creation. Mine has been no exception. Yet without the particulars of place and person, without the finely evoked atmospheres and brilliant minor vignettes, the novel's amount of brooding debate might have become intolerable. Its pleasures in any event would have been different ones. Page by page, *Lord Jim*'s consistent great appeal largely depends on its changing of the lens, on its sudden shifts from a distant and often nebulous moral perspective to a grossly and superbly material foreground. Marlow's tendency to make such shifts is his most personal and most useful mannerism. It lends reality to the unsubstantial reveries, as gross substance is bound to do, yet invites us to look at them more critically. But most of all it offers the pleasure of a creative surprise. Thus (to take a fine example of sudden rescue from the vague and vast) Cornelius interrupts Marlow's revery, which once again has indulged its fondness for the old problem of "illusion":

". . . I have that feeling about me now; perhaps it is that feeling which has incited me to tell you the story, to try to hand over to you, as it were, its very existence, its reality — the truth disclosed in a moment of illusion.

"Cornelius broke upon it. He bolted out, vermin-like, from the long grass growing in a depression of the ground. I believe his house was rotting somewhere near by, though I've never seen it, not having been far enough in that direction. He ran towards me upon the path; his feet, shod in dirty white shoes, twinkled on the dark earth: he pulled himself up, and began to whine and cringe under a tall stovepipe hat. His dried-up little carcass was swallowed up, totally lost, in a suit of black broadcloth." [14]

Conrad's success with such minor figures is (as we look back on the earlier work and forward to *Nostromo*) one of the substantial advances registered by *Lord Jim*. Cornelius, Marlow remarks, merely skulks on the "outskirts" of the story. But the account of his trembling attempt to get rid of Jim is fine dramatic writing. Through a slight narrative distance (we are never told in so many words what Cornelius intends) we watch him try to sell Jim protection for eighty dollars, then hover outside the house in the darkness, apparently waiting to see him killed. We know his intentions by his behavior when Jim appears unexpectedly: the way he ducks sideways as though shot at, his panic as he clings to the rail of the verandah, his "faint shriek" when Jim appears again.

Criticism, it may be, pays too little attention to the vivid minor figure, and to the pleasure and actualizing effect of surprise. *Lord Jim* obviously depends very heavily on intellectual surprise, as the reader is compelled to make large and sudden adjustments and resolve conflicting demands. But the lesser surprises are important too. The German captain of the *Patna,* for instance, reaches us through a series of surprises. He is created by them. He is dramatically introduced, after a long elevated passage on the pilgrims coming aboard the *Patna,* by his brief remark: "Look at dese cattle . . ." And a surprise may be most effective when it proves to be true in an unexpected way. The fanciful metaphor to convey his voice has its exactness: "From the thick throat of the commander of the *Patna* came a low rumble, on which the sound of the word *schwein* fluttered high and low like a capricious feather in a faint stir of air." Presently we see him (who also is being taken "unawares") slide into the harbor office and Archie Ruthvel's presence: "something round and enormous, resembling a sixteen-hundred-weight sugar-hogshead wrapped in striped flannelette, up-ended in the middle of the large floor space." And finally we see him drive off in the gharry to the astonishment of his subordinates, the monstrous fatness somehow squeezed into that "little box on wheels":

". . . but it only sank with a click of flattened springs, and suddenly one venetian blind rattled down. His shoulders reappeared, jammed in the small opening; his head hung out, distended and tossing like a captive balloon, perspiring, furious, spluttering. He reached for the gharry-wallah with vicious flourishes of a fist as dumpy and red as a lump of raw meat. He roared at him to be off, to go on. Where? Into the Pacific, perhaps. The driver lashed; the pony snorted, reared once, and darted off at a gallop. Where? To Apia? to Honolulu? He had 6,000 miles of tropical belt to disport himself in, and I did not hear the precise address. A snorting pony snatched him into 'ewigkeit' in the twinkling of an eye, and I never saw him again . . ." [15]

A connected account of *Lord Jim* (unless it is to rival the novel in length) is bound to neglect such fine particulars. Thus a discussion of Chapter 14 must mention Jim's loss of his certificate and the cynicism of Chester's offer. But our living experience of the chapter is no little affected by the plaintiff in the assault case: "an obese chocolate-coloured man with shaved head, one fat breast bare and a bright yellow caste-mark above the bridge of his nose, sat in pompous immobility: only his eyes glittered, rolling in the gloom, and the nostrils dilated and collapsed violently as he breathed." It is affected infinitely more, of course, by the brief portrait of Captain Robinson, who had once been reduced to cannibalism. Chester's story is made vivid in classical fictional ways:

". . . a boat of Her Majesty's ship *Wolverine* found [Robinson] kneeling on the kelp, naked as the day he was born, and chanting some psalm-tune or other; light snow was falling at the time. He waited till the boat was an oar's length from the shore, and then up and away. They chased him for an hour up and down the boulders, till a marine flung a stone that took him behind the ear providentially and knocked him senseless. Alone? Of course . . ." [16]

This is fine enough, and credible enough. But the great fictional stroke was to interrupt Chester's talk with the appearance of Captain Robinson himself, a doddering and "amiable" old man:

"An emaciated patriarch in a suit of white drill, a solah topi with a green-lined rim on a head trembling with age, joined us after crossing the street in a trotting shuffle, and stood propped with both hands on the handle of an umbrella. A white beard with amber streaks hung lumpily down to his waist. He blinked his creased eyelids at me in a bewildered way. 'How do you do? how do you do?' he piped, amiably, and tottered. 'A little deaf,' said Chester aside." [17]

The naked chanting Robinson and the Robinson with amber-streaked white beard, the plaintiff with his one fat breast bare and eyes rolling in the gloom, the monstrously fat captain of the *Patna* and the monstrously fat Doramin, the slinking Cornelius and his twinkling white shoes, Gentleman Brown and the "sunken glare of his fierce crow-footed eyes" — all alike remind us of the old paradox: that the successfully achieved grotesque has a kind of fictional reality that the flat and commonplace seldom attains. Conrad will show even more of this novelistic creativity, this intense visual and dramatic surprise, in *Nostromo.*

Chapter Six

NOSTROMO

NOSTROMO (1904) is in some ways a more difficult and more baffling novel than *Lord Jim*. Through many chapters the plight of the reader is precisely that of Captain Mitchell's privileged listener who appears near the end, to be "stunned and as it were annihilated mentally by a sudden surfeit of sights, sounds, names, facts, and complicated information imperfectly apprehended . . ." And the reader may often want to respond to the abrupt allusions as that outraged listener did: "Abominable Pedrito! Who the devil was he?" For at the outset we are cut suddenly adrift in the midst of an unexplained riot, and with no way of telling time. Captain Mitchell's comment on the coffee served at the Amarilla Club gives us, on page 479 of the novel's 566, our first real chance to mark off days on a calendar. And even this information is buried at the end of a paragraph vividly evoking the ceremonial arrival of this coffee at the club: on three mules, escorted by mounted peons. Life (as form, color, movement) repeatedly reaches us before any coherent understanding of it. The reader must collaborate not only in the writing of a novel, now, but also in the writing of a country's history.*

* A brief summary of *Nostromo* may be useful to the reader who has not read it recently: The Occidental Province of the Republic of Costaguana is dominated by the Gould Concession, financed in part by the American capitalist Holroyd. Charles Gould idealizes his San Tomé silver mine as a civilizing force which will bring progress to the contented but backward city of Sulaco. But silver, the incorruptible metal, is a corrupting influence both politically and morally. Its fascination separates Gould from his wife Emilia, who must at last agree with Dr. Monygham that there is no peace in "material interests." The San Tomé mine attracts politicians from the interior and provokes a revolution. Martin Decoud, skeptical boulevardier

The disruptions of chronology and bedeviling distortions of emphasis would suggest a further movement toward the sophisticated "art novel" and its minute attention to the reader's response. But this is on the whole not true. In the breadth of its canvas and in the nature of its preoccupations *Nostromo* is much closer than *Lord Jim* to the nineteenth-century realistic novel and to the Edwardian double-decker study of society. There is little danger now of art violating life through overelaboration, or of technique artfully concealing a paucity of material. The danger to *Nostromo* is the opposite: that so much imagined and felt life might finally violate art and understanding, and dismiss technique as irrelevant; that the material might exhaust the author. And there is in fact a sharp falling-off from the first half to the last. F. R. Leavis is quite right in his estimate of *Nostromo* "as one of the great novels of the language." [1] But he suggests a much more controlled performance than we actually have.

There are other links with *Lord Jim* than the use of the impressionistic method. The great difference is that *Nostromo* is not to the same degree an "interior" novel, either for the characters or for the reader. An essential Conradian story is reënacted by Dr. Monygham, who betrayed friends under torture, spent years in self-destructive isolation and remorse, and found redemption at last. But we are not asked to become intimately involved in his story, nor even allowed to look at it closely. We are offered instead the accomplished facts of

---

and journalist, falls in love with the patriotic Antonia Avellanos, and fathers the idea of a separate Occidental Republic. At a crucial hour in the revolution Nostromo (leader of the "people" who will undertake any mission for the sake of prestige) is enlisted to save bars of San Tomé silver. He takes them to a desert island in the Placid Gulf, accompanied by the political refugee Decoud. Their lighter survives a collision with a troopship, but is supposed to have been sunk. Nostromo buries the silver, and leaves Decoud on the safe island. But he, finding his skepticism powerless against complete solitude, commits suicide. Nostromo realizes the silver could be his. Corrupted by solitude, he resents a social order which "uses" him but gives him no proper reward. He returns occasionally to the island for silver, and "gets rich slowly." But, by coincidence, a lighthouse is erected on the island — to be kept by Giorgio Viola and his daughters Linda and Giselle (Nostromo's sacred and profane loves). Nostromo, stealing to his silver by night, is mistaken by Viola for a despised suitor of Giselle; and is shot.

sardonic personality, profound skepticism concerning men and their motives, courageous loyalty when put to the test. And this is as close as we come, in *Nostromo,* to Conrad's usual interest in marginal crime and self-imposed punishment. The novel recognizes unconscious motives and self-deceptions (Charles Gould's especially) but its treatment of them — its psychology, in a word — is classical rather than Freudian. Reason and folly play a larger part than unconscious or half-conscious compulsion; reasoning on political affairs occupies more pages than solitary introspection. The novel's mysteries are rarely those of communication between two men, or of one man's communication with himself. Its most considerable interior action (Decoud's drift toward suicide) is explicitly attributed to a failure of intellect. Decoud commits suicide because he is an isolated skeptic.

Nostromo does pursue *Lord Jim*'s interest in the "dream," in the ego-ideal and its aura of illusion. Each of the major characters is immersed in the "destructive element" and must idealize something — if only, as with Dr. Monygham, a conception of his disgrace. The novel examines both these vulnerable idealizations and various types of opposing skepticism. What does skepticism do to human capacity? Stein's enigmatic conjunction of *illusion* and *action* is developed again, and the two are opposed to paralyzing *thought.* The situation is complex, and we shall have to return to it. Conrad doubtless does at a certain point repudiate (try to separate himself from) Decoud's skepticism. But he very markedly sympathizes with it too. And the novel's own view of history is skeptical and disillusioned, which for us today must mean true. The history of Costaguana is the sum of its inhabitants' follies: their self-bemusing idealisms and self-intoxicating manifestoes, their vanities, greeds, cowardices, deceptions and self-deceptions. And it is a little more than this sum. Certain institutions or instruments (notably capitalism, imperialism, revolution, political discourse itself) are regarded as inherently destructive or futile. In *Nostromo* the unconscious (given a little less than its due in the stories of individual men and their close relationships) finds in history its stunning revenge. For this history escapes very far the puny wills of men, and their intentions either good or bad.

Nostromo is less interior than *Lord Jim* in one further way. It does deliberately baffle and irritate the reader, and does compel him to explore and organize the fragmentary. But it makes nothing like *Lord Jim*'s effort to induce in the reader sharp conflicts of sympathy and judgment. The materials for such conflicts are there, as they are in all life. But we are allowed to respond to them more freely than before. The novel does not try to keep so close a finger on our pulse. Or, to put the matter differently, Costaguana and its inhabitants seem to exist fairly independently of us. Conrad's Author's Note is a lovely arabesque in which real reality and fictional reality come closer and closer together; it is no little justified by the novel it introduces. For Costaguana exists. And exists more palpably and visibly in this frankly written history than does Patusan in Marlow's personal, more informal rendering.

Others among Conrad's novels may be psychologically subtler and more penetrating; several others show a more controlled artistry. But *Nostromo* is without question Conrad's greatest creative achievement: the successful creation (from a few books read and a "short glance" at Central and South America a quarter of a century before) of a city, a country, a history. In its absurd rhythm of exploitation and misrule, of revolution and counterrevolution, Costaguana may evoke almost any South or Central American republic; its trials are as contemporary as yesterday's *coup d'état* in Honduras or Haiti or the Guatemalan intervention of a few years ago. The forces of deception and self-deception are the same as those at work anywhere. The land has a sufficient generality to permit, as Robert Penn Warren has said, "one of the few mastering visions of our historical moment and our human lot." [2] Yet for all that it comes to us more vividly and more concretely — from the dust and the shining tracks by Viola's inn to the white head of Higuerota — than any actual South American republic we may read about. Or than the actual and remembered places described in the Malayan novels.

Nothing in Costaguana is not credible, unless it be that symbolic lighthouse on the Great Isabel; the realism of *Nostromo* is so successful that we are tempted to give it no thought. But it seems evident that Conrad himself gave considerable energy (perhaps more energy than thought) to the task of creating an authentic and unchallengeable world. Some of his methods are standard, time-honored, and uninteresting: the plausible voice of Captain Mitchell to get us started and to establish that all to follow is "true history"; the reasonable sprinkling of Spanish words and reasonable number of picturesque servants in the background; and, regrettably, more description of furniture and décor than is usual in his work. But all this substantiates rather than creates. In *Nostromo* the impressionistic method — though it may also reflect the author's evasive temperament, or mirror the subject's complexity, or baffle and buffet the reader — serves first the great humble fictional aim of creating reality in depth: of suggesting, behind the incident it flashes down to observe, a hundred similar incidents unrecorded.

Certain descriptions in an older manner are frankly "written"; the blocks are wearily piled into place, the eye is rather desperately on the object. And even where there is an attempt to suggest very informal narrative (as of one Costaguanero writing to another) the details may accumulate too rapidly. The severe strain under which Conrad worked to create his world, and win his reader's assent, shows through rather noticeably in the first impressionistic treatment of Charles Gould (pages 48–49). The small local and verifying particulars ("Castillan, as the natives say" . . . "not said of him in the mocking spirit of the Llaneros" . . . "the Camino Real of popular speech," etc.) are obviously designed to carry us without protest through the experience of acquiring very rapidly a great deal of important information: the fact, for instance, that the Goulds had been "liberators, explorers, coffee-planters, merchants, revolutionists," or that Charles was the only representative of the third generation. Characteristically, the information on the ancestral Goulds is offered as a digressive aside set off by dashes, and the reference to a third generation is immediately undercut: "third generation in a continent possessing its own style of horsemanship . . ." This evasiveness and irony, this systematic slighting of the essential, may remind us of Marlow. But the next two paragraphs, subtly juxtaposing Charles Gould on horseback and the equestrian statue of Charles IV, are much more deliberately constructed than most of Marlow's. They ask us, further, to record too many visual impressions, down to the white eye of Gould's "slate-coloured beast." The overwrought two-page vignette gradually moves from broken to periodic rhythms, from loose syntax to formal. It suggests a question which Conrad must have asked himself again and again: Is this novel to be a spoken or a written narrative, a story or a history?

But this passage is uncharacteristic: it achieves little because it attempts so much. The usual actualizing digression — the digression that exists to give absolute authenticity to the surrounding narrative and world — operates in a very different way. For one thing, it offers little information. What we have instead, with a sudden approach of the camera and a marked slowing of time, is a vivid picture of a characteristic and perhaps absurd incident, a few moments of *vis comica*. Thus in Chapter 4 we may not be ready to believe that old Viola had fought with Garibaldi; or to believe in the existence of his inn enough to care what happens there; or in fact to believe that such a place exists. But then the narrative closes to a very particular but recurrent situation: the old man backing out of the door holding a frying-pan that has caught fire, and in his rage muttering the name of Cavour; and his wife Teresa issuing anxiously from another door ("Giorgio! thou passionate man! Misericordia Divina!"); and the hens making off in all directions; and the "young English face" appearing at a window while the mulatto Luis hides; and the Indian girls staring "dully from under the square-cut fringes on their foreheads"; and the smell of burnt onions in the "drowsy heat, enveloping the house." The scene conveys little information and nothing important happens in it. But it catches our attention in a way that charges it with life. Conceivably it prepares us to believe in this city of Sulaco we have not yet visited, a mile or so away.

Nostromo thus carries further than usual a classical stratagem: to actualize the whole through the glittering fragment, the important through the peripheral or the irrelevant. And it recognizes that a successful visualizing of the strange or the ridiculous may lend more reality than a successful visualizing of the obvious and ordinary. We are introduced to the San Tomé mine community (divided into Village One, Village Two, Village Three) through Don Pépé's ability to distinguish the miners "not only by their flat, joyless faces" but by the infinitely graduated shades of dark skin. The paragraph evokes the two shifts mingling in a confusion of naked limbs: the Indian boys, the screeners and ore-breakers smoking long cigars, the heads of gangs with brass medals on their bare breasts, and one half of the crowd swallowed by the mountain while the other half moves in long files to the bottom of the gorge and to the numbered villages. Yet all this remains a little blurred, inhuman, distant. Are these miners only exploited animals? Is this mine only another literary mine? We return to Don Pépé, who shared with Father Romàn this ability to distinguish among indistinguishable dark bodies:

> It was only the small fry that puzzled him sometimes. He and the padre could be seen frequently side by side, meditative and gazing across the street of a village at a lot of sedate brown children, trying to sort them out, as it were, in low, consulting tones, or else they would together put searching questions as to the parentage of some small, staid urchin met wandering, naked and grave, along the road with a cigar in his baby mouth, and perhaps his mother's rosary, purloined for purposes of ornamentation, hanging in a loop of beads low down on his rotund little stomach. The spiritual and temporal pastors of the mine flock were very good friends.[3]

This then is one of *Nostromo*'s methods: to humanize two moderately important characters and to actualize a great mine through a cigar in a baby's mouth and the beads on his rotund stomach. It is in a way the obverse of a method that vivifies a general climate of oppression by a swift parenthetical reference to atrocity: "(their bodies were afterwards stripped naked and flung into the plaza out of the windows by the lowest scum of the populace)." Yet we are essentially dealing with the same creative temperament that refuses to give the normal, logical, expected emphasis: a temperament that insists on changing the lens, insists on varying distances, and by the same token *keeps its distance*. There are times when the distortions of emphasis baffle the reader to no purpose. But it is equally true that the weakest parts of *Nostromo* are those which record action straightforwardly, without the distance lent by time or narrating irony, without the authorial distance implicit in such distortion.

It would be inaccurate and even absurd to suggest that all of *Nostromo*'s innumerable digressions exist to authenticate the country and the narrative. Some (though far fewer than in *Lord Jim*) serve as reflectors, for moral illustration or contrast; others, we shall see, fill out the community and complete the moral spectrum. But there are also certain digressions which seem to exist for some poetic effect of phrasing, management, grouping. Life, as often occurs in Flaubert, is for the moment subordinated to the rhythm of sentence or paragraph. The Flaubertian introduction of Signora Teresa, for instance, is charming, but distinctly more literary than that of her husband old Viola:

> Her voice was a rich contralto. When, with her arms folded tight under her ample bosom, she scolded the squat, thick-legged China girls handling linen, plucking fowls, pounding corn in wooden mortars amongst the mud outbuildings at the back of the house, she could bring out such an impassioned, vibrating, sepulchral note that the chained watch-dog bolted into his kennel with a great rattle. Luis, a cinnamon-coloured mulatto with a sprouting moustache and thick, dark lips, would stop sweeping the *café* with a broom of palm-leaves to let a gentle shudder run down his spine. His languishing almond eyes would remain closed for a long time.[4]

These then are differences from *Lord Jim:* that the first

part of *Nostromo* is more concerned with background reality, but also more concerned with written poetic effects. There are of course times, in Conrad as in Flaubert, when the aims coincide: when an exceptional attention to poetic phrasing and grouping achieves a more exact human meaning. The scene of Charles Gould's proposal is excellent in the manner of Flaubert. The two brief extracts to follow come from just before and just after the proposal. The first conveys a suspension of life, to which the bell gives a strange reality; the second dramatizes with remarkable compactness the ritual Conradian gesture of impotence, and so (perhaps unconsciously) anticipates Gould's desertion of his wife for the mine. Both passages are effective, though the first seems more literary than the second. But both illustrate more concern for written (not spoken) effect than we are accustomed to in Conrad:

> And then they stopped. Everywhere there were long shadows lying on the hills, on the roads, on the enclosed fields of olive trees; the shadows of poplars, of wide chestnuts, of farm buildings, of stone walls; and in mid-air the sound of a bell, thin and alert, was like the throbbing pulse of the sunset glow. Her lips were slightly parted as though in surprise that he should not be looking at her with his usual expression.
>
> When her feet touched the ground again, the bell was still ringing in the valley; she put her hands up to her hair, breathing quickly, and glanced up and down the stony lane. It was reassuringly empty. Meantime, Charles, stepping with one foot into a dry and dusty ditch, picked up the open parasol, which had bounded away from them with a martial sound of drum taps. He handed it to her soberly, a little crestfallen.[5]

The major theme of idealization is developed through the central personages: the Goulds and Martin Decoud, Nostromo, Dr. Monygham. But the novel's overwhelming sense of created life and no small share of its human wisdom, its *connaissance du coeur humain,* is conveyed by the vignettes of lesser characters, some of them exceedingly minor. The extreme compression of these biographies or glimpses of character in action, and their vividness of selected detail, contributes as much as anything to the novel's authority: to the sense it gives of completely knowing its world. In this respect *Nostromo* is more than most novels a history: seeming to know much more than it has time to tell, reluctantly compelled to choose one incident or personage from a hundred.

These vignettes or glimpses, which populate the land, may be very brief. The pervasiveness of political corruption (the first fact of Costaguana life, almost a natural resource) is brilliantly suggested in a scene involving the refusal of a bribe. The father of Charles Gould (who would like to escape the fatal privilege of the San Tomé mine concession) has offended the Finance Minister, sometime gambler, cheat, and robber, and cannot go to him directly with a bribe. His representative reaches a "florid person" of French extraction "who was accommodated with lodgings within the walls of a secularized convent next door to the Ministry of Finance." This woman exists for less than a page but with extraordinary vividness: good-natured, refusing on principle to accept a bribe for something she cannot accomplish, but annoyed because she must lose the money and the opportunity to practice her profession of selling influence. She is obviously accustomed to look on those who bring her bribes with an amused and affectionate irony. Every word of her few speeches in French create a character and personality; and, as by an irradiation of life, create the political world in which she moves:

"No; it's no go. *Pas moyen, mon garçon. C'est dommage, tout de même. Ah! zut! Je ne vole pas mon monde. Je ne suis pas ministre — moi! Vous pouvez emporter votre petit sac.*"

For a moment, biting her carmine lip, she deplored inwardly the tyranny of the rigid principles governing the sale of her influence in high places. Then, significantly, and with a touch of impatience, "*Allez,*" she added, "*et dites bien à votre bonhomme — entendez-vous? — qu'il faut avaler la pilule.*"

After such a warning there was nothing for it but to sign and pay.[6]

The corrupt and the cynical are many. At the other end of the political spectrum, fewer yet perhaps as endemic to the Costaguana scene, are those who put their whole faith in words rather than bribes: the self-beguiling intellectuals, the constitutionalists, the theorists on political rectitude. (Words, to be sure, proclamations and manifestoes, are the common currency of oppressors and oppressed, and the bread of daily life; the "growling mutter" of the mine comes to Charles Gould's heart "with the peculiar force of a proclamation.") The novel's view of the thoughtful parliamentarian, confronting power with intellect, is pitying and ironic. Don José Avellanos stands apart from the rest of the theorists, having survived the tortures of the dictator Guzman Bento; he has received the novel's all-important seal of courage. But he is old, and "overtaxed by so many years of undiscouraged belief in regeneration." His life in pursuit of political rectitude has produced the famous and contradictory speeches, also the manuscript and first sheets of the "History of Fifty Years of Misrule," presently to be used as wadding for guns. His chief political success was to bring about the provisional reform dictatorship of Don Vincente Ribiera. As for Ribiera, he "was more pathetic than promising, this first civilian Chief of the State Costaguana had ever known, pronouncing, glass in hand, his simple watchwords of honesty, peace, respect for law, political good faith abroad and at home — the safeguards of national honour." The benevolent dictatorship ends as the mule carrying Ribiera expires under him at the edge of Sulaco. And Don Juste Lopez, President of the Provincial Assembly, can respond to the effrontery of Gamacho and Fuentes only by "a dazed smoothing of his beard and the ringing of the presidential bell." Any resistance to Pedro Montero would be useless, Don Juste feels. But perhaps democracy may yet be saved by words and forms:

Official courtesies must not be neglected, if they are gone through with a bleeding heart. The acceptance of accomplished facts may save yet the precious vestiges of parliamentary institutions. Don

Juste's eyes glowed dully; he believed in parliamentary institutions — and the convinced drone of his voice lost itself in the stillness of the house like the deep buzzing of some ponderous insect.[7]

These are the futilities, of which Conrad takes a fairly Flaubertian view. The realities are corruption, power, savagery, greed, cowardice, the San Tomé mine including its North American financing; also idealism and courage. In the historical background, still shadowing the lives of those who survive, is Guzman Bento, who "ruled the country with the sombre imbecility of political fanaticism": the "Citizen Saviour of the Country" whose Army of Pacification devastated and united the land. The vignette (pages 137–139) is a brief and brilliant one. At the tail of the Army of Pacification Bento carried about a captive band of his political opponents, "a diminished company of nearly naked skeletons." The final refinement of his sadism was clemency: "to enjoy his power . . . by seeing his crushed adversaries crawl impotently into the light of day out of the dark, noisome cells of the Collegio." A retrospective view, much later in the book, shows one such adversary crawl out with maimed feet and ceaselessly trembling body: Dr. Monygham. For years he is haunted by the memory of Father Beron, the army chaplain who presided over the tortures and confessions.

Guzman Bento's political descendants are cruel, but timeservers and poltroons rather than fanatics. Pedro Montero's "army" of half-savage Llaneros is not contemptible. These are ignorant, proud, strong fighting men of a "haggard fearlessness" and with "scorched eyes." And even Montero's brother the General and backwoods hero has a saving stupidity and grotesque magnitude, who could spell out the print of newspapers and so knew he had performed the "greatest military exploit of modern times." But Pedro — Pedrito with his "genius for treachery" — has emerged from the garrets of Parisian hotels, where he had served the Costaguana Legation, possibly as waiter or lackey, possibly as inferior scribe. His ambition formed by reading in those garrets is to be another Duc de Morny and, with his brother as Dictator or even Emperor, to demand a share in every enterprise as the price of his protection. He is escorted into Sulaco by the Señores Fuentes and Gamacho, onetime Moderates who at the first rumors of a Montero victory showed a "subtle change of the pensive temper" and, on confirmation of the news, "blossomed into convinced Liberals." One of Fuentes' first acts — while Gamacho orates in the plaza, the "uncouth howlings of an inferior sort of devil" — is to try to turn Montero against the orator. Colonel Sotillo is another revolutionary leader: turncoat, coward, and liar. "Like most of his countrymen, he was carried away by the sound of fine words, especially if uttered by himself." He feigns sickness rather than talk to his terrible ally Montero; he runs out of the room with a "yell of alarm" when Captain Mitchell leans forward angrily. The book's two most craven figures come face to face as Sotillo tries to extort information from the bound and already hanging Señor Hirsch. Presumably Hirsch spits in Sotillo's face in a paroxysm of fear rather than in defiance. And presumably Sotillo — springing back "with a low cry of dismay, as if aspersed by a jet of deadly venom" — shoots him in terrified self-defense.

Such are the men who initiate revolutions and profit from them, or who take over the revolutions begun on idealistic grounds. But there are also the brave and the faithful. The novel's division of its humanity into the cowardly and the brave is certainly less conscious than some of its other polarities (skeptic–idealist, complex–simple, scoundrel–dupe) but possibly as important. Don Pépé, General Barrios, Hernandez, Father Corbelàn and to some extent Father Romàn form an interesting group; they might be heroes of the later Hemingway. Don Pépé and Father Romàn may seem developments of the simple extrovert and faithful-retainer type. But the five belong together as veterans of the wars, or who have had some contact with savage life, the "wild life" of the interior. They are incapable of betrayal yet have been, in various senses, outlaws. And now they find themselves in paradoxically respectable positions or as trusted old men. They are brave.

The austere moralistic and intellectual side of Conrad sometimes blinds us to his sympathy for the adventurous and the brave. Don Pépé (who carries faint overtones of Don Quixote) has the "vein of genuine humanity so often found in simple old soldiers of proved courage who have seen much desperate service." He is "the fighter." But now he is the paternal administrator of the mine's villages, and walks about "girt with a great sword and in a shabby uniform with tarnished bullion epaulettes of a senior major." He is absolutely dependable. So too is Father Romàn, card player and great snuff-taker who had "shriven many simple souls on the battlefields of the Republic." So too, apparently, is Hernandez the robber turned general, now that he is pledged to Father Corbelàn.

Father Corbelàn himself (though presently to be the country's first Cardinal-Archbishop) has enjoyed the wild life as much as any of the others. He has the esoteric scar which in Conrad may indicate sympathy or approval; his appearance suggests "something unlawful behind his priesthood, the idea of a chaplain of bandits." According to rumor he had baptized whole nations of Indians, living with them like a savage himself. "It was related that the padre used to ride with his Indians for days, half naked, carrying a bullock-hide shield, and, no doubt, a long lance, too — who knows? That he had wandered clothed in skins, seeking for proselytes somewhere near the snow line of the Cordillera." He comes out of the wilderness to advocate the rights of the Church with the same passion. He refuses compromise, rejects the offer of the episcopal palace, and prefers "to hang his shabby hammock amongst the rubble and spiders of the sequestrated Dominican Convent." We know him in the present as the beautiful Antonia's uncle and as the stern critic of Martin Decoud's skepticism and General Barrios' drunkenness.

The figure of General Barrios, as presented in a first vignette (pages 161–164), is a singularly attractive one; it has all the reality that skillful and sympathetic caricature lends. Barrios too is a man's man. Like the others, he is unmarried, and prefers unceremonious gatherings where he can talk about the old days and his "genuine love of that wild life": jaguar-hunts, encounters with wild bulls and crocodiles, adventures in the great forests. He is brave and incapable of betrayal because "too much of a real soldier"; he has the desirable token wound, covered by an eyepatch. But the vice to which he has to accommodate himself is gambling. Through the night before one battle he gambled away horses, pistols, accoutrements, and finally his sword, sent to a town in the rear and pledged for five hundred pesetas. In the morning he discovered he "could lead his troops into battle very well with a simple stick in his hand." So later (since his gold-laced uniforms are almost always in pawn) he assumes a disdain of military trappings. And we see him thus for the first time: half-drunk, chatting while the embarked soldiers await him:

General Barrios, in a shabby blue tunic and white peg-top trousers falling upon strange red boots, kept his head uncovered and stooped slightly, propping himself up with a thick stick. No! He had earned enough military glory to satiate any man, he insisted to Mrs. Gould, trying at the same time to put an air of gallantry into his attitude. A few jetty hairs hung sparsely from his upper lip, he had a salient nose, a thin, long jaw, and a black silk patch over one eye.[8]

He too is a Costaguanero; and, in Conrad's moderately exclusive world, one of the saved.

This is a wise book, and no little of its wisdom reaches us through these brief vignettes, with their distilled understanding of character in action. But *Nostromo* is also a philosophical novel: a meditation on politics, on history, on motivation. Is it, as I believe, a pessimistic and skeptical meditation; and therefore a true one? The instances are glaring of the generous-minded who have read into Conrad's narratives their own tenderness and faith. But the contrary danger exists that the disillusioned, reading as tendentiously, should discover only their own disillusionment with political process. *Nostromo*'s prophecies of 1904 would seem to have been confirmed to a remarkable degree, and not only in South America. Or does this mean that we misread its prophecies from the vantage point of our mid-century ruin? Robert Penn Warren's brilliant introduction to the Modern Library edition (which sees a less ironic treatment of "idealization" than I do, and a less pessimistic view of capitalism) has repeatedly led me to question my conclusions. And the essay has in fact led me to modify certain opinions on the novel's structure. But my view of the novel's ethics and politics remains unmodified: that *Nostromo* is a deeply skeptical novel.

To weigh the value of idealization and illusion means weighing, also, the value of skepticism and reality. And any definition of the novel's position or attitude must depend to a considerable degree on how we interpret Martin Decoud. The problem is a special one, to which we must presently return. But there are other skeptics in *Nostromo* besides Decoud, and others who place some faith in the efficacy of skepticism. There is first of all the omniscient narrator who (after commenting on Nostromo's reaction to Señora Viola's death) brings up the matter rather gratuitously: "The popular mind is incapable of skepticism; and that incapacity delivers their helpless strength to the wiles of swindlers and to the pitiless enthusiasms of leaders inspired by visions of a high destiny." The history of popular misfortune in Costaguana is a history of credulity, as generation after generation is taken in by slogan and glowing manifesto. "Liberals!" even Charles Gould complains. "The words one knows so well have a nightmarish meaning in this country. Liberty — democracy — patriotism — government. All of them have a flavour of folly and murder."

Does skepticism, protecting us from folly, also prevent us from acting at all? Such would seem to be the meaning of Decoud's death, and of the aphorism that holds action the enemy of thought and the friend of flattering illusion. But the general skepticism of Dr. Monygham and the political skepticism of Father Romàn do not prevent them from acting and acting loyally; and even the thought-paralyzed Decoud turns out to have accomplished a good deal. Characteristically,

Conrad makes it difficult to know how to value the disillusionment of Father Romàn.

[He was] saddened at the idea of his flock being scattered or else enslaved. He had no illusions as to their fate, not from penetration, but from long experience of political atrocities, which seemed to him fatal and unavoidable in the life of a State. The working of the usual public institutions presented itself to him most distinctly as a series of calamities overtaking private individuals and flowing logically from each other through hate, revenge, folly, and rapacity, as though they had been part of a divine dispensation. Father Romàn's clear-sightedness was served by an uninformed intelligence; but his heart . . .[9]

The rhetorical uncertainties (clear-sighted but uninformed, from long experience not from penetration) suggest Conrad felt more sympathy with this nihilism than seemed to him proper.* And what is his attitude toward Mrs. Gould (the novel's unequivocal heroine) when she reaches its most succinct skeptical recognition? "There was something inherent in the necessities of successful action which carried with it the moral degradation of the idea."

The history of Costaguana is largely determined by individuals, and by their idealizations as well as by their cupidities and lusts; men compose the state. Yet these seem to be, in *Nostromo,* two separate areas for inquiry: first, man's propensity to self-deception and his need to "idealize" his existence; second, the failure of institutions to work and the failure of history to make sense. The protagonists and their illusions stand a little to the forefront of a turgid and disordered congeries of event.

The meanings of the words "ideal," "idealize," and "ideal conception," whether used by Decoud or another, are by no means immutable. The sense in which Dr. Monygham made an "ideal conception of his disgrace" is dark and elusive, but

* We are finally concerned with the novel's attitudes (to which the imagination and the unconscious have contributed their devil's share) rather than the author's rational convictions. But it is interesting to speculate on these, irrecoverable though they may be because of the windings of irony and the complexities of structure.

at least it involves the "imaginative exaggeration of a correct feeling." It does not imply self-deception, much less self-flattery. But Decoud suggests (speaking of Charles Gould's idealization of the mine) both distortion of reality and unconscious moralistic self-deception. Gould "cannot act or exist without idealizing every simple feeling, desire, or achievement. He could not believe his own motives if he did not make them first a part of some fairy tale." He must, Decoud remarks, endow his "personal desires with a shining robe of silk and jewels"; must see life as a "moral romance." [10] And Decoud's contempt for that "utter sentimentalist" Holroyd, the San Francisco financier, is grounded in his awareness of the man's need to moralize his game of power — who "would not drop his idea of introducing, not only justice, industry, peace, to the benighted continents, but also that pet dream of his of a purer form of Christianity." Decoud speaks as forcefully as anywhere in the novel when he refers to "the sentimentalism of the people that will never do anything for the sake of their passionate desire, unless it comes to them clothed in the fair robes of an idea."

How much credence are we to give this skeptical, attractive voice with its distinctly Conradian rhythm and rhetoric? The question is raised by Decoud's solitary vigil on the Great Isabel, and death. Thereafter he cannot speak for the author or anyone else. But someone does appear at once, the chief engineer, who can speak at least for Decoud. The degree to which he echoes Decoud suggests that Conrad shared no little of this skepticism; or, at least, could not "turn off" a congenial voice and flow of thought:

"The introduction of a pure form of Christianity into this continent is a dream for a youthful enthusiast, and I have been trying to explain to you why Holroyd at fifty-eight is like a man on the threshold of life, and better, too. He's not a missionary, but the San Tomé mine holds just that for him . . . Upon my word, doctor, things seem to be worth nothing by what they are in themselves. I begin to believe that the only solid thing about them is the spiritual value which everyone discovers in his own form of activity —"

"Bah!" interrupted the doctor, without stopping for an instant the idle swinging movement of his legs. "Self-flattery. Food for that vanity which makes the world go round." [11]

In daily life we may approve this tendency to moralize and idealize all impulse; or we may, as I do, find it deeply repugnant. What is the novel's attitude toward it? Warren's important discussion of this problem refers back to *Lord Jim*'s famous passage on the "destructive element" and on the dream into which man is born. "By the dream Conrad here means nothing more or less than man's necessity to justify himself by the 'idea,' to idealize himself and his actions into moral significance of some order, to find sanctions." [12] But does Conrad therefore approve this necessity under all circumstances, and even when it involves gross egotism and self-deception? To argue thus, and to suggest approval of the "true lie" at all times and even when directed toward oneself, is to destroy at one stroke Conrad's healing lucidity and irony.* Warren remarks that we see the process of imperialism "absolutely devoid of 'idea' " in "Heart of Darkness"; presumably he refers to the pilgrims or "explorers." But the grandiloquent moralizings of Kurtz, which feed his vanity in solitude, lead to conduct even more abominable. The "idea" and the very process of moralistic self-deception here corrupt. My own feeling is that Conrad does not limit our choice (as Warren implies) to an inhuman naturalism or a self-deceptive idealism, to animal savagery or "illusion." *Nostromo* seems rather to distinguish between the self-deluding, self-flattering victim of his own illusions and the genuine clear-headed idealist; between, say, Charles Gould and his wife. But also I think the novel makes much more allowance than Warren

* Would Conrad imply that Pedro Montero is more admirable because he sometimes rationalizes his greed? Was Kurtz more admirable because he wrote the pamphlet? Is a nation or group bent on exploitation or power more admirable because it invents, professes, and even comes to half-believe an idealistic purpose? A defense of the "true lie" can hardly fail to become a defense of propaganda and of moralistic pretense or fantasy in the conduct of public affairs. I do not think Conrad makes such a defense. The "true lie," *nota bene,* is especially reserved for women in his books. They are "out of it" and must be protected—which could mean that they are not worthy of receiving the truth!

does for those who do something "for the sake of their passionate desire"; who without illusion but also without meanness pursue it. They need not be cynics, after all, nor mere healthy animals. I should even include Father Corbelàn among them, that passionate man — driven by something stronger than vanity and other than religious obligation.

The skepticism concerning historical and political process is less equivocal; it seems, at times, total. There is first of all a total distrust of political discourse, spoken or written. All governments however corrupt seek the "peace," "progress," and "security" of Sulaco; all journalism and all propaganda is deceitful. But *Nostromo* insists, as *1984* will, that the deception is often self-deception and the rhetoric self-intoxicating. Even the chief engineer is affected. "It was as if something subtle in the air of Costaguana had inoculated him with the local faith in 'pronunciamientos.' " For the young Goulds the passing of the silver escort to the harbor was "like another victory gained in the conquest of peace for Sulaco"; their friend, the historian Don José, expatiates even in their presence "upon the patriotic nature of the San Tomé mine." Conrad separates himself from the Decoud who repudiates patriotism because "the narrowness of every belief is odious," but less so from the Decoud who says patriotism in this country was "hopelessly besmirched . . . had been the cry of dark barbarism, the cloak of lawlessness, of crimes, of rapacity, of simple thieving." I am not sure that he separates himself at all from the Decoud who feels political journalism is a degrading profession, and who dislikes evoking the enthusiasms which will send ignorant people out to die. The parrot's cry "Viva Costaguana!" defines the country's excited preoccupation; Decoud's *"Gran' bestia!"* defines the methods of its journalism. Amused or perhaps embittered by the "boastful tumult" and self-deceptions of the politicians gathered at the Casa Gould, he shouts it into the room — *"Gran' bestia!"* his journalistic epithet for Montero — "with all the strength of his lungs." But the politicians, not recognizing the irony, turn toward him "with an approving expectation."

The political skepticism of *Nostromo* goes much farther

than this. In places it suggests, simply, that reason and good will are relatively powerless before dumb or hidden process; that history escapes man's intentions and his will. What are the true causes of "history"? Pedro Montero's reading of light historical literature in the Paris garret is one; Decoud's love for Antonia is another. But there would be no thriving Occidental Republic without the eleven-story Holroyd building in San Francisco. Certain employees there suppose "the Holroyd connection meant by-and-by to get hold of the whole Republic of Costaguana, lock, stock, and barrel." The truth is that Holroyd took up the country as a hobby, even took up the man Gould rather than the country, and made the journey south because his doctors insisted he take a vacation. Yet who can really know the truth? Holroyd's ancestry had given him "the temperament of a Puritan and an insatiable imagination of conquest." So behind the individual's whim and moral heritage lies a nation's manifest destiny. The last sentence of Holroyd's remarkable prediction is the most important one:

"Of course, some day we shall step in. We are bound to. But there's no hurry. Time itself has got to wait on the greatest country in the whole of God's Universe. We shall be giving the word for everything: industry, trade, law, journalism, art, politics, and religion, from Cape Horn clear over to Smith's Sound, and beyond, too, if anything worth taking hold of turns up at the North Pole. And then we shall have the leisure to take in hand the outlying islands and continents of the earth. We shall run the world's business whether the world likes it or not. The world can't help it — and neither can we, I guess." [13]

These then are some of the contradictory forces flowing together, in Costaguana, to bring forth the historical events: from one side chance, unpredictable dreams and illusions, whim, folly; from the other a vast predetermined economic movement. But the two conceptions of history that insist on them are not contradictory: they alike discount man's reason as a force and alike deny a rational orderly consecutiveness of event. The chronological dislocations and almost insoluble complications of the first part of the novel thus dramatize a theory of causality. They suggest too that since one manifestation is much like the next one, it little matters which "came first." The main events of the Sulaco disorders (which we retrospectively discover lasted only a few days) give an impression of occuring over weeks or even months; conversely, events which occurred years apart seem contemporary. Costaguana is a country in which "everything merely rational fails"; literally, then, its history is absurd.

It is inviting to universalize this country, which in many ways seems truer and more contemporary than the England of *The Secret Agent* or the Geneva and Russia of *Under Western Eyes*. And it is reasonable to suppose that Conrad was thinking of lands as far removed from each other as nineteenth-century Paraguay and Carlist northern Spain and imperial Russia (as well as say Venezuela or some Central American republic) when he wrote of an endemic moral darkness breeding "monstrous crimes and monstrous illusions," and of the "indolence of the upper classes and the mental darkness of the lower" as "fundamental causes." But his thematic insistence is on the "moral romance of capitalism" (with its inherent tendency to confuse power and goodness, profit and welfare) as it affects a small, still undeveloped, and anarchic land. It is the fatality of the country, Decoud complains, to be exploited by foreign speculators while the natives cut each other's throats. But Charles Gould argues that only capitalism — "material interests" — can stop the throat-cutting:

"What is wanted here is law, good faith, order, security. Any one can declaim about these things, but I pin my faith to material interests. Only let the material interests once get a firm footing, and they are bound to impose the conditions on which they alone can continue to exist. That's how your money-making is justified here in the face of lawlessness and disorder. It is justified because the security which it demands must be shared with an oppressed people. A better justice will come afterwards. That's your ray of hope." [14]

The classic defense could hardly be put more succinctly. But what do the material interests actually accomplish, and by what methods? Granted that Holroyd looks upon God "as a sort of influential partner," and granted too Charles Gould's ambition to "redeem" the mine — the Gould Concession must work in an imperfect world of men and manners and must stoop for its weapons. The story is subtly equivocal. The Concession does bring a position of "privileged safety" to the miners, but at a cost of individuality and personal freedom. They live in the three numbered villages protected by an armory, an armed body of sereños, and under the benevolent absolute authority of Don Pépé. They are safe on visits to Sulaco, even have a relative immunity to arrest, but because they wear a kind of uniform, the colors of the mine. The San Tomé mine is a state within a state. Did it, with its bribes, increase or diminish the over-all corruption? The evidence (especially on pages 115–116) is ambiguous, since the chronology is obscure; we cannot be sure whether the mine profited from, reacted against, or contributed to the increasing cynicism. My guess is that Conrad intended a contrast between the naked cynicism and "brazen-faced scramble" for loot in the hinterland and the subtler methods practiced in an Occidental State controlled by the mine. The former killed all enterprise; the latter encouraged at least a nepotistic energy. There would thus be a choice of evils. But surely one evil is replaced by another evil (or at least by a dangerous precedent) when the Gould Concession finances the revolution which brought Don Vincente Ribiera into his five-year dictatorship with a mandate of reform.

So far as Dr. Monygham is concerned, and finally Mrs. Gould herself, there is a corruptive fatality in the "material interests":

> "No!" interrupted the doctor. "There is no peace and no rest in the development of material interests. They have their law, and their justice. But it is founded on expediency, and is inhuman; it is without rectitude, without the continuity and the force that can be found only in a moral principle. Mrs. Gould, the time approaches when all that the Gould Concession stands for shall weigh as heavily upon the people as the barbarism, cruelty, and misrule of a few years back." [15]

And Mrs. Gould,

There was something inherent in the necessities of successful action which carried with it the moral degradation of the idea. She saw the San Tomé mountain hanging over the Campo, over the whole land, feared, hated, wealthy; more soulless than any tyrant, more pitiless and autocratic than the worst Government; ready to crush innumerable lives in the expansion of its greatness.[16]

These passages occur very near the end of the novel's chronological time. *The time approaches* . . . In my interpretation they look forward to a period when — as in Guatemala yesterday, as in the Middle East today — the conflicts induced by capitalist exploitation outweigh the benefits accrued. But according to Warren we may read them hopefully, keeping in mind Charles Gould's prediction that a better justice will come afterwards. "The material interests have fulfilled their historical mission, or are in the process of filling it . . ." [17] The difference would seem to lie in how far the novel looks into the future. We can respect Warren's serious statement — "nothing is to be hoped for, even in the most modest way, if men lose the vision of the time of concord" — without admitting that *Nostromo* dramatizes or even implies it. The horizon offered by the book itself seems to me, simply, Dr. Monygham's dark one.

What are we to say of Sulaco within the dramatized lapse of time? Certainly the society at the end of the book is preferable to that at the beginning, as Warren argues, if we take as beginning the savage old days of Guzman Bento's tyranny and as end the quiet moment when Dr. Monygham makes his prediction. Or is the "end" that referred to by the narrator who momentarily speaks in the first person: a Sulaco with cable cars, foreign merchants with modern villas, a vast railway goods yard, warehouses, and "serious, organized labour troubles"? He remarks, of the earlier Sulaco, that the "material apparatus of perfected civilization which obliterates the individuality of old towns under the stereotyped conveniences of modern life had not intruded as yet . . ." The old debate — the values of modern comfort against those of individuality and ancient culture — is suggested but not solved. On the large subject of "progress" even imagery offers an uncertain testimony:

> . . . the sparse row of telegraph poles strode obliquely clear of the town, bearing a single, almost invisible wire far into the great campo—like a slender, vibrating feeler of that progress waiting outside for a moment of peace to enter and twine itself about the weary heart of the land.[18]

Martin Decoud remains to be dealt with; and no small part of the impression of skepticism left by *Nostromo* comes from him. His consciousness, as Leavis says, seems to permeate and even dominate the book. And if the novel succeeds in "repudiating" Decoud with sufficient force, this must certainly affect our response to the over-all vision. Warren remarks that Conrad "repudiates the Decouds of this world" and Leavis that "we can have no doubt" about the judgment on Decoud's skepticism. But both go on to recognize that the creative situation is more complex than this. Indeed it is! We cannot say that Conrad repudiates skepticism by repudiating Decoud; we cannot even say (without further qualification) that Conrad develops some creative sympathy for Decoud while disapproving of him. The characterization obviously belongs with those in which a writer attempts to separate out and demolish a facet of himself; attempts to condemn himself by proxy. But there are certain signs of an even more special relationship than this; *there is, generally, a marked discrepancy between what Decoud does and says and is, and what the narrator or omniscient author says about him.* This suggests that some of the irony is directed at a personage who is not fully in the book or not in it at all; a Decoud-self conceived but not dramatized. To put matters bluntly: Conrad may be condemning Decoud for a withdrawal and skepticism more radical than Decoud ever shows; which are, in fact, Conrad's own. May we not alter Leavis' proposition — that *Nostromo* was written by a Decoud who wasn't a complacent dilettante and who was "drawn toward those capable of 'investing their activities with spiritual value' " — to say that it was written by an even more skeptical Decoud who recognized, to be sure, the immobilizing dangers of skepticism?

Critics have generally dwelt on what the narrator or author says about Decoud, if only because it is so quotable. The book's mannerism of recurrent ironic epithets is repeatedly directed against him: he is "the boulevardier," "the exotic dandy of the Parisian boulevard," "the dilettante in life," "the spoiled darling of the family," "the brilliant Costaguanero of the boulevards," etc. And the account of his suicide includes a large amount of decisive repudiation.[19] Decoud "died from solitude and want of faith in himself and others"; he "was not fit to grapple with himself singlehanded"; "the affectations of irony and skepticism" had driven forth his thought "into the exile of utter unbelief." And he died a "victim of the disillusioned weariness which is the retribution meted out to intellectual audacity"; he "disappeared without a trace, swallowed up in the immense indifference of things." Some of the force of Conrad's "repudiation of skepticism" may be taken away by that last phrase. If Decoud experiences a total cosmic skepticism, the surviving narrator here certainly shares it! It is useful to recall, too, that only ten days but 194 pages separate the Decoud we left on the Great Isabel and the Decoud who commits suicide.

For how indifferent, inactive, and uncommitted is the real Decoud, whom Warren describes as thinking "himself outside of the human commitments"? If we subtract the ironic epithets, authorial summaries, and solitary suicide, a quite different person emerges. So far from believing in or caring about nothing, he has an ideal of lucidity and of intellectual honesty, he is very much in love, and he is (quite apart from his love for Antonia or from his attitude toward the current political situation) a patriot. His bitter reaction to the slurring remarks of young Scarfe and his sudden outburst to Don José are hardly those of an indifferent man:

"There is a curse of futility upon our character: Don Quixote and Sancho Panza, chivalry and materialism, high-sounding sentiments and a supine morality, violent efforts for an idea and a sullen acquiescence in every form of corruption. We convulsed a continent for our independence only to become the passive prey of a democratic parody, the helpless victims of scoundrels and cut-throats, our institutions a mockery, our laws a farce—a Guzman Bento our master! And we have sunk so low that when a man like you has awakened our conscience, a stupid barbarian of a Montero—Great Heavens! a Montero!—becomes a deadly danger, and an ignorant, boastful Indio, like Barrios, is our defender." [20]

How are we to weigh these impassioned tones against Decoud's claim that he is not a patriot, or against his desire (enunciated by the narrator once) to carry Antonia "away out of these deadly futilities of pronunciamientos and reforms"? The paradox is like that of Conrad himself, though I offer it as illustration rather than "source": a deeply patriotic and even excited feeling toward Poland doubled by intellectual distrust of fanaticism. Decoud very properly sees propaganda journalism as "a sort of intellectual death," yet becomes the editor of a local newspaper; he sees accurately enough that the political situation in Costaguana is comical, yet brings the small arms to Sulaco; he ridicules the excited discussions of the legislators in the Gould salon, yet fathers the Occidental Republic. "Another revolution, of course. On my word of honour, Mrs. Gould, I believe I am a true *hijo del pays,* a true son of the country, whatever Father Corbelàn may say. And I'm not so much of an unbeliever as not to have faith in my own ideas, in my own remedies, in my own desires." He is, to borrow his own words, one of those who *will* do something for the sake of his passionate desire, and even though it not come "clothed in the fair robes of an idea."

The creative situation is thus exceedingly complex, even if we put aside possible direct biographical connections. On the one hand there is a Martin Decoud who, in spite of the epithets, receives no little of his creator's sympathy and approval: the apparently idle and indifferent young exile who returns home to participate in inflammatory journalism, obeys his loved one's commands, and fathers a revolution, yet all the while (through his lucid insight into men's motives) maintains intellectual integrity. He is at once spectator and actor, and he achieves a kind of immortality in the commemorative medallion and Antonia's undying love. But there also has been present, perhaps all the time, the idea or image (though not in the events of the book itself) of another Decoud or another self: immobilized in total physical isolation and in the exile of utter unbelief, who sees no reason for action, who is virtually incapable of it. This is the dramatically invisible Decoud now and then belabored by epithet, and whose suicide we are allowed to witness: "his sadness was the sadness of a skeptical mind." Is it hard to believe, in spite of Conrad's magnificent rhetorical evocation of his solitude, that the active and loving Decoud would commit suicide so soon? The remarkable thing is that we believe as much as we do. For the two Decouds are, indeed, two very different men, two different "potential selves."

A few words, finally, on structure, technique, craft.

> In *Nostromo* Conrad is openly and triumphantly the artist by *métier,* conscious of French initiation and of fellowship in craft with Flaubert. The French element so oddly apparent in his diction and idiom throughout his career (he learnt French before English) here reveals its full significance, being associated with so serious and severe a conception of the art of fiction.[21]

My admiration for the creative achievement and my sympathy with the political vision are such that I wish Leavis' comment were true, or his further remark that the melodrama is "completely controlled to the pattern of moral significance." Both comments are far from true of the whole book. Technically speaking, *Nostromo* represents an important step in that deformalization of the novel which will attract the twentieth century's greatest talents. Its best pages, moreover, show an audacity and, yes, severity of technique as impressive as that of *Lord Jim;* the first sixty pages constitute an almost impenetrable barrier to the lazy reader. But these generalizations, and the larger ones on density of creation and seriousness of theme, apply to not much more than the first half of the book. On returning to *Nostromo* after a year or more it is shocking to discover how much that one remembered at all (and how much of the material discussed by critics) comes in the first two hundred and fifty or three hundred pages. *Nostromo* is in fact a great but radically defective novel, and its greatest defect is that it is at least two hundred pages too long. This is not a matter of generalized diffuseness. The two hundred or more pages in excess come in the last two hundred and sixty.

The crucial change in the creative situation occured, I suspect, in the middle of Chapter 7 of Part II, with the end of Decoud's long letter to his sister: that is, on page 249. At this point an ironic, elliptical, austere yet intense attitude toward the material gives way to a more naïve dramatic interest in the unrolling events; the historian becomes a roving camera or (still less successfully) a subjective reporter of intense emotional experience. For the author, then — at page 249 of its 564 pages — the novel changes in character. But the remainder of the second section (i.e., to page 304) is memorable as well as exciting: the long account of Decoud's and Nostromo's voyage on the lighter through the unearthly blackness of the Placid Gulf, and the collision with Colonel Sotillo's steamer, whose anchor sweeping past carries off the craven hiding Señor Hirsch, to be interrogated, tortured, and killed.

The story could not, of course, have ended at this point. But the real *Nostromo,* the book one remembers and the book critics talk about, has largely been achieved by the beginning of Part III. The land has been fully created. The large themes too have been developed: the fatality of revolution, which liquidates its own best elements; the fatality of capitalism, which destroys or corrupts even as it creates; the paradoxical effects of idealization, and Charles Gould's "circumvallation" by incorruptible metal; the effect on history and politics of fanaticism, rationalism, skepticism. So too, with one or two exceptions, we know the people as well as we shall ever know them; presumably we are even in a position to predict Dr. Monygham's loyalty and Nostromo's slow corruption. The essential creative fact is that Conrad had, by page 304, discovered and explored his material.

What indeed of the essential *Nostromo* would be lost if we simply lopped off those last two hundred and sixty pages? Not much more than the following: Decoud's arbitrary but movingly written philosophical suicide (pages 496–501), the excellent chapter on the arrival of Pedro Montero (pages 384–393) and perhaps certain other pages of politics, the sudden revelations and tragic ironies of Captain Mitchell's wandering narrative (pages 473–489). In general the rest is either inferior or repeats effects already achieved. The last fifty pages on Nostromo's plight (after the lighthouse has been built on the Great Isabel, close to his buried silver) are audaciously conceived. The one large symbol and the multiplying ironies close in on him ineluctably, once he is compelled to place the Violas on the island; the whole ends with a fine grand-opera effect and last crescendo sentence. Yet all this, really (and given the inevitably embarrassed treatment of sexual passion) is unworthy of the novel that has gone before. "The incorruptible Nostromo breathed her ambient seduction in the tumultuous heaving of his breath." This at least will not do. Nostromo led Conrad into the book and gave it its title.[22] But he is, both as symbolic Man of the People and as exemplar of idealized vanity, the novel's "lost subject." And it is perhaps just as well.

It may be a thankless activity: to hack away at the rough edges of a great book. But this is more than a rough edge. It is better to state frankly that the third part of *Nostromo* is for the most part good intelligent popular fiction on a quite different level from the first two parts. The diminished seriousness and dwindling creative energy is accompanied by much technical clumsiness and by lapses into a kind of phrasing characteristic of Conrad's last books. Style is, we cannot repeat too often, not the man but the artist; it is our primary evidence of glowing or failing energy, of intense or relaxed imagining, of congenial or uncongenial situation. A few examples (and they have no counterpart in the first 250 pages) will at least indicate that something was going wrong. The *as, as to* constructions (very common in the last novels) suggest a weary gathering up of discrete materials; certain others suggest that Conrad was thinking in French or, at least, had momentarily lost his touch with English idiom. All of the passages reflect, in one way or another, embarrassment or lack of confidence in the presence of material intended to be very exciting:

Sotillo's temperament was of that sort that he experienced an ardent desire to beat him; just as formerly when negotiating with difficulty a loan from the cautious Anzani, his fingers always itched to take the shopkeeper by the throat. As to Captain Mitchell, the suddenness, unexpectedness, and general inconceivableness of this experience had confused his thoughts. Moreover, he was physically out of breath.

The facts of his situation he could appreciate like a man with a distinct experience of the country. He saw them clearly. He was as if sobered after a long bout of intoxication.

The word had fixed itself tenaciously in his intelligence. His imagination had seized upon the clear and simple notion of betrayal to account for the dazed feeling of enlightenment as to being done for, of having inadvertently gone out of his existence on an issue in which his personality had not been taken into account.

"Hullo!" exclaimed the doctor, looking up with a start. He could hear the Capataz stagger against the table and gasp. In the sudden extinction of the light within, the dead blackness sealing the window frames became alive with stars to his sight.

"Of course, of course," the doctor muttered to himself in English. "Enough to make him jump out of his skin."

Nostromo's heart seemed to force itself into his throat. His head swam. Hirsch! The man was Hirsch! [23]

Such prose as this may indicate fatigue, indifference, or the absence of an imaginative challenge. Or it may indicate a losing struggle with intractable material and method. The over-all weakness of the third section is puzzling, and all the more puzzling because certain pages are brilliantly successful. What dramatic situation in the novel, or "creative situation" for the novelist, does the inhibiting? The recurrent symptom of uncertain or uselessly wavering point of view ought to tell us something; at least, it has no little to do with the reader's discomfort. My own conclusion is that point of view in the very largest sense — the *literal* distance in space and time from which the action is seen by the imagination — is responsible for most of Conrad's difficulties. And through most of Part III no narrating consciousness (point of view in the technical sense) was available capable of controlling distance efficiently.

For distance, when we are concerned with imaginative creation, is not simply a figure of speech; it may to some degree be measured. Through the important chapters (1–10, pages 307–503) we are concerned, primarily, with the critical hours following the departure of the lighter, though the tenth chapter takes us ahead for the death of Decoud and some years ahead for Captain Mitchell's retrospective view. But in fact we have (so far as the imagination is concerned) a real present time and a full obligation to report it only in the chapters that take place at Viola's house (pages 307–322, 461–472) and in the chapters that take place in the Custom House (pages 323–351, 422–461). The structure is this: the narrative reports a very few things happening slowly in the Custom House, then breaks away for a selective view of the larger historical events occurring (but only so far as the imagination is concerned) in the past (pages 351–422), then returns to the Custom House for further full reporting of things happening in an imagined present.

I am persuaded this is more than a matter of distinguishing between "scenic" and "panoramic" methods, though the scene does imply presentness and the panorama does imply a surview of the past. It would be more accurate to say that the imagination has been trapped in space and time. For the present time of the Custom House action involves, very literally, a present place; the larger historical events are imagined as taking place *elsewhere,* and can be reported as from a distance. Finally the one new character and new consciousness in these chapters is that of Colonel Sotillo, who remains in the Custom House, and who gets a disproportionate attention. This is where the creative imagination is, so to speak, located: close to Colonel Sotillo and his nervousness, in the Custom House, in a slowly moving present time. It is planted there so firmly that any movement — to the town, to the mine — seems awkward and difficult. Indeed Part III might well have been called "The Custom House" rather than "The Lighthouse," since it dominates and disrupts two hundred pages. The Custom House is the solid immovable object on which the novel nearly founders; the dark immediate place in a present time from which, desperately, Conrad's imagination strains away.*

But if the Custom House is the imagination's unfortunate "post of observation," the novel's post of observation (the technical point of view) is constantly changing. This is no longer a matter of the sudden, large, and of course deliberate shifts that go into the impressionism of Part I, but rather of amateurish and clumsy shifts within a single scene. Many of these seem inadvertent; others are made for transparent reasons of convenience. Either way they would suggest an indifference to technique: an indifference to harmonious movement and to skillful management of the reader. In the first chapter of Part III the point of view changes at least ten times in five pages and often for no good reason.† But even

* These inferences are, of course, highly speculative. Even if it were possible to describe such a situation with complete accuracy, it would be impossible to describe it briefly. Conrad's imaginative concern with the death of Hirsch is obsessive, even sadistic. Perhaps Hirsch has something to do with the imagination's apparent "imprisonment" in the Custom House?

† A summary of the changes will give some idea of the roughness: (1) The chapter begins (p. 307) with two paragraphs of *omniscient* summary and clarification: truly omniscient since it reports both what the European press reaction will be and what Captain Mitchell intends to do in the next hours. (2) The point of view changes (307) to *Dr. Monygham*'s limited view for fourteen lines, presumably to authorize a closer look at the workmen and the Albergo. An omniscient narrator could have taken it as well. (3) It

this chapter, written on the threshold of that imprisoning Custom House, does not show some of the major difficulties and embarrassments to appear in later ones. It does not have to report violent physical action; it does not have to convey intense passion, intense fear, or the intense shock of discovery; it does not have to build a merely physical or dramatic suspense. But it does suggest the kind of difficulty caused by Conrad's refusal to commit himself to a consistently omniscient view, or to a retrospective narrator, or to the limited view of one character only; his narrative is compelled to blunder back and forth among these three points of view and sometimes others. The chapter comes under the author's control, and the wavering ceases, only when Dr. Monygham and the chief engineer begin to talk, ironically and philosophically, about conscious and unconscious motives. The

changes (308) within a paragraph, but for four lines only, to the *workmen*'s view of Dr. Monygham. There is no apparent reason for this change. (4) It changes (308), for fourteen lines, to a *sound camera*'s report of dialogue (so-called because almost totally objective, as the original point of view was not). (5) It changes radically (308), for sixteen lines, to an *omniscient* commentary on the chief engineer's plan. (6) It changes (309), for twenty-three lines, to the *chief engineer*'s own summary of his activities, and of the railroad's usefulness to its friends — this passage, like the preceding one, offering a disguised authorial "harking back to make up." (7) It changes (310), for thirty lines, to the *sound camera*'s report. (8) It changes radically (310), for seventy lines, to the *chief engineer*'s reflections on Dr. Monygham, these shading quickly into the *community*'s view of his story — an omniscient view, or almost so, which speaks succinctly of the doctor's years of isolation. Are the rumors that he betrayed his friends at the time of the Great Conspiracy true? We now see the importance of that "almost." The novel does not have to tell us, because of the nominal restriction to the *chief engineer*'s view. (9) It changes slightly (312), for fourteen lines, to the *chief engineer*'s reflections on Viola and the Albergo. (10) For the remainder of the chapter (312–322) the point of view remains fairly constant, except for a few authorial or omniscient interjections: it is a *sound camera* recording the conversation of Dr. Monygham and the chief engineer. But the real situation is very different from this nominal or technical one. Both persons offer essential information and raise important questions; they are talking for our convenience. But the chief engineer inheriting the detached lucid view and meditative rhetoric of Decoud (whom the novel had abandoned on page 302) becomes an important vehicle for the author's analyses of character and moral situation. The most awkward fact about this sudden and apparently strong author-identification with the chief engineer is that we have had little chance to know him before. He comes importantly into the book, presumably, because Decound is no longer available.

secret once again is distance, and the authority to indulge an ironic evasiveness. Unfortunately the point of view that might have solved Conrad's difficulties — the Faulknerian overriding consciousness and voice, free to blend with other consciousnesses without losing irony and free to blend with other voices without losing richness — had not yet been invented. But the historian who speaks in the best parts of *Nostromo* helped prepare the way.

The paradox (nearly always overlooked by critics) is that the skillful, innovating Conrad often showed less than average skill when trying to employ the narrative methods of the standard realistic novel; he became, suddenly, amateur. But if he finds, or allows himself to take, the right distance, the brilliance and assurance at once return. The great chapter of Pedrito Montero's arrival (pages 384–393) is straightforward enough. But it is reported by an ironic observer who is also a thoughtful historian, who makes no pretense of "planting" his observations in one of his characters, and who makes no effort to create an illusion of time passing very slowly. He keeps his imaginative distance! And keeping it — authorized thus to change focus and timing as he pleases, authorized to move freely from the scenic to the meditative and back, authorized to select — he is all the more capable of fine particulars. Here is the end of the chapter; and the end of that day for the National Guards and their new friends and allies of Montero's cavalry. This (as against the lamentable prose of the Custom House chapters) is Conrad writing with authority:

The National Guards were thinking of siesta, and the eloquence of Gamacho, their chief, was exhausted. Later on, when, in the cooler hours of the afternoon, they tried to assemble again for further consideration of public affairs, detachments of Montero's cavalry camped on the Alameda charged them without parley, at speed, with long lances levelled at their flying backs as far as the ends of the streets. The National Guards of Sulaco were surprised by this proceeding. But they were not indignant. No Costaguanero had ever learned to question the eccentricities of a military force. They were part of the natural order of things. This must be, they concluded, some kind of administrative measure, no doubt. But the motive of it escaped their unaided intelligence, and their chief and orator, Gamacho, Commandante of the National Guard, was lying drunk and asleep in the bosom of his family. His bare feet were upturned in the shadows repulsively, in the manner of a corpse. His eloquent mouth had dropped open. His youngest daughter, scratching her head with one hand, with the other waved a green bough over his scorched and peeling face.[24]

It is time to comment, briefly, on the structure of Part I; and to qualify certain exasperated remarks made on it long ago.* The novel "almost unreadable" in its richness and difficulty is preferable, after all, to the novel unreadable because crudely oversimple: A *Nostromo,* not to mention an *Absalom, Absalom!* or a *Light in August,* merely reminds us that some books must be read more strenuously than others. A Faulkner novel reminds or forewarns us of this from its first page. But *Nostromo* begins with a deceptively clear statement of symbol and theme, and it ends, however symbolically or tragically, in simple romantic narrative. Between the easy beginning and the easy end comes the most audacious of Conrad's experiments: the first part. This is a more radical example of spatial form than *Lord Jim* for the one reason that it does not pretend to be the oral narrative of a free wandering memory. *Nostromo* goes to great lengths to avoid effects of logical composition. Yet it is,- frankly, a history; a written book.

* In my monograph *Joseph Conrad,* pp. 25–26: "In spite of its brilliant opening pages, the first part of *Nostromo* and the third and fourth chapters of the second part stand badly in need of a detached narrator . . . It is highly probable that when Conrad began *Nostromo* he did not forsee where his own interest in the subject would lie. The tone alters considerably with the arrival, after a hundred and fifty pages, of a character with whom Conrad could identify himself: the Marlovian Martin Decoud. Prior to his coming, the book professes to be a portrait of a community achieved through both space and time. It is as though a flashlight were playing fitfully and at random in a dark room, full of still objects and moving people, the forces of history. As the flashlight plays back and forth it picks out objects and persons, and rests for a moment on each. Every image is startling in its visual clarity; in its precise detail and beauty. But it remains for the unequipped spectator to reassemble the scattered images and give them form."

Martin Decoud's letter to his sister (Part II, Chapter 7) comes much closer to the impressionism of Marlow in *Lord Jim;* its difficulty is, so to speak, a normal difficulty. Decoud avoids bookish plotting and he assumes some knowledge in his reader. On the other hand, he also makes an effort to place the events in time and to establish an order among the forces, thoughts, and feelings described. The writing of such a letter at such a juncture is a convention, of course, and a rather less plausible convention than Marlow's speaking whole novels aloud. Attempts to rationalize this novel-like letter are unimportant and even irrelevant. For the letter, dealing for the most part with events that had happened the day before, contains some of the book's most vivid writing. It provides Conrad a congenial method and distance, and a chance to speak with his own voice.

The first part is infinitely more difficult, and one great source of this difficulty is chronology. It has been my sad experience, each time I have tried to disentangle the time-scheme of *Nostromo,* to come up with a different result. Some of the difficulty is caused by a moment of extreme carelessness or of Faulkerian perversity. For the banquet attended by Ribiera occurs eighteen months before the Sulaco riots (pages 34, 130) but the riots occur about six months after a "visit" which presumably refers to the banquet (page 145) — unless we are to assume that the briefly flaring Monterist revolution lasted a year or more. It is as difficult to know how many hours intervened between the embarkation of General Barrios and the Sulaco riots as to know how many years went into the regeneration of the San Tomé mine. The literal chronology of *Nostromo* (working from that parenthetical reference to the third of May) is presumably irrecoverable. It is perhaps enough to recognize again that many of these events which seem to occur over months — from the departure of Barrios, through the escape of Ribiera, the riots, the plan for a new revolution and Occidental Republic, the departure of Decoud and Nostromo, to the return of Nostromo, the death of Hirsch, the arrival of Pedrito Montero — actually occur within a few days. But this infinite lengthening out of present time has little effect on the reader of Part I, since he gets almost no glimpses of a genuine present.

We may exclude as irrelevant the "real" present time referred to on page 95 by a first-person narrator; we may exclude too the unspecified later times of Captain Mitchell's narrative and Nostromo's death. The basic fictional present time begins on page 147 on the day of General Barrios' departure with the troops, and continues through the long evening and night of political planning (pages 151, 160–161, 164–172, 173–222); it is resumed on the afternoon of the riot near Viola's house (11–14, 14–15, 16–17, 18, 21, 22–23, 26–28); it is resumed again, the next day, with Decoud's writing of his letter (223–249) and his departure with Nostromo in the lighter. Perhaps the essential fact about this fictional present, before page 173, is that almost nothing happens in it. It seems, rather, a pretext and starting-place for historical retrospect, for meditative digression, or for evocation of a "timeless" Sulaco. The reader of Part I, which ends on page 131, experiences this basic present time for only thirteen pages.

Matters are even more complicated than this, however. For we have at least two other fictional present times— "present" not merely because they come to us scenically, but because they too serve as pretexts or starting-places for digression. One of these is the day of the banquet on the *Juno,* which occurred eighteen months before the riots (pages 34–36, 39, 117–131); the other comprises, years earlier, that conversation late at night between Mrs. Gould and her husband which elicits his important defense of "material interests" (69–74, 82–85). It is entirely possible that an alert first reader of *Nostromo* might take the day of the banquet on the *Juno* to be the basic (i.e., latest) fictional present time. To do so he need only forget or minimize that casual "eighteen months before."

But even such a summary as this does not suggest how very precarious is the reader's foothold in these elusive presents. For what exactly does the reader receive, experience, see in them? An inexplicable glimpse of Nostromo's cargadores pursuing an unidentified mob, the Viola family waiting for Nostromo, a distant glimpse of rioters and a closer glimpse of runaway horses, a brief family conversation. And, from the present of eighteenth months before, Mrs. Gould and her apparently trivial conversation with a railway chairman. And (after seventy-eight pages of digression and retrospect) the briefest notice of Ribiera's pathetic speech and Montero's brutal one. And (from the present of that evening conversation of the Goulds, years before) an important though short discussion of the mine's moral justification. Part I ends (pages 127–131) with its most vivid and only uninterrupted scene: as the vain Nostromo on horseback parries with the girl Morenita, then allows her to cut the silver buttons from his coat. But this scene turns out, as we look back, to have little relevance to the rest of the book; we would know Nostromo's vanity without it.

We are likely to reach the essential, rather, through a digression within a digression. The fifth chapter of Part I (radiating from that banquet on the *Juno*) is characteristic in its method and difficulty; much more than half of the chapter is vivid, packed, and fairly obscure digression. Only an elaborate chart could record its windings, and its numerous contradictory assaults on the reader's attention. But an impression of the method may be derived from a step-by-step summary of the chapter's approach to certain important information about Costaguana and Charles Gould: (1) We meet, hovering near the vividly evoked Mrs. Gould, the "chairman of the railway board." He speaks of his hard trip across the mountains and of Sulaco's old-fashioned atmosphere; he seems to exist in the novel only as a minor, imperceptive outsider. (2) The chairman reflects in a wandering fashion on the resistance of certain aristocrats to the railroad; on the government's commitment to support it, if necessary by force; on Ribiera as the railroad's "creature"; on the arrangements for this banquet — to which General Montero has insisted on coming. (3) We return, after three paragraphs of omniscient comment on General Montero and other matters, to the railway chairman. But he is no longer on the *Juno*! Instead we see him at dinner in the surveying camp near Higuerota, and with the engineers there. (4) The omniscient narrator or author comments on the engineers and their strength; then returns abruptly to a striking night scene, with the chairman and the chief engineer talking, one infers, about the railroad's difficulties. The link between the omniscient narrator's generalizations and a sudden line of dialogue — "We can't move mountains!" — comes only *after* that line. It is the white Higuerota soaring "out of the shadows of rock and earth like a frozen bubble under the moon." (5) The conversation proceeds briefly but deviously to the engineer's statement of Charles Gould's political influence on the people of the province. Thus (to recapitulate) the digressive reflections of a character whom we do not know at all, the railway chairman, brings us our first body of genuine information on the political situation of the country; and, a page or so later, in a digression recalling his journey, the chairman's conversation with an engineer brings us our first substantial knowledge of Charles Gould. It would be hard to imagine a novel going farther out of its way to avoid logical composition and expository directness.

This then is one aim and one achievement: to avoid obvious authorial organization of the material. What else does the extraordinary impressionist experiment of Part I accomplish? It certainly does establish a historical and novelistic authority; it continually implies that more scenes, persons, events, and forces exist than these few we are allowed to glance at; and by implying this successfully "creates" them. Thus we have the illusion of a solid land existing and a teeming life continuing even after we are compelled to look away. This fact, together with the extraordinary effort we must make to apprehend and organize, gives us the sense of actively discovering a world. In *Lord Jim* the impressionistic method draws us in, implicates us, and asks us to judge a marginal and unfinished case. In *Nostromo* we work as hard but are much less personally and morally involved. Instead we are asked to discover an existing land and help write its history. It could be argued, again, that the chronological dislocations and distortions of emphasis may reflect a theory of history as repetitive yet inconsecutive, devoid of reason, refusing to make sense. The method would then reflect the material in an extreme example of organic or imitative form.

All this may in some measure be true. Yet I am not sure the procedures of Part I can be defended pragmatically in these terms. They do not seem to be, as they were in *Lord Jim,* indispensable to meaning. What they achieve, rather, is the subjection of the reader to a new, strange, and largely frustrating experience; or, to put things more conventionally, they achieve certain odd and original fictional effects. We have, as in *Lord Jim,* a combat between author, material, and reader. But the reader's main effort is now largely to gain some foothold, assume some habitual stance, put himself in a less vertiginous relationship to what he observes. The first part of *Nostromo* invites and then frustrates the normal objectives of readers to an astonishing degree. A reader's first objective may be to identify with one figure and then use him as a post of observation. But each opportunity — Captain Mitchell, Giorgio Viola, Nostromo, Sir John, Mrs. Gould, Charles Gould — is withdrawn almost as soon as offered. So too it is a normal if unconscious ambition of the reader to live vicariously through an imagined experience; to live through scenes. But every promised scene is here broken off, at most after a few pages. The reader is never allowed to settle down and enjoy. And so too, if only to combat that vertigo, the reader incorrigibly longs to locate himself in time and space, and incorrigibly wants to apprehend experience in its order and degree of importance. But this longing is frustrated from beginning to end of the first part. The common reader's notorious general aim — to enter into the book and become one of its characters — is carefully and austerely baffled. The novelist (shifting scene, time, emphasis, focus, post of observation) maliciously chops at his hands.

Nostromo is, surely, one of the most uneven of the great English novels. A first seeming paradox (within the first two parts) is that this ample creation of life and most serious vision of the historical and political process is conveyed by an experimental and necessarily unpopular method. (This is less of a paradox to us, who have survived *Ulysses,* than it would have been to a reader of 1904.) But it remains a paradox within the novel since the diverging impulses to obfuscate and to clarify are both so strong: *Nostromo* offers a more disordered actuality than any of Conrad's earlier novels, but also far more explicit definition of theme and analysis of motive. The larger paradox is that the experimentalism and the intense, austere, serious drama of Parts I and II should have surrendered, in Part III, to a relaxed method and a much more popular story. There is no reason to believe that Conrad, on reaching page 250 or 300, decided to popularize his novel or attenuate his theme. We can refer instead to his own account of his struggle for the creation and assume a temporary exhaustion. In novel-writing the surrender to the obvious and the easy is not always — even, not usually — conscious. In any event, we can assume that *Nostromo* was from beginning to end a more exploratory performance than *Lord Jim.* For that very reason it exposes more clearly (or fails to conceal through rhetoric and narrative device) what Conrad could not yet do well: above all, the handling of dramatic action and the rendering of intense emotion imagined as occuring in a present place and time.

When all this has been said, and the paradoxes and failures of energy and lapses noted (enough of them to crush a slighter book) — the novel substantially remains, in the great dark truth of its political vision and the consoling lucidity of its understanding of human beings. It is, as Warren shows, the central novel of Conrad's career: "As the earlier fiction seems to move toward *Nostromo,* so later fiction seems to represent, by and large, specializations and elaborations of elements that had been in suspension in that work." [25] It brings to a close one of the most astounding periods of creative energy in the career of any novelist: a ten-year period that produced, in addition to the collaborations with Ford Madox Ford and in addition to several minor stories: *Almayer's Folly, An Outcast of the Islands,* a large part of *The Rescue, The Nigger of the "Narcissus," Tales of Unrest, Lord Jim, Typhoon,* "Youth," "Heart of Darkness," "The End of the Tether," "Amy Foster," "Falk."

Chapter Seven

TWO VERSIONS OF ANARCHY

THE *Secret Agent* (1907) and *Under Western Eyes* (1911) stand appealingly between the visionary, experimental early masterpieces and the sentimentalities of *Chance* and *Victory*. This does not mean that Conrad (tired as he certainly was, ridden by sickness and debt) had already entered into an uninterrupted decline. Neither of these fine political novels shows such lapses in language as occurred in the third part of *Nostromo;* neither shows the clumsiness which comes from radical imaginative fatigue. But they are transitional books in the over-all movement from an eccentric to a popularized art and from a highly personal view of humanity to a normalized one. This is true even though the astounding complications of *Chance* are still to come. For already much of the personal rhythm, audacity of rhetoric, and strangeness of perspective have been lost. In part "lost," no doubt; in part deliberately sacrificed to the recognition that things must be made easier for the reader; and in part repudiated. It is obvious that Conrad made a conscious effort to chasten and simplify style, to subdue temperamental evasiveness and control digressive fantasy. And some of this effort (though Conrad's mind and letters now turned rather desperately to the question of finding a larger public) must be attributed to sincere artistic conviction. *The Secret Agent* and *Under Western Eyes* are intelligent, carefully planned novels showing a major change from the impressionist to the realist method. They also show a new mastery of suspenseful plotting, a new power to dramatize scene and crisis directly, a full command of pure nonidiosyncratic English.

In a word they show, *The Secret Agent* especially, control. *The Secret Agent* is, among Conrad's full-length novels, the first easy one and perhaps the only one to know fairly well what it is doing from the first sentence to the last. But even the great first and fourth parts of *Under Western Eyes* (where darker energies are engaged) are comparatively straightforward.

Such a normalizing of method might well betoken and reflect a normalizing of attitude; or, as it is sometimes miscalled, a maturing of attitude. The artist sees matters less obsessively but also less freshly; the world falls back into the place common sense gives it. There are several indications that such a normalizing was occurring in Conrad, who in 1907 was fifty years old. The political subject was given fairly uninhibited and fantastic treatment in the stories of *A Set of Six;* the material of "The Informer" and even of "An Anarchist" would be used in certain pages of *The Secret Agent.*[1] But by then the vision of moral anarchy and latent violence had come under full control and achieved expository clarity. The very turn to the political subject means a normalizing of interest, after all; so too does the turn to comedy with its implications of a rational or social norm and its objective interest in behavior. *The Secret Agent* is macabre comedy, and it would be possible to present it as the very darkest of Conrad's books: a version of modern life and modern man untouched by grace in any form except that of British legality; a vision (in his own words) "of a monstrous town . . . a cruel devourer of the world's light"; a book about mankind's petty weakness and infirmity of spirit. And yet it is comedy: the public, the nonsolipsistic art. The entirely rational author watches with amusement and scorn the respectability of the criminal and the laziness of the violent, and watches Verloc's blind egoism bring on his own ludicrous destruction.

The interest in politics and the turn to a kind of comedy are accompanied, in *The Secret Agent,* by another sign of normalization: the close attention and sympathy given Winnie Verloc, and the very fact that she has been so successfully created. Conrad claimed she was the book's imaginative center.[2] But the portrait is not entirely free of the old misogyny; the attention at last becomes (like that of Comrade Ossipon himself) a terrified, "scandalized" attention. *Under Western Eyes* rather shows the real advance toward an understanding at once mature and compassionate of women; there is not a trace of gratuitous or obsessive denigration in the lifelike portraits of Nathalie Haldin, Mrs. Haldin, Tekla, or even Sophia Antonovna. Some of this new assurance and security in the presence of the female menace may be due to the Jamesian position and Jamesian tone of the narrator: a man clearly too old for a serious romance with Nathalie, and whose role is to *watch* her affectionately. Misogynous reveries are less likely where at least one spokesman for the author has withdrawn from the start. As for Razumov (with whom Conrad certainly identified more closely) — his nominal interest in Nathalie, as soul to be damaged or woman to be loved, cannot be taken very seriously. The matter is above sex. She is instead another major witness in his interior drama of self-scrutiny and self-destruction.

These easier and more conventional realistic novels were, nevertheless, commercial failures. Conrad blamed some of this failure on the "sordid surroundings" of *The Secret Agent* and on the "detachment" of *Under Western Eyes*. But it may be that they failed for the very reason that makes them so accessible to us: that they were some twenty years ahead of their time and, *The Secret Agent* especially, virtually created the genre of the serious psycho-political mystery novel. They recognized that the melodramatic fringe of society (the world of connivance between police and petty criminal, of *agent-provocateur* and police informer, of thought-crime and torture and confession, of anarchist and revolutionary exile) could also be, symbolically and morally, at the very heart of society and corrupting it. But the genteel reader in a confident Edwardian England could hardly be expected to take such "recognitions" seriously, or to accept Conrad's very dim view of humanitarian gesture, or to see a real connection between international affairs and introspective torments. *The*

Secret Agent dealt, after all, with a few Soho crackpots and *Under Western Eyes* with a few Russian crackpots in Geneva! The actual events (an attempt to blow up the Greenwich Observatory, the assassination of Plehve) were safely in the past.[3] It has taken the fiction of Greene, Moravia, Flaiano, Koestler, and others, not to mention the Second World War and its aftermath, to connect fully private conscience and public political crime; to convince us that the moral anarchies and cynicisms and betrayals on which Conrad insisted are realities not ornaments of a fiction. And are never safely in the past.

Various readers have remarked on *The Secret Agent*'s anticipation of Graham Greene, and on the Dostoevskian character of *Under Western Eyes*. But Greene is not Dostoevsky. It is well to make this distinction at the outset, and to recognize that *Under Western Eyes* is the greater novel of the two. Mr. Leavis' preference for *The Secret Agent* (which leaves it not far short of that summit of the English novel *Hard Times*) is to be explained, I suppose, by a preference for neatness of construction and for explicit development of a morally serious theme. But *Under Western Eyes* is more than this, more than a work of fine satirical intelligence. It is, except for the brief *Shadow Line,* the last book in which Conrad was importantly involved and also the last in which he could, importantly not sentimentally, involve his readers. It contains those unpredictables and audacities which may indicate very strong engagement and which, if they turn out to be true and persuasive, provide one of the surest ways of distinguishing the work of powerful imagination from the intelligent imitation of life. And *Under Western Eyes* is tragedy. It is tragedy dealing beyond its private issue with the most contemporary of the ancient conflicts, the essential one: that between the individual ethic of personal loyalty and the public "ethic of state." The particular occasion of a man fallen under the shadow of Russian autocracy is also contemporary enough. The novel's enormous personal achievement is to have done so much justice to Russia and things Russian. It reminds us, as we recall Conrad's hatreds and disgusts, how great must have been the share of conscious imaginative integrity as well as how great the devil's share of unconscious sympathy.

The Secret Agent (subtitled "A Simple Tale") is a work to be enjoyed, and to be enjoyed thoughtfully. But it is not an intimate personal experience to be shared and survived, nor a political treatise to be endlessly reread and debated. "After all, you must not take it too seriously. The whole thing is superficial and it is but a tale. I had no idea to consider Anarchism politically, or to treat it seriously in its philosophical aspect . . . The general reflections whether right or wrong are not meant as bolts . . . They are, if anything, mere digs at the people in the tale." [4] Such disclaimers as these can be irritating, as when a difficult symbolist claims he wants only to "tell a story." But Conrad seems to be speaking with some sincerity in this letter to Galsworthy; or when, to his publisher, he describes the novel as purely a work of imagination without social or philosophical intention.[5] This is doubtless too strong a statement. But the word *entertainment* comes to mind in the honorable sense given it by Graham Greene: an exciting story for thoughtful readers, and in which the most serious and most intimate human concerns (such as alcoholism and bodily degradation, political loyalty and international conflict, even religious conversion and neurotic self-destructiveness) are put to dramatic and "entertaining" use. This does not mean that Greene does not intend quite sincerely his wry general reflections and religious asides, but simply that they subserve the major aim of original and successful entertainment. (I would not even except the sincere *Quiet American,* a fine dramatized essay, though I would except large portions of the great *Power and the Glory.*) Briefly, one of the appeals of Greene's fiction derives from the expository play of an interesting and sardonic mind. But the books were not written for the sake of this expository play. Nor were they written to convert readers.

The situation in *The Secret Agent* is similar. The novel

does have its genuine seriousness of theme; it does express certain strong and austere convictions, recognizably the author's. But it neither explores these convictions for subtle ramification and nuance, nor ever seriously challenges them. Instead, the convictions are simply and forcefully affirmed. Thus the notable absence of strong emotional involvement with any one character is accompanied by a relative absence of subtle intellectual conflict. The Gides and the Thomas Manns, lovers of intellectual play for its own sake, are capable of questioning their own assumptions even in some of their more impersonal novels. But with Conrad, it appears, only a tragic or intensely personal story or at least a very large one (such as *Nostromo*) could induce these intellectual challenges and self-scrutinies. Only a deep introspective drive, that is, could disturb the smooth cluster of ideas on the surface. Such slight author-identification as exists in *The Secret Agent* is clearly with the Assistant Commissioner — especially when (tired of desk work) he leaves his office to take a personal hand in the investigation and experiences a pleasing sense of loneliness and "evil freedom." His life too is divided into an adventurous past and a present of being chained to a desk. He is committed to British respect for legality, order, liberty. But he knows the excitement of the "game" between policeman and outlaw. "He stepped back into the full light of the room, looking like the vision of a cool, reflective Don Quixote, with the sunken eyes of a dark enthusiast and a very deliberate manner." This may well be the author in a succinct if unconscious self-portrait. Yet the Assistant Commissioner evokes none of the major emotional involvement and hence none of the profound intellectual conflict we feel in the portrait of Razumov. The author's relationship to the Assistant Commissioner is rational and without uneasiness. Therefore he may be used to put, clearly and unevasively, what the author has to say about secret agents:

"No, Sir Ethelred. In principle, I should lay it down that the existence of secret agents should not be tolerated, as tending to augment the positive dangers of the evil against which they are used. That the spy will fabricate his information is a mere commonplace. But in the sphere of political and revolutionary action, relying partly on violence, the professional spy has every facility to fabricate the very facts themselves, and will spread the double evil of emulation in one direction, and of panic, hasty legislation, unreflecting hate on the other." [6]

This is clear expository dialogue, justified perhaps by Sir Ethelred's insistence on lucid simplicity. But it differs in no significant way from what Conrad might have said in an essay or letter to the *Times*. A more promising fictional situation occurs when the obsessed Professor pushes certain ideas of the author to a dangerous extreme, as in the discourse on the weak as a source of evil.[7] This is a form of ironic self-evaluation Gide carried very far, but there is not much of it in *The Secret Agent*. More frequently the omniscient author qua author states his position unequivocally: tells us that revolutionists are "the enemies of discipline and fatigue," or react fanatically to seeming injustice, or are guided by vanity, "the mother of all noble and vile illusions, the companion of poets, reformers, charlatans, prophets, and incendiaries." Significantly the Professor and the author-narrator sound very much alike when they make one of the novel's important points, that the terrorist and the policeman "both come from the same basket." [8]

It is necessary to acknowledge, then, that *The Secret Agent* is not (so far as ideas are concerned) a work of exploration and discovery. It dramatizes positions already securely held and carries no farther than a casual essay might have. This short novel simply cannot be compared with *The Possessed* as a tragic study of moral anarchy and revolutionary psychology. But the ideas, once we have acknowledged the modesty of their pretentions, do contribute a great deal to the solidity and force of the entertainment. The asides on indolence, vanity, and so forth furnish footnotes to the continuing dramatized paradoxes: that the revolutionary or the double agent may be the laziest and most domesticated of bourgeois, that the policeman may have the mind of a criminal. The conservative assumptions concerning human nature, some of them to reappear in Graham Greene, were by no means banal in 1907, perhaps are not so today: that sympathy, "which is a form of fear," may turn easily to rage and violence; that humanitarian and revolutionary ardors may derive from indolent egoism. The degenerate Stevie in his morbid horror of pain and in his indiscriminate compassion is a symbolic extreme both of the visionary and of his victim. The spectacle of a beaten horse (or dream of one, as in Dostoevsky) may be one cause of a crime.

This is not a tragic world of noble defeats and vast forces overthrown. *The Secret Agent*'s vision is of "a mediocre mankind" in an "imperfect society": flabby, debased, eternally gullible. The Stevies and other weaklings are always available, to be used and abused by the Verlocs and the Karl Yundts. "With a more subtle intention, he (*Yundt*) took the part of an insolent and venomous evoker of sinister impulses which lurk in the blind envy and exasperated vanity of ignorance, in the suffering and misery of poverty, in all the hopeful and noble illusions of righteous anger, pity, and revolt." And this poor humanity, whether we look to the left or to the counterrevolutionary right, is overcome by fatness as by a plague. It is the sign of a universal spiritual indolence. Michaelis the humanitarian idealist is "oppressed by the layer of fat on his chest" and is round "like a distended balloon." Verloc has an "air of having wallowed, fully dressed, all day on an unmade bed"; his "vast bulk" offends his Embassy employers, who believe a pretended anarchist should be both unmarried and lean. Sir Ethelred the Secretary of State is also vast in bulk and stature, has a double chin, thick neck, and puffy lower lids. Even the blind terrorist of skinny hands, Karl Yundt, suffers from gouty swellings. The "determined character" of Chief Inspector Heat's face is "marred by too much flesh."

Such then is Conrad's almost neo-Humanist view of revolutionary ardor, and his more personal view of counterrevolutionary zeal; both views are unquestionably sincere. It is most accurate, however, to look on them as important parts of the "entertainment," and to take the vision of a monstrous town in the same light: this "slimy aquarium from which the water had run off," this "immensity of greasy slime and damp plaster," this London. The rather gratuitous horror of the charwoman Mrs. Neale — "aproned in coarse sacking up to the arm-pits" — takes its place in an artistic composition of somber effects as it could not, comfortably, in a more ambitious philosophical novel. The reader remains as coolly detached from Mrs. Neale, presumably, as from Stevie's wonderful "steed of apocalyptic misery" whose lean thighs move "with ascetic deliberation." The particular nature of Conrad's "entertainment" is to hold the reader at a relatively fixed distance of amused scorn from persons and situations that, in an ordinary fiction, would evoke strong sentimental responses. Its prevailing tone is one of ironic hauteur and control. The sum of so many instances of calculated coldness may well be, as in Swift's "Modest Proposal," a serious and tenable compassion. But the function of the irony, page by page, is to repudiate any generous response to misfortune and disaster.

The Secret Agent is in several ways an astonishing leap into an entirely different kind of art, and not least in this absolute control of an ironic style operating in comparatively short and simple sentences. The style is elevated, but in the special sense of being elevated above the miseries and squalors it describes; of remaining cool, scornful, calculating, aloof. "His prominent, heavy-lidded eyes rolled sideways amorously and languidly, the bedclothes were pulled up to his chin, and his dark smooth moustache covered his thick lips capable of much honeyed banter." This is almost the first glimpse of Mr. Verloc. And the detached style refuses to become excited or compassionate at the moment of his death:

But they were not leisurely enough to allow Mr. Verloc the time to move either hand or foot. The knife was already planted in his breast. It met no resistance on its way. Hazard has such accuracies. Into that plunging blow, delivered over the side of the couch, Mrs. Verloc had put all the inheritance of her immemorial and obscure descent, the simply ferocity of the age of caverns, and the unbalanced nervous fury of the age of bar-rooms. Mr. Verloc, the Secret Agent, turning slightly on his side with the force of the blow, expired without stirring a limb, in the muttered sound of the word "Don't" by way of protest.[9]

His body becomes, immediately, "the mortal envelope of the late Mr. Verloc reposing on the sofa," and Mrs. Verloc the murderess becomes "his widow."

The particular chill humor of *The Secret Agent* derives from such elevation of passion and suffering to abstraction and from such reduction of the human being to a function or formal status. With each new use, the standard tags — Michaelis as the "ticket-of-leave apostle" or Ossipon as "nicknamed the Doctor" — become more denigrative. Karl Yundt ("the terrorist") is not just blind. He has "extinguished eyes" in which an expression of "underhand malevolence" survives. He is not an old and feeble man out for a walk but a "spectre" taking "its constitutional crawl," helped by an "indomitable snarling old witch." Winnie Verloc contemplates with satisfaction the propriety of her respectable home, ensconced "cosily behind the shop of doubtful wares." "Her devoted affection missed out of it her brother Stevie, now enjoying a damp villeggiatura in the Kentish lanes under the care of Mr. Michaelis." The word "villeggiatura" is hardly one she would use or even know; it takes on the more ironic force because, as the reader knows and Winnie does not, Stevie was blown up that morning. On the same page Mr. Verloc, who will very shortly be murdered, preserves an "hieratic immobility" at the touch of an unexpected and lingering kiss. Comrade Ossipon's cold and scientific habit of speaking of Stevie as "the degenerate" is less malicious than some of Conrad's linguistic modes. The merciless style marches ahead with an extraordinary assurance to its final view of Ossipon:

"I am seriously ill," he muttered to himself with scientific insight. Already his robust form, with an Embassy's secret-service money (inherited from Mr. Verloc) in his pockets, was marching in the gutter as if in training for the task of an inevitable future. Already he bowed his broad shoulders, his head of ambrosial locks, as if ready to receive the leather yoke of the sandwich board.[10]

The great menaces to such a style are, of course, self-conscious coyness and polysyllabic humor; language, separating itself from an attitude to be expressed, may take pleasure in its own self-indulgence. But this almost never happens in *The Secret Agent*. We have instead a "voice" which is an attitude, and which controls to an unusual degree its distance from the material. (Hence the two serious intrusions of a different authorial consciousness and voice, in the remarks on Alfred Wallace's book and on the Italian restaurant, are fairly startling.)[11] In any event this controlled and relatively bare style did function for Conrad as a congenial point of view or narrating consciousness; style became, as it were, an interposed narrator. It satisfied the needs provided for in earlier novels by literal removal in time and space or by the screening Marlovian voice. As a result Conrad was able to carry through for almost the first time long dramatic scenes occurring in a fictional present; to achieve, even, excellent scenes of violent action, violent emotion, and violent comic discovery. *The Secret Agent* strongly contradicts our assumption (hitherto justified) that Conrad was least successful where he tried to do what most journeyman novelists can do. This is, in a way, his most "professional" novel, and it appears that for this difference and for this new ease style, a deliberately cultivated new style, must be thanked or blamed. It provided him at all times with that historian's detachment he found so congenial. We have seen that Conrad could dramatize physical action and crisis so long as he imagined it occurring in the past. We now see he can dramatize such action and crisis in a fictional present, provided he sees it through scornful eyes that are not exactly his own. The style is a mask.

The professional ease and expertness show themselves in an almost flawless plotting: the events so contrived as to cause the characters a maximum discomfort, and to extract from the dramatized experience a maximum ironic significance. And the knowledge of these events withheld or offered in such a way as to make possible the greatest suspense and the most rewarding macabre comedy. It seems strange to speak of Conrad in these journalistic and conventional terms. But these are the terms that apply; the novel is an "entertainment." (The fifth chapter, in fact, is excellent detective fiction of a kind that would become very conventional.) Given the fact that this is a story of mystery and suspense, and that certain information must therefore be withheld, *The Secret Agent* makes things as easy as possible for its readers, and as grimly amusing. The reader is allowed to proceed through eighty straightforward pages before encountering a major interruption. Evidence may be concealed, but drama is not evaded. The satisfying discomfitures of Mr. Vladimir and Mr. Verloc and Comrade Ossipon are dramatized not reported.

The "surprises" are prepared with great care. The death of Stevie, which happens between the third and fourth chapters, is not formally revealed until near the end of the ninth; and the eighth chapter (a disguised flashback, which suggests Stevie is still alive) is certainly deceptive. Meanwhile enough clues have been dropped to make the final revelation seem inevitable and the death itself meaningful. From the beginning we have seen Stevie — the very type for Conrad of dumb, gullible, sentimental humanity — react neurotically to the overheard conversations of the anarchists. The death of Verloc, which he is to bring upon himself through the astonishing but overlong eleventh chapter, has been prepared from the end of the third. The "funereal baked meats for Stevie's obsequies" are also for his own; the sharp carving knife and its possibilities were carefully hinted at almost two hundred pages before. The literary but still sinister business of putting out the light at the end of the third chapter virtually becomes, when repeated at the end of chapter eight, a sharp warning. The price of such total control is, of course, an occasional effect of contrivance. This realistic novel is by no means as true to life as the visionary impressionistic chiaroscuros, nor as conducive to serious psycho-moral involvement. But there is a certain pleasure to be derived from contemplation of the "well made." It is no paradox to say that this first "entertainment" among Conrad's longer novels is also a very artful performance. Comedy is control.

The eleventh chapter (described by Leavis as "one of the

most astonishing triumphs of genius in fiction") is rich moral comedy, though it ends with the plunge of a knife. The misunderstanding is caused not by misinformation but by vanity, and Verloc rather than his wife takes the initiative in each important step toward his murder. For one of the first times we see Conrad extend a successful dramatic scene over many pages (too many, probably) and try to wring from it the last measure of drama, irony, meaning. The scene is too fully and too carefully explicated. However, it would be idle to quibble over such a fine and unexpected performance. I would simply propose that the twelfth chapter, and the farcical collision of Mrs. Verloc and Comrade Ossipon, is an even greater success.

Here, to be sure, we have misinformation with a vengeance. The opportunistic Ossipon assumes that Verloc not Stevie was blown up in the Greenwich Observatory attempt, and now he is on his way to pay his respects to the widow. A discreet courtship of the money can come later. But she (terrified by the vision of being hanged "amongst a lot of strange gentlemen in silk hats") is rushing away from her crime. They literally collide in the dark street. The astonished, scandalized, and presently terrified Ossipon hears Mrs. Verloc abuse her husband's memory, profess interest in himself, suggest the police have already solved the bombing and that Verloc had connections with an Embassy. And beg him to save and hide her. But he does not understand that she is disjointedly confessing murder, and he must discover the body for himself. His final horror, as he learns that Winnie had killed her husband and that her brother "the degenerate" had carried the bomb, is a scientific one. He gazes into her face like adamant "as no lover ever gazed at his mistress's face . . . He gazed at her, and invoked Lombroso, as an Italian peasant recommends himself to his favorite saint." His remark to Winnie that the brother resembled her (which she interprets tenderly) presages his leap from the railway carriage. The macabre comedy is so successful, and Ossipon's growing horror and disgust so vivid, that it effectively destroys much of our sympathy for Winnie. We may come to share his view.

But this is not too high a price to pay for such a show of fictional virtuosity.

For *The Secret Agent* is finally, and admirably, that: a work of virtuosity. This entertaining and easy book may well be the coldest and most restrained of Conrad's serious novels — a work so "cold" that even some of his strongest preoccupations (such as the sense of isolation, such as the political conservativism) serve, chiefly, as materials for an ironic design.

Under Western Eyes, however, is a great tragic novel. It is Conrad's final and in some ways most moving treatment of his central story of betrayal and self-punishment. The terms of "The Secret Sharer" are now reversed. The Razumov who chooses to protect society and who betrays the outlaw brother and double Victor Haldin has betrayed himself first of all. But it is rather with *Lord Jim* that *Under Western Eyes* demands to be examined, if only because the two novels are more comparable in length and density. Once again we have the story of a not uncommon man whom chance and suffering render extraordinary; who suddenly has to face a boundary-situation and most difficult choice; whose crime both makes and breaks him. The act of betrayal, carrying him out of one solitude and into another, lends him a somber magnitude and new moral awareness, and compels him to destroy himself at last. Responses will vary among different readers and different generations as to which act of betrayal was the more fundamental, Razumov's or Lord Jim's. (In the early 1950's, in America, neither the informing on Haldin nor the employment as a police spy would have seemed anything but commendable to certain readers.) But the plot of *Under Western Eyes* builds more impressively than *Lord Jim*'s, after the betrayal occurs, and offers a less equivocal pattern of redemption. *Under Western Eyes* never threatens to descend into popular adventure and romance, as *Lord Jim* occasionally does.

Why then does it occupy a slightly less commanding position in the Conrad canon? Presumably because it is distinctly the less original novel of the two. The study of Razumov's guilt and of the Russian temperament generally cannot fail to remind us of Dostoevsky, though Conrad's is a different and far more orderly manner. And there is a much less impressive dramatization of certain psychological processes than in *Lord Jim*. The art of *Under Western Eyes,* moreover — its manipulation of the reader through structure and texture, plot and reflexive reference — is more conventional. It does not to the same degree stand between the reader and the material to control that reader's response. *Under Western Eyes* is Conrad's best realistic novel. But it is not an "art novel" of infinite complexity, and it does not, like *Lord Jim,* change and greatly expand on second and subsequent readings.

Razumov in himself (considered, that is, apart from the narrator's musings on him) is psychologically a fuller and more important creation than Lord Jim. Or, at least, he is a more interesting person. The initial betrayal and the half-conscious stages leading to it are dramatized with great subtlety and economy. For the decision to inform on Haldin is no sudden accident of failing will or swift forestalling vision. At the outset Razumov is "as lonely in the world as a man swimming in the deep sea." He has seen his father Prince K—— once. Once too he saw his half-sisters descend from a carriage, and "felt a glow of warm friendliness towards these girls who would never know of his existence." For he has only the "immense parentage" of Russia, and no more intimate conscious longing than for the silver medal offered by the Ministry of Education for a prize essay. He combines, rather curiously for Conrad, the vulnerable solitary and the sane hard worker. "Razumov was one of those men who, living in a period of mental and political unrest, keep an instinctive hold on normal, practical, everyday life. He was aware of the emotional tension of his time; he even responded to it in an indefinite way. But his main concern was with his work, his studies, and with his own future." Some day, perhaps, he will be a "celebrated old professor."

This is the unawakened man. His stable existence is shattered in the worst possible way when Haldin appears in his room to acknowledge the assassination and ask for help. "The sentiment of his life being utterly ruined by this contact with such a crime expressed itself quaintly by a sort of half-derisive mental exclamation, 'There goes my silver medal!' " He is all the more indignant when Haldin tells him one of the reasons why he was chosen for this confidence: he had no family to suffer in the event his complicity came out. "Because I haven't that, must everything else be taken away from me?" Yet he sets out on his errand of mercy to find the driver Ziemianitch, impelled by instinctive loyalty to a fellow student and perhaps even by his "personal longings of liberalism." The account of his approach to political conversion on that night is brief but extremely convincing: his egoism and fear create the doctrinal commitment which alone can rationalize the betrayal. Thus the inert drunken Ziemianitch, whom he beats in frustrated rage, provokes meditations on power and the "stern hand." And Razumov's personal plight ("done for" between "the drunkenness of the peasant incapable of action and the dream-intoxication of the idealist incapable of perceiving the reason of things") is by implication national.

At this point, "conscious now of a tranquil, unquenchable hate," he has his first phantom vision of Haldin lying on his bed as if dead. The half-conscious mind at least is approaching that decision to betray. "Must one kill oneself to escape this visitation?" In rage he stamps his foot on the snow, and under it feels the "hard ground of Russia, inanimate, cold, inert, like a sullen and tragic mother hiding her face under a winding-sheet." He experiences an intuition of Russia's "sacred inertia," which must not be touched, and of absolute power which must be preserved for the great autocrat of the future. Within, some "superior power had inspired him with a flow of masterly argument." The superior power is his ability to rationalize and generalize selfish aims. It interweaves, indeed masterfully, his concern with his possibly ruined career and his awareness of Haldin as a disruptive political force; his selfish rage and his theory of the throne. He is disturbed in his reflections by the yell of one sledge-driver to another, "Oh, thou vile wretch!" But the phrase drives him on rather than deters him. Immediately afterward he experiences his hallucination of Haldin lying in the snow across his path. He forces himself to walk over the breast of the phantom — and decides to give Haldin up. Betray him? "All a man can betray is his conscience. And how is my conscience engaged here; by what bond of common faith, of common conviction, am I obliged to let that fanatical idiot drag me down with him?" His decision, as the narrator remarks, "could hardly be called a decision. He had simply discovered what he had meant to do all along." And when the long evening is ending (after he has informed on Haldin, after Haldin has left his room) he hears himself say "I confess"; and thinks of himself as on a rack. This is, surely, great dramatic writing. But the drama is largely within.

For the remainder of the novel Razumov is always on a rack; or on the two racks of fear and guilt. There are times when it is difficult to distinguish between the two, and if the analysis of guilt is more impressive, the dramatization of fear is more exciting. The greatest actual menace is a Dostoevskian *dédoublement* and consequent reckless volubility and snarling uneasiness. Razumov watches appalled his own indiscretions and temptations to confess. Even before Haldin is arrested, he speaks to General T—— with dangerous violence. The rack turns after the police visit to his room and more swiftly through the interview with Councillor Mikulin. Even as he talks Razumov is appalled by his own flow of hasty words, and during the interview has a frightening vision of "his own brain suffering on the rack — a long, pale figure drawn asunder horizontally with terrific force . . ." And when he becomes a police spy (having found no other answer to Councillor Mikulin's sinister question "Where to?") the real danger is immeasurably increased.

In Geneva he is unwisely talkative with Peter Ivanovitch and with Sophia Antonovna, who had been sent to Geneva to verify an identity. He stupidly insists on the distrust of the exiles, but he had largely invented that distrust; he is aware of his savage curtness and cannot control it. "Even as he spoke he reproached himself for his words, for his tone. All day long he had been saying the wrong things. It was folly, worse than folly. It was weakness; it was this disease of perversity overcoming his will." From the first moment he behaves unwisely in front of the killer Necator, who will presently burst his eardrums. In the grand traditional pattern Razumov, literally menaced by death, is throughout his own worst enemy. When he has finally won outward impunity he must, because of that other rack of guilt, confess what no one would have ever discovered.

The two racks turn in unison. It would be hard to conceive a plot more successfully combining dramatic suspense and psycho-moral significance. Through the second and much of the third part the reader has no certain knowledge that Razumov, welcomed in Geneva as the late Haldin's friend and associate, is actually a police spy. The motives for his presence might as plausibly be inward ones: a self-destructive tempting of fate; a compulsion to confront those most likely to destroy him; even, an unconscious effort to appease guilt through reenactment of the crime. "Ah, Peter Ivanovitch, if you only knew the force which drew—no, which *drove* me towards you! The irresistable force." Razumov is thinking of Councillor Mikulin. But the reader is likely to think of a generalized self-destructiveness, and the reader not Razumov would be right. That *is* the hidden motive, hidden even from him. Thus Razumov, in his "satanic" game of suggesting yet concealing a second and truer meaning from Peter Ivanovitch, stumbles with unconscious irony upon a third and truest one. Only he can do the "work" of redeeming himself through confession; he has indeed been impelled, by the strongest of psychic drives; he does not stand before Ivanovitch confessed, but someday he will. And a "blind tool" he may well be, though at the end he will go as far as possible toward converting compulsion into moral choice. But Razumov, of course, has no idea he is saying all this:

"You have been condescending enough. I quite understood it was to lead me on. You must render me the justice that I have not tried to please. I have been impelled, compelled, or rather sent — let us say sent — towards you for a work that no one but myself can do. You would call it a harmless delusion: a ridiculous delusion at which you don't even smile. It is absurd of me to talk like this, yet some day you will remember these words, I hope. Enough of this. Here I stand before you — confessed! But one thing more I must add to complete it: a mere blind tool I can never consent to be." [12]

By delaying as long as he does the formal revelation that Razumov is Mikulin's agent, Conrad preserves a sympathy that would (with a more abrupt procedure) have been lost. We must see Razumov suffer before we see, nakedly, this second of his crimes. And the "deceptive" impression that Razumov is obeying a psycho-moral compulsion is not deceptive at all. He has been sent to Geneva to write incriminating reports on the exiles. He will write instead his diary and condemning self-analysis.

The novel's anatomy of guilt is Dostoevskian, which means that it is true; the difference is that Conrad's method is infinitely more selective. His dramatization of the phantom, for instance, and its slow attenuation from sharp hallucination to symbolic force and allusion, is remarkably tactful and convincing. The original vision on the snow (coinciding with the decision to give Haldin up) is reported in a cool, matter-of-fact prose. It is a "phenomenon," and Razumov tackles it calmly. But when he reaches his room, and finds Haldin lying on his bed as though already dead, he reflects: "I have walked over his chest." He touches Haldin's shoulder and at once feels "an insane temptation to grip that exposed throat and squeeze the breath out of that body, lest it should escape his custody, leaving only a phantom behind." The vision during the Mikulin interview of his own brain suffering on the rack is also of this Haldin-phantom. And shortly after that interview (as we glance ahead to Part IV) Razumov sees Haldin as a "moral spectre infinitely more effective than any visible apparition of the dead." He thinks that the specter cannot haunt his own room, through which the living Haldin had blundered; supposes, glancing at the bed, that he would never actually see anything there. But only two pages later he does.

Through much of the second and even third parts we have little chance to see the phantom, since we long watch Razumov from the outside. But we note his stammering "compelled" remarks to Madame de S—— that he too had had an "experience," had once seen a phantom. The interview with Sophia Antonovna, treated more subjectively, shows that the phantom has become featureless; is becoming, so to speak, a component of mental discourse. "He had argued himself into new beliefs; and he had made for himself a mental atmosphere of gloomy and sardonic reverie, a sort of murky medium through which the event appeared like a featureless shadow having vaguely the shape of a man; a shape extremely familiar, yet utterly inexpressive, except for its air of discreet waiting in the dusk." Razumov thinks of it as "not alarming." But this quiet prose certainly conveys alarm, and on the next page his allusions to Madame de S——'s spiritualist powers and to the "cold ghost" of a tea seem mildly obsessive. The phantom, which had been "left behind lying powerless and passive on the pavement covered with snow," is perhaps most powerful when embodied in Mrs. Haldin and Nathalie on the long night of confessions. "The fifteen minutes with Mrs. Haldin were like the revenge of the unknown." There is something Razumov cannot understand in her manner; she is as white as a ghost; she falls into an incomprehensible silence. But the terms are naturalistic; Haldin continued to exist, but "in the affection of that mourning old woman." Razumov strides from the room, leaving her behind; it is "frankly a flight." But he comes upon Nathalie. "Her presence in the ante-room was as unforseen as the appearance of her brother had been." And the time for a full confession has come.

The phantom (whether as hallucination, psychic symbol, or shorthand notation of anxiety) does not have the major part in the story of Razumov's torment. The ferocious ironies of his situation, rather, constitute that major part: to be honored by his fellow-students for a supposed complicity in the assassination; honored by Haldin himself for his "unstained, lofty, and solitary" existence; welcomed by the Geneva exiles with respect and by Nathalie Haldin with a dedicated passion, and who has, thanks to the betrayal, the only real conversation with his father in his whole life. Razumov's immediate response (waking chilled on the morning after Haldin's capture) is not fear or shame but a plausible mental stagnation and inertia. His "conservative convictions . . . had become crystallized by the shock of his contact with Haldin." However, his notes and books have become a "mere litter of blackened paper." He compels himself to go to the library, but an "infinite distress . . . annihilated his energy." The apathetic state passes, after the interview with Councillor Mikulin, into an actual psychosomatic illness, briefly and brilliantly described.[13] He emerges from it to find things "subtly and provokingly" changed. But he continues to suffer from ennui, the fitfulness and dread when outside alternating with a total inertia when at home. One might suppose the room would become "morally uninhabitable." But this does not happen, perhaps because Razumov has now entered into his second and testing solitude:

> On the contrary, he liked his lodgings better than any other shelter he, who had never known a home, had ever hired before. He liked his lodgings so well that often, on that very account, he found a certain difficulty in making up his mind to go out. It resembled a physical seduction such as, for instance, makes a man reluctant to leave the neighborhood of a fire on a cold day.[14]

The portrait is psychologically and dramatically true. But it cannot be conveyed through summary, nor reduced to the shortcuts of psychological discourse. The very great scene of Razumov's confession to Nathalie Haldin cannot (though we recognize such elements as the phantom) be abstracted at all. The scene is as it were irreducible. Even the furnishings of the little anteroom, with its remorseless light and its hooks recalling the hook on which Ziemianitch was found hanging, seem part of the inward experience. The drama is intensified by the unconscious irony of the teacher of languages, who thinks he is to witness a love scene: "The period of reserve was over; he was coming forward in his own way." Razumov is indeed coming forward; but "watching himself inwardly, as though he were trying to count his own heart-beats, while his eyes never for a moment left the face of the girl." He exists, speaks under the greatest conceivable strain. For this is now a matter of life and death, of moral life or death. The great spectacle is of the mind breaking willfully not compulsively through its long habit of evasion, calculating its moves, pausing long enough to ask about the efficacy of remorse; and circling down to the truth. The denunciation of self does not involve a blind jump from one state of being to another. The final speeches, on the contrary, bring into play and as it were into the open all the essentials of Razumov's being, and all the terms of his conflict. His triumph is a genuine one.

For the crime which had broken Razumov has now fully made him. Thus he has the strength necessary, after leaving Nathalie Haldin, to add certain confessions to his diary and then go before the assembled revolutionists at the house of Julius Laspara, there to put his back against the wall and make his public confession. "He was the puppet of his past," yet also a free agent to some degree. The comment made later by Sophia Antonovna applies well enough to both confessions:

> Well, call it what you like; but tell me, how many of them would deliver themselves up deliberately to perdition (as he himself says in that book) rather than go on living, secretly debased in their own eyes? How many? . . . And please mark this — he was safe when he did it. It was just when he believed himself safe and more — infinitely more — when the possibility of being loved by that admirable girl first dawned upon him, that he discovered that his bitterest railings, the worst wickedness, the devil work of his hate and pride, could never cover up the ignominy of the existence before him. There's character in such a discovery.[15]

The written confession (pages 358–362) raises the one serious question concerning the characterization's over-all authenticity and firmness. For the Razumov of these pages, whose voice and style are fairly convincing, claims to have been a much more cynical person, in his relationship with Nathalie Haldin, than we have had any reason to suspect. A few sentences (which I draw together from two pages of the novel and which therefore falsify their texture and pace) will indicate how very much is claimed:

> I was given up to evil. I exulted in having induced that silly innocent fool to steal his father's money. He was a fool, but not a thief. I made him one. It was necessary. I had to confirm myself in my contempt and hate for what I betrayed . . . Listen — now comes the true confession. The other was nothing. To save me, your trustful eyes had to entice my thought to the very edge of the blackest treachery . . . And do you know what I said to myself? I shall steal his sister's soul from her. When we met that first morning in the gardens, and you spoke to me confidingly in the generosity of your spirit, I was thinking, 'Yes, he himself by talking of her trustful eyes has delivered her into my hands!' If you could have looked then into my heart, you would have cried out aloud with terror and disgust . . . Perhaps no one will believe the baseness of such an intention to be possible . . . every word of that friend of yours was egging me on to the unpardonable sin of stealing a soul . . . I returned to look at you every day, and drink in your presence the poison of my infamous intention.[16]

The conception is a powerful one: Dostoevskian if not Russian, perhaps simply human. Moreover, it is at least logically consonant with a psychology which sees in reënactment one of the spirit's few ways of coping with unappeased guilt. One function of the phantom is to remind us, and Razumov, that Haldin must be killed again and again. And the conception appears plausible enough if we go outside the novel to speculate on the possibilities for evil of a man who has done what Razumov has already done. And yet it seems (coming so late in the story) rhetorical, arbitrary, untrue. One reason may be that symbolic reënactments are rarely as conscious as this. A more important reason is that we have known Razumov only as a man on the two racks of fear and guilt. He has had little time for anything else. But most of all, the claims seem untrue to everything we have seen of his relationship with Nathalie Haldin.

The very first meeting was a brief one. But her first remarks to Razumov — "You are Mr. Razumov" . . . "Can't you guess who I am?" . . . "Victor — Victor Haldin!" — are enough to send him reeling against the wall of the terrace. (Later, Razumov is "tempted to flight at the mere recollection" of that meeting.) His response to the first interview in the narrator's presence is a curious irritability and an "unrefreshed, motionless stare, the stare of a man who lies unwinking in the dark, angrily passive in the toils of disastrous thoughts." There is no reason to believe, here, that the "disastrous thoughts" are other than those prompted by fear and guilt. Furthermore, not all our view of Razumov's relationship with Nathalie Haldin is from the outside. Whatever intentions he had to "steal the soul" would surely have come out on the occasion of Peter Ivanovitch's request that he, *la personne indiquée,* bring Nathalie to the Chateau Borel group. Tekla explains to him, a few minutes later, why such a contact would be ruinously disillusioning for her. The occasion for evil is thus propitious. But Razumov's inward reaction is a vague one of *dédoublement,* loathing, uneasiness.

Was the diabolism confessed in writing then only an afterthought, a new idea discovered this late in the novel and too attractive to expunge? The more probable explanation is that Conrad, writing here in Razumov's name for the first time, returned imaginatively to his original plan for the novel. It was to have been entitled *Razumov,* and would have involved much more melodrama. And it would have dramatized a much greater cynicism:

> 2d in Genève. The student Razumov meeting abroad the mother and sister of Haldin falls in love with that last, marries her and, after a time, confesses to her the part he played in the arrest of her brother.

The psychological developments leading to Razumov's betrayal of Haldin, to the confession of the fact to his wife and to the death of these people (brought about mainly by the resemblance of their child to the late Haldin), form the real subject of the story.[17]

The temptation to steal the soul may be described as another "lost subject."

Otherwise, the characterization of Razumov is altogether impressive. It would be futile to try to define with exactness the creative situation behind it. There are depths below depths in these matters, and a symbolic repudiation of self may turn out to be, finally, a secret justification. But the situation was certainly an intense one, involving no small degree of intellectual identification with Razumov, informer and police spy. It is as though an officer sharing far more of Conrad's convictions than Jim had leaped off the *Patna*. The author recognizes the egoistic sources of Razumov's conversion, and he does not share the mystical absolutism of his new faith. But he lends to Razumov the very language of his own scorn of visionaries, even the favorite and personal *secular:* "Visionaries work everlasting evil on earth. Their Utopias inspire in the mass of mediocre minds a disgust of reality and a contempt for the secular logic of human development." He would agree with Razumov that "twenty thousand bladders inflated by the noblest sentiments and jostling against each other in the air are a miserable incumbrance of space, holding no power, possessing no will, having nothing to give."

Thus the reasoned political credo Razumov writes immediately after Haldin's arrest could serve as Conrad's own:

History not Theory.
Patriotism not Internationalism.
Evolution not Revolution.
Direction not Destruction.
Unity not Disruption.[18]

The student Razumov at the outset shows, moreover (and in the Author's Note as well as in the text), the supreme maritime virtues of sanity and steadiness. Even the betrayal of Haldin, seen in the context of Conrad's respect for law and distrust of revolution, could be said to correspond with certain authorial convictions.

But only with convictions, and only with certain of these. The energizing conflict derives from the fact that Razumov, this sane conservative scorner of visionaries and servant of law and victim of revolutionary folly, is (when he informs on Haldin) dramatized as committing a crime; he has violated the deepest human bond. This implication seems to me unarguable. If it were not present, the rest of the novel would be morally meaningless. And it is of course the suffering guilty man (rather than the "ordinary young man" with "sane ambitions" of the Author's Note) who elicits the prolonged act of novelistic sympathy. "You have either to rot or to burn," Sophia Antonovna remarks in a different context. The Razumov of the opening pages (whose "main concern was with his work, his studies, and with his own future") rots. He has not yet entered the moral universe, and he enters it by committing the crime. But thereafter he elicits as much sympathy (not approval) as any of Conrad's protagonists. The achievement of this dramatic sympathy is all the more remarkable, of course, because Razumov is not just any betrayer of the human bond. He is also a Russian.

"The most terrifying reflection (I am speaking now for myself) is that all these people are not the product of the exceptional but of the general — of the normality of their place, and time, and race . . . The oppressors and the oppressed are all Russians together; and the world is brought once more face to face with the truth of the saying that the tiger cannot change his stripes nor the leopard his spots." Thus Conrad wrote of his characters years afterward, and three years after the Revolution, in his Author's Note. But the novel itself shows no little ambivalence, and perhaps its greatest act of imaginative integrity (i.e., fidelity to such truth as the dream discovers) is its marked creative sympathy with Russia and Russians, a sympathy which extends even to some of the revolutionary exiles. "I think that I am trying to capture the very soul of things Russian," Conrad wrote to Galsworthy. But he was at least briefly captured by that soul, and on the devil's side without knowing it. The narrator, to be sure, makes certain negative statements which Conrad would have signed in an essay or preface: on the spirit of Russia as the spirit of cynicism; on Russian scorn of the practical forms of political liberty; on her "terrible corroding simplicity in which mystic phrases clothe a naïve and hopeless cynicism"; on her detestation of life, "the irremediable life of the earth as it is . . ." [19] But the novel's over-all tone is compassionate, and especially toward the sufferings reported by Tekla and Sophia Antonovna.

"Sometimes I think that it is only in Russia that there are such people and such a depth of misery can be reached." There runs throughout a counterpoint of East and West, which is in part a counterpoint of the suffering and the secure. "It is a very miserable and a very false thing to belong to the majority," Nathalie Haldin says, and the narrator pleads in defense of England's "bargain with fate" that she too has had tragic times. The contrast, if not between those who burn and those who rot, is between those who burn and those who have escaped from the fire. The teacher-narrator (at times much less sympathetic to Russia than is the novel as a whole) once seems almost to speak for its own uneasy conscience: "It is not for us, the staid lovers calmed by the possession of a conquered liberty, to condemn without appeal the fierceness of thwarted desire." Russia exists, to borrow Rathenau's famous phrase, in the soul-saving "abyss of sin and suffering."

The counterpoint becomes necessarily, and perhaps unluckily for the West, a counterpoint of Russia and Switzerland. And in the area of cool judgment there can be little doubt as to Conrad's preferences. They are for the order and stability of Swiss democratic institutions, as for the stolid decency of the English narrator. But Geneva is the "respectable and passionless abode of democratic liberty," and the narrator himself composes a very tendentious contrast whose sympathies go in an entirely different direction. He considers the Bastions, where Nathalie Haldin and Razumov will meet:

I saw these two, escaped out of four score of millions of human beings ground between the upper and nether millstone, walking under these trees, their young heads close together. Yes, an excellent place to stroll and talk in. It even occurred to me, while we turned once more away from the wide iron gates, that when tired they would have plenty of accomodation to rest themselves. There was a quantity of tables and chairs displayed between the restaurant chalet and the bandstand, a whole raft of painted deals spread out under the trees. In the very middle of it I observed a solitary Swiss couple, whose fate was made secure from the cradle to the grave by the perfected mechanism of democratic institutions in a republic that could almost be held by the palm of one's hand. The man, colourlessly uncouth, was drinking beer out of a glittering glass; the woman, rustic and placid, leaning back in the rough chair, gazed idly around.[20]

The counterpoint of Swiss and Russian would seem to be, as we consider all the references to Geneva and consider all of the narrator's complacencies, not merely one of the secure and the suffering, but also of the respectable and the anarchic, the decent and the messy, the complacent and the compassionate, the mercenary and the mystical, the "saved" and the tragic, the abstract and the human. The narrator's own obtuseness is one of the great sources of this created sympathy for the damned. His mumbling about "Western readers" and about "a lurid, Russian colouring" at the moment of the Haldins' most intense grief increases sympathy for the Russians generally. And his astonishment because the revolutionists visit the deafened Razumov throws an unfavorable light on his own automatic moralism, and a final light on their unexpected compassion.

Irving Howe's argument that the novel is weakened because it develops too little sympathy for the revolutionaries strikes me, in fact, as seriously mistaken.[21] It would be unreasonable to demand much for the squeaky-voiced killer Necator (himself a police spy, as it turns out) or for Julius

Laspara. But Tekla in her appointed role as nurse and companion of the punished sinners (she herself recruited by a "saintly apple-woman") is a familiar Dostoevskian figure of compassion. Her narrative to Nathalie Haldin (pages 149–155) is a moving account of suffering "inside Russia." It subtly prepares us, moreover, for Razumov's own fate, and on a second reading functions as very striking reflexive reference. (Her humble offer of her services to Razumov reveals an ear for feminine speech and feminine logic — or, it may be, a compassionate imagination rather than ear — not evident in the earlier novels.) And even the "wrong headed" Sophia Antonovna, as Conrad calls her in his Author's Note, wins some of the affection he normally accords durable old soldiers. For this is what she is: the white-haired veteran of revolution who had begun going to the secret societies at sixteen, and who had cut her hair as a "first step towards crushing the social infamy."

A novelistic sympathy for these women is natural enough. But there may also exist, in addition to such sympathy and in addition to a normal unconscious sympathy with the outlaw, a creative sympathy with the exceptional buffoon or exceptional object of contempt. Such may be the truest meaning of Milton's alliance with Satan, or of Shakespeare's with Iago and Richard III. And Dostoevsky's power to dramatize the fool as from within, many fools in fact, is one of the sure tokens of his genius. There is some of this in Conrad. He groups the feminist Peter Ivanovitch and Madame de S—— as "fair game" in his Author's Note. "They are the apes of a sinister jungle and are treated as their grimaces deserve." But the ironic account of Peter Ivanovitch's absurd heroic progress across Siberia, engirdled by his chain ("that simple engine of government") is one of the summits in Conrad's work.

It has a quality of vividness, humor, and phrasing that only imaginative sympathy can achieve. Mere scorn could not conceive the disastrous dropping of the file, or the faint jingling of the chain, or the "naked tawny figure glimpsed vaguely through the bushes with a cloud of mosquitoes and flies hovering about the shaggy head," or the leaves and twigs in his tangled hair that astonish his rescuer. Indeed mere scorn could hardly dramatize so well a fatuousness which describes the events leading up to his obtaining of the file as an "obscure episode . . . in the history of ideas in Russia." The retrospective narrative and image of Ivanovitch and his cloud of mosquitoes notably affects our present view of him riding in a landau with Madame de S—— in Geneva: "the 'heroic fugitive' . . . sitting, portentously bearded and darkly bespectacled, not by her side, but opposite her, with his back to the horses. Thus, facing each other, with no one else in the roomy carriage, their airings suggested a conscious public manifestation." We may borrow the word. It may be that the imaginative sympathy (combined of course with the deepest scorn) is for Ivanovitch as a total, realized manifestation of a type.

Cosas de Russia . . . This novel, if we are to believe either the classics of Russian fiction or the enigmatic accounts of current events, does come remarkably close to the "very soul of things Russian." The brief glimpses of life in St. Petersburg are most convincing. So too are Victor Haldin, with his strange speech on the "divine" resignation of the Russian soul; and the long bony student living on the fringe of conspiracy, and the contradictions of "Madcap" Kostia; and the fanatic General T——, and the weary Prince K—— with his aura of Western culture. Nathalie's vision of unity and her contempt for political parties are Russian; so too is her mystical vision of a time of concord. "Listen, Kirylo Sidorovitch. I believe that the future will be merciful to us all. Revolutionist and reactionary, victim and executioner, betrayer and betrayed, they shall all be pitied together when the light breaks on our black sky at last." Will Russians in their "land of spectral ideas and disembodied aspirations" turn always to autocracy and turn "at last from the vain and endless conflict to the one great historical fact of the land"? In any event the trial of Councillor Mikulin reminds us that much that has seemed grotesque in the Soviet system is, simply, Russian:

> Later on the larger world first heard of him in the very hour of his downfall, during one of those State trials which astonish and puzzle the average plain man who reads the newspapers, by a glimpse of unsuspected intrigues. And in the stir of vaguely seen monstrosities, in that momentary, mysterious disturbance of muddy waters, Councillor Mikulin went under, dignified, with only a calm, emphatic protest of his innocence — nothing more. No disclosures damaging to a harassed autocracy, complete fidelity to the secrets of the miserable *arcana imperii* deposited in his patriotic breast, a display of bureaucratic stoicism in a Russian official's ineradicable, almost sublime contempt for truth; stoicism of silence understood only by the very few of the initiated, and not without a certain cynical grandeur of self-sacrifice on the part of a sybarite.[22]

Under Western Eyes is not, like *The Secret Agent,* a small and symmetrical triumph of controlled form. It sets itself few technical boundaries, yet occasionally overflows even these to leave momentary impressions of clumsiness. Certain scenes in the second and third parts, carried on the "deluge of dialogue," are much too long. In this middle section of the novel, moreover, Conrad sometimes fails to conceal his embarrassment in the presence of acute problems of point of view. And the elderly teacher of languages and unprofessional narrator (who shows himself such an expert novelist through most of the first part) creates unnecessary obstacles by raising the question of authority. For this naturally leads us to examine and question his. Should he not rather have pretended to that truest authority which has nothing to do with Jamesian logic, and which he phrases very well in the second sentence below?

> Wonder may be expressed at a man in the position of a teacher of languages knowing all this with such definiteness. A novelist says this and that of his personages, and if only he knows how to say it earnestly enough he may not be questioned upon the inventions of his brain in which his own belief is made sufficiently

manifest by a telling phrase, a poetic image, the accent of emotion. Art is great! But I have no art, and not having invented Madame de S——, I feel bound to explain how I came to know so much about her.[23]

The source and breadth of a narrator's information is of little importance as such. An example of looseness will serve, which would doubtless have caused James to groan. The nominal authority for the early St. Petersburg chapters is Razumov's diary, a diary which for the reader scarcely exists. This authority is obviously exceeded when the narrator enters Prince K——'s study, there to discover him "sitting sadly alone." The one thing of importance here violated, however, is the reader's intimate identification with Razumov. The instance is trivial and serves to remind us that Conrad too could forget about that diary. (Though it presumably was a protective, interposed instrument of no little use to his imagining.) A far more radical clumsiness — a clumsiness almost amusing in such a great novel — occurs in the first pages of Part III, as the narrator shuttles back and forth between Razumov's subjective view and his own eyewitness report. And there is to be sure the classic moment of awkwardness when (page 317) the narrator walks into his own narrative by coming into Razumov's line of vision.

But these are small flaws in the surface of a major success. The narrative method evidently worked, since it helped or at least permitted Conrad to dramatize his major scenes, rather than report them; and helped him to achieve his meaning without recourse to *The Secret Agent*'s heavy verbal irony. The method (in its combination of the meditative and the dramatic, the personal and the objective) is in part a development of that used in *Lord Jim*. It represents a serious effort to extend the possibilities of first-person narration without losing most of its generic advantages.* The teacher of lan-

* Among the generic advantages: eyewitness credibility and the authority of spoken voice, ease and naturalness of time-shift and transition, freedom to select only a few details or incidents. It can be a great relief to have one's "omniscience" formally limited, as it must be here.

guages is, unlike the Marlow of *Lord Jim,* the only narrator of the novel. But he manages to function at certain times as third-person omniscient observer, at other times as first-person eyewitness-participant. The first part, though based on a "document," is as forthright and as economical as the opening chapters of *Lord Jim.* It can evoke the assassination in a few paragraphs (here really relying, of course, on more than the document) and can present Razumov and his plight in a few pages.

The relative expertness of *Under Western Eyes* shows itself in the swiftness with which Conrad escapes nominal limitations, and converts a narrow point of view to, functionally, an ampler one. Thus the narrator who begins by disclaiming "the possession of those high gifts of imagination and expression" achieves, by page 12, all the dramatic power of the traditional observing point of view. Already he has made us forget that "documentary evidence" and even made us forget himself. So too Haldin's narrative-within-narrative report (through dialogue) of the assassination becomes, after only a few lines, a direct dramatizing of the event: intervening voices are silenced. In Part II Conrad again quickly disposes of his nominal authority (that Nathalie Haldin is telling the narrator about her visit to the Chateau Borel) and substitutes a dramatic third-person account of the event. We thus at least escape the weary game of quotation marks within quotation marks that mars *Lord Jim* and especially *Chance.* The particular technical compromise was one designed to satisfy both the reader (with his desire for dramatic immediacy) and the author (with his need for a literal detachment in space or time). Through certain scenes the reader appears to be experiencing life directly in a fictional present. But for the writer these protective screens still secretly existed: that the time is really past, that the imagination is at double or triple remove from the scene, that voices and documents are interposed.

The curious interruption and leap forward to the "later on" of Councillor Mikulin's trial is a clue, if we needed one, that this vivid and violent drama is (for Conrad's imagination) in the past. But it is the narrator's function as obtuse participant and observer to give, from page 100 on, a strong sense that we are in a fictional present time: watching new persons unexpectedly appear and unexpected events unroll, speculating on Razumov's status, and living through the very drama of ambiguity and discovery. The teacher of languages again protests, at the outset of the second part, his lack of professional skill. He "would not even invent a transition," he says — while accomplishing with ease the major transition from Councillor Mikulin's "Where to?" to the society of Nathalie Haldin and her mother.

At this point the narrative contracts to a very slow-moving present. We must wait some thirty-five pages for a further hint that Razumov and Nathalie Haldin may meet, sixty-seven pages for them to come face to face, seventy-two pages for those words that will send Razumov reeling against the wall. The delay is doubtless excessive. But some delay was certainly needed to make acceptable the melodramatic *donnée:* that Razumov will be sought out and admired by the sister of the man he betrayed. The illusion of presentness also permits the narrator's blundering unconscious ironies. For he is reconstructing a time when the first part of his narrative was unwritten. So in his fussy, innocent way he too can send Razumov reeling, as when he bluntly remarks: "There was something peculiar in the circumstances of his arrest. You no doubt know the whole truth . . ." The last interview of Razumov and Nathalie Haldin is, as much as any scene in fiction, happening "now." And for the reader watching that scene the narrator's presence may seem unimportant; may even be forgotten. But his presence, and the fact that this interview nominally occurred in the past, were extremely important to Conrad. They permitted him to keep his saving distance, and so permitted him to write coherently of violence and without embarrassment of passion.

One of the great dangers of an obtuse narrator and Jamesian fool is, of course, the invitation to write imperceptive prose for the sake of accurate characterization. The danger would seem most severe where the general mode is realistic, as it is in *Under Western Eyes.* But this is a problem that James, Gide, Mann, Ford, and others have solved, and Conrad here solves it with little waste of time. A few brief passages suggest in their phrasing the narrator's old-maidish side. It comes out even in his comments on his lack of professional skill. "In the conduct of an invented story there are, no doubt, certain proprieties to be observed for the sake of clearness and effect." But from such a passage the narrator moves very quickly to an efficient, evocative prose not unlike that of James. "Mr. Razumov's record, like the open book of fate, revives for me the memory of that day as something startlingly pitiless in its freedom from all forebodings." Only a few pages after this he attains the major accent and lucid controlled irony of the Peter Ivanovitch portrait. Admittedly such a narrator was incapable of the strange rich connotative effects and subtly disturbing rhythms of *Lord Jim.* And perhaps Conrad too was incapable of them by now. But this self-effacing and more rational prose has the great merit of not interfering with the drama of ideas or with the drama of betrayal and redemption. The narrator's style was natural to Conrad, as the style of *The Secret Agent* was not. And it is probably capable of accomplishing a greater variety of effects. The prose style too points to the remarkable control Conrad kept, in *Under Western Eyes,* over very strong personal feelings. This exciting novel is also a triumph of intelligence.

Conrad himself remarked that the old teacher of languages was useful to him in several ways, and so must be useful to the reader: "in the way of comment and by the part he plays"; as an eyewitness to "produce the effect of actuality"; as a friend and listener for Miss Haldin, "who otherwise would have been too much alone and unsupported to be perfectly credible." [24] Conrad succeeds, we may repeat, in making the narrator's comment nearly always dramatic: a difficult and important achievement. His editorials on the Russian character and on Western rectitude may well reflect Conrad's cool views. But they are so timed and so phrased as to help create sympathy for the despised and the damned. And this too is, to recapitulate, a triumph of art and integrity. For the Russians also are human. "The obligation of absolute fairness was imposed on me historically and hereditarily, by the peculiar experience of race and family, in addition to my primary conviction that truth alone is the justification of any fiction which makes the least claim to the quality of art or may hope to take its place in the culture of men and women of its time."

This slightly graceless sentence from the Author's Note holds for me an accent of high sincerity.

Chapter Eight

CHANCE AND AFTER

IN *The Shadow Line* (1917, written in 1915) Conrad returned to the story of his first command for a final inward journey and small masterpiece of psychological symbolism. It is a very special case, and was described by Conrad himself as virtual autobiography. How true this was is open to question. But perhaps his view of the task — the imaginative stance taken, the obligation to "report" sensation faithfully — explains why *The Shadow Line* escapes the sentimentalities and even puerilities of the other late works. At least three circumstances favorable to a tiring writer were present. He did not have to invent plot and setting, the problem of narrating consciousness was easily solved, and the story was freed from the land entanglements of love and prosaic urban environment. Conrad may not have grasped conceptually the whole meaning of *The Shadow Line,* which seems to dramatize, among other things, the throwing off of immobilizing neurotic depression. But his imagination understood well enough the work it was about, and therefore prompted a firm grouping of incident and a plain style of the highest distinction. *The Shadow Line* shows one of the several Conrads not far from his best.

Otherwise, the novels after *Under Western Eyes* are inferior: *Chance* (1913), *Victory* (1915), *The Arrow of Gold* (1919), *The Rescue* (1920, begun 1896), *The Rover* (1923), and the unfinished *Suspense* (1925). And those after *Chance* are radically inferior. Thus Conrad's period of commercial success as a novelist exactly corresponds with his period of failing power. Criticism is coming around to this view of the later books, especially with the recent books of Douglas Hewitt and Thomas Moser; hence there is no present obligation to discuss say *The Rover* at length. But the gross overvaluation of *Victory* is of such long standing that it will not be easily corrected. *Victory* is Conrad for the high schools and the motion pictures, the easiest and generically the most popular of the novels. And the easiest, incidentally, for the teacher or critic blocking out themes, plot lines, symbols. The position of F. R. Leavis — that *Victory* is inferior to *Nostromo* yet "among those of Conrad's works which deserve to be current as representing his claim to classical standing" [1] — is presumably the common one. But the novel is very badly written and very roughly imagined.

The ultimate psychological and perhaps biological *why* of Conrad's anticlimax may well be undiscoverable. It is clear that the normalizing of attitude and method increased with age, until both positive attitude and transparent method were at times indistinguishable from those of popular magazine romance. But is this normalizing to be regarded chiefly as a cause of the imaginative collapse, or as one of its notable effects? And how shall we say where such an undeliberate normalizing leaves off and where deliberate or undeliberate vulgarization for commercial reasons begins? In André Gide the imaginative decline occurs once the very strong impulse to confess and appease guilt has been satisfied. Perhaps Conrad too, by 1912, had expelled most of his demons. In any event his fiction, bereft alike of certain unconscious drives and of the old conscious austerity, came presently to depend upon a kindly and often relaxed sensibility.

Meanwhile, however, Conrad had become famous and successful; and presumably less amenable to criticism. The extraordinary uncorrected lapses in syntax and diction in the last novels tell us, if they tell us nothing else, that his editors were afraid of this proud and difficult older man. "I am very willing indeed to accede to your request, except as to the specimen pages. No one sees my manuscript till it is ready for the printer. A specimen page is nothing. A piece of literature is not a bag of wheat and I should think that in the case of a writer of my standing as an artist, even the very booksellers ought to feel a certain amount of confidence as to the character of the wares they are going to receive." [2] It is pleasing to see Conrad, after his years of failure, in a position to utter such a rebuke. But the rebuke suggests (especially since the work in question was *The Arrow of Gold*) that Conrad would have to be his own critical editor. And the power of self-criticism, to judge both by the work and by certain letters, was by now seriously lacking.

One reason for the imaginative decline and collapse is not obscure at all: physical and mental fatigue. His efforts of the great decade (to and including *Nostromo*) should have been enough to exhaust a ruggeder constitution and more stable temperament than Conrad's. His own sickness and the sickness of wife and children compounded, together with actual financial worry and debt, the debt of expended energy. "I am sinking deeper and deeper," Conrad wrote to Galsworthy in 1907. "The state of worry in which I am living, — and writing, — is simply indescribable. It's a constant breaking strain. And you know that materials subjected to breaking strain lose all elasticity in the end, — part with all their 'virtue' on account of profound molecular changes. The molecular changes in my brain are very pronounced. It seems to me I have a lump of mud, of slack mud, in my head." [3]

It is not surprising to find the young naïve heroes of *The Arrow of Gold* and *Suspense* think and behave like tired old men. They share old Peyrol's sense of living in a dream and his old-man's concern with finding something to do in order to get through the day. The two young men of these novels seem in fact to be the same old one. The "Monsieur George" of Conrad's romantic Marseilles adventure finds his "occupation" is gone when his toilet is finished. Was it a fact, Cosmo Latham wonders in *Suspense,* "that he had lost all wish to travel? However, he let Spire take the packet to the post and during the man's absence took a turn or two in the room. He had got through the day. Now there was the evening to get through somehow."

Dictation is, of course, the crutch of the tiring writer who also happens to be successful enough to get away with anything. And Conrad's later prose does not allow us to forget that parts, apparently very large parts, of these later novels were dictated. Perhaps we need look no further than this for clues to certain clumsy idioms and constructions. But it is also worth noting, especially of *The Arrow of Gold* and *Suspense,* that the most serious lapses in syntax and diction occur toward the end of these works. We can see within these novels (and within *The Rover,* prior to a fine recovery at the very end) the unmistakable signs of increasing fatigue.

The gross characteristics of the anticlimax, behind the one great sign of failing language, are at least three:

1. *The sentimental ethic.* The normalization — the new optimism and achieved equanimity — remove the very foundation of Conrad's best work: his tragic sense of individual moral failure in a world of men. Love and even passionate love between the sexes now replace the old preoccupation with loyalty to the community, to the brother, to one's self. But Conrad could not, as Moser has abundantly demonstrated, take seriously these new values he professed to believe; his plots and his imagery discredit them. The late novels can be gloomy enough. But evil and failure, in this new cleansed moral universe, are presumed to come from the outside rather than from within.

The heroines notably have been victims of social or individual terrorism. Flora de Barral in *Chance* was neglected by her father and rejected by her governess, who deliberately sought to leave a psychic wound. The Lena of *Victory* was the victim of an underprivileged childhood, then became the prey of Schomberg. Rita de Lastaola in *The Arrow of Gold* had been terrified, both as a child and as a woman, by the neurotic Ortega, and the child-bride Adèle de Montevesso of *Suspense* by her vindictive and jealous husband. Arlette in *The Rover* has suffered the most obvious (and least plausibly conveyed) of the traumatic experiences: she has witnessed the death of her parents during the Terror in Toulon. These are the women to be pitied, protected, saved — though now and then they seem alarmingly able to take care of themselves.

The author's protestations concerning feminine mysteriousness, intuition, and the like are simply more numerous than before.

A stronger indication of real change in attitude is made by certain passages evoking the concept of the "true lie." In the early work, women were to be protected from the dark truth, and from the corrosive power of cynical masculine understanding. They were left with their fond illusions and told true lies. But now in certain passages the roles appear to be reversed; men must be protected from the realism of women. The Marlow of *Chance* has, if we are to take him at his word, come as far as possible from the Marlow who lied to protect Kurtz's Intended:

"The women's rougher, simpler, more upright judgment, embraces the whole truth, which their tact, their mistrust of masculine idealism, ever prevents them from speaking in its entirety. And their tact is unerring. We could not stand women speaking the truth. We could not bear it. It would cause infinite misery and bring about most awful disturbances in this rather mediocre, but still idealistic fool's paradise in which each of us lives his own little life — the unit in the great sum of existence. And they know it. They are merciful." [4]

The heroes are, to complete the sentimental ethic, essentially innocent. They are also uninteresting and immature. Though nominally capable of passion, they are really incapable of any significant action. *Chance* offers an intelligent if wavering criticism of Captain Anthony's chivalric immaturity. But at times it takes his good intentions at face value. Of the later heroes only Peyrol of *The Rover* could conceivably have committed a crime, and he only in the now revolved lawless unemasculated days.

2. *The narrator or central consciousness as dullard.* The Conrad who conceived the various evocative narrating voices of the early novels fell, at the end, into one of the worst of the realistic traps: to employ narrators or observers who by definition or by profession are unequipped to tell their stories effectively. Some of the imprecise and flabby rhetoric must

simply be blamed on the author's failing command of language. But some of it too must be blamed on a realist's respect for the way a dullard would speak: roughly, bluntly, without grace of style. Even Marlow has been turned into such a casual and uninteresting speaker.

"She was amazing in a sort of unsubtle way; crudely amazing—I thought. Why crudely? I don't know. Perhaps because I saw her then in a crude light. I mean this materially—in the light of an unshaded lamp. Our mental conclusions depend so much on momentary physical sensations—don't they?"[5]

None of the multiplying narrators of *Chance* (certainly not the original "I") is given the privilege of consistently rich language. And *Victory,* before dispensing with a narrator altogether, offers a dullard within a dullard, Davidson within the "I." The youthful narrator of *The Arrow of Gold* defines his own limitations of perspective succinctly: "I was the exception; and nothing could have marked better my status of a stranger, the completest possible stranger in the moral region in which those people lived, moved, enjoying or suffering their incomprehensible emotions." Old Peyrol, though central observer rather than narrator in a novel which badly needed a narrator, confers his dullness of perception and language on all the scenes we see through his eyes, or on all but fragments of the last one. His own limitations are truly radical ones:

He had done that thing no further back than two o'clock the night before, not twelve hours ago, as easy as easy and without an undue sense of exertion. This fact cheered him up. But still he could not find an idea for his head. Not what one would call a real idea. It wouldn't come. It was no use sitting there.[6]

Suspense too has no narrator, and the novel takes even greater liberties with the natural laxity of omniscient narrative than *The Rover* does. Cosmo Latham is usually our post of observation, however. A few sentences concerning him will suggest his limitations as a hero, and the kind of imprecise authorial language he provoked:

Cosmo had no inborn aptitude for mere society life. Though not exactly shy, he lacked that assurance of manner which his good looks and his social status ought to have given him . . . Often during talk with some pretty woman he would feel that he was not meant for that sort of life, and then suddenly he would withdraw into his shell. In that way he had earned for himself the reputation of being a little strange. He was to a certain extent aware of it, but he was not aware that this very thing made him interesting.[7]

3. *Failure of imaginative power and imaginative common sense*. This was not primarily a matter of failure to invent good stories or to conceive significant dramatic crises, but rather an inability to dramatize scenes which had been intelligently conceived. The imagination refused to act; refused to do anything with the material before it. This was true even in a literal sense, and Conrad came to have more and more trouble with the mere stage mechanics of getting a person in and out of a room. He could still work with ease and authority when retrospective and spoken narrative was possible. But he was more embarrassed than ever when left face to face with his characters in a present place and time. He could not move them, and sometimes seemed unable to see them. This failure is occasionally betrayed by a telltale attention to minutiae of behavior and expression. *The Rover* — the feat of "artistic brevity" Conrad hoped to accomplish before he died — contains an extraordinary number of waste motions.

But there is also a radical lack, at times, of what must be called imaginative common sense. That is, Conrad now and then conceived situations, persons, and conversations without realizing that they would be, when rendered active in a particular context, absurd. A gulf existed between conception and dramatic imagination. In *Victory,* for instance, Heyst's instructions to Lena concerning signals of communication between them were no doubt carefully planned. But Lena's chance of understanding and remembering them would seem small. "Wait in the forest till the table is pushed into full view of the doorway, and you see three candles out of four blown out and one relighted — or, should the lights be put out here while you watch them, wait till three candles are lighted and then two put out. At either of these signals . . ." The example is humble but significant. The same failure of common sense becomes more serious when it appears in the presentation of character and in the reporting of dialogue. Instances are scattered through the later novels; the Ricardo of *Victory* may serve. The conception is of a very masculine figure of almost animal sensuality. But Ricardo's rhetoric is consistently childish or feminine: "He's spying from behind them now, I bet — the dodging, artful, plotting beast!" Or, as he addresses Lena in a moment of passion: "You marvel, you miracle, you man's luck and joy — one in a million!" Perhaps it is this effeminacy rather than the animal metaphor which makes Ricardo's charge at Lena's curtain unforgettably ridiculous:

> Ricardo drew back one foot and pressed his elbows close to his sides; his chest started heaving convulsively as if he were wrestling or running a race; his body began to sway gently back and forth. The self-restraint was at an end: his psychology must have its way. The instinct for the feral spring could no longer be denied. Ravish or kill — it was all one to him, as long as by the act he liberated the suffering soul of savagery repressed for so long. After a quick glance over his shoulder, which hunters of big game tell us no lion or tiger omits to give before charging home, Ricardo charged, head down, straight at the curtain.[8]

Chance is (always excepting *The Shadow Line*) the only later novel worth much attention on its merits. It won for Conrad a measure of commercial success at last, partly because it exploited a staple sentimental plot of popular fiction ("I've never had such a crushing impression of the dependence of girls — of women") and partly because it was skillfully publicized by Alfred A. Knopf, then a young employee of Doubleday. The very real falling off from *Under Western Eyes* is certainly not a matter of decline into facile method, nor even wholly a matter of tragedy surrendering to pathos. The game of multiplying narrators is complicated enough. But it is vitiated by the fact that each of these narrators is an uninteresting person. No one, however, is as uninteresting as Captain Anthony. He initiates the line of immature, passive, irritable, unintelligent heroes that will continue immediately in Powell and culminate in the tired drifting Cosmo Latham of *Suspense*.

Luckily Captain Anthony's full entrance into the book is deferred more than two hundred pages, and he is prematurely killed off. His melodramatic death, to make way for the aging Powell and to round off the book, may well wring easy tears from certain readers. But the absurd final pages of *Chance* should simply be subtracted and ignored, as the final pages of certain Victorian novels are subtracted and ignored. The whole last chapter, in fact, is of interest chiefly to the psychologizing critic, who may wonder whether Conrad truly subscribes to Marlow's sermon on coupling:

"Pairing off is the fate of mankind. And if two beings thrown together, mutually attracted, resist the necessity, fail in understanding and voluntarily stop short of the — the embrace, in the noblest meaning of the word, then they are committing a sin against life, the call of which is simple. Perhaps sacred. And the punishment of it is an invasion of complexity, a tormenting, forcibly tortuous involution of feelings, the deepest form of suffering from which indeed something significant may come at last, which may be criminal or heroic, may be madness or wisdom — or even a straight if despairing decision." [9]

This is doubtless a commendable and intelligent statement, even if the surrounding scene suggests that successful pairing-off is accompanied by a deathly stillness. But the word *sacred* is alarming. It will begin to recur oddly in the late novels, as the word *secular* recurred in the early ones. "They stood side by side, looking mournfully at the little black hole made by Mr. Jones's bullet under the swelling breast of a dazzling and as it were sacred whiteness." The underlying misogyny which may still secretly exist is doubled, at a disagreeably explicit level, by a growing Thackerayan tenderness. The series of bruised maidens of the later work (beginning with Alice

Jacobus of "The Smile of Fortune" and Flora de Barral in *Chance*) prompt an interesting combination of clinical, sentimental, and at times sadistic imagining. The danger of course is that the sentimental note should prevail.

Chance is, however, an intelligent novel, and especially so where it maintains a firm critical awareness of Captain Anthony's sentimentality. The attitude toward pity remains at times that of the early Conrad: pity, involving "the egoism of tenderness to suffering." Marlow remarks that the "man was intoxicated with the pity and tenderness of his part." But Anthony's first feeling toward Flora was not one of pity alone. "It was something more spontaneous, perverse, and exciting. It gave him the feeling that if only he could get hold of her, no woman would belong to him so completely as this woman." And the "I" interlocutor agrees that "the very desolation of that girlish figure had a sort of perversely seductive charm, making its way through his compassion to his senses." After the marriage the essential fact is that of a "sublime delicacy" and renunciation, the generosity of an "immense" vanity, a magnanimity that crushes. Captain Anthony's "amazing and startling dream" is to "take the world in his arms — all the suffering world — *not to possess its pathetic fairness* but to console and cherish its sorrow." [10] And for long he takes no one in his arms. The criticism of Captain Anthony's self-intoxicating idealism distinctly recalls the criticism of Lord Jim's. The two figures, if we subtract the sympathetic comments of the narrators, seem in some ways very similar. The very great difference between them lies in what they have done or left undone. For Jim has at least jumped off the *Patna,* has at least faced the inquiry. And at least has gone to Patusan. The essential fact about Captain Anthony is that he has refrained from sexual intercourse with his wife.

The satirical view of Captain Anthony might well have made an interesting Jamesian portrait, strengthened by the subtly suggested linking of magnanimity and psychic impotence. His vitality, we are told near the end, has been "arrested, bound, stilled, progressively worn down, frittered away by Time." And his determination not to stumble over the corpse of the father may suggest a determination not to fail sexually. Unfortunately, however, Marlow and Conrad refused to take a consistently satirical view of their hero, and lacked the materials for a significant conflict of judgment and sympathy. Perhaps Anthony was a good manly fellow after all? A single passage will suggest how a misplaced and debilitating sympathy undercut satire to propose a second and more vigorous Captain Anthony. The next to last sentence in the following simply surrenders the understanding which the other sentences show:

"If Anthony's love had been as egoistic as love generally is, it would have been greater than the egoism of his vanity — or of his generosity, if you like — and all this could not have happened. He would not have hit upon that renunciation at which one does not know whether to grin or shudder. It is true too that then his love would not have fastened itself upon the unhappy daughter of de Barral. But it was a love born of that rare pity which is not akin to contempt because rooted in an overwhelmingly strong capacity for tenderness — the tenderness of the fiery predatory kind — the tenderness of silent solitary men, the voluntary, passionate outcasts of their kind. At the same time I am forced to think that his vanity must have been enormous." [11]

The critical and ironic spirit is thus undermined by another and more sentimental one, prepared to take Captain Anthony very seriously. But at its best *Chance* shows a fine theoretical and as it were Jamesian intelligence, producing not a few Jamesian tones and turns of phrase. It also shows, in certain chapters, a fine dramatic intelligence: a power, that is, to dramatize personality emerging under stress, and character exposed in action. Not infrequently a novel has one real story to tell, which may be different from the story it chooses to emphasize. And this is true of *Chance*. The third and fourth chapters of the first part (Marlow's retrospective narrative of the de Barral financial empire and its crash, and the consequent abandonment of Flora by the governess and her "nephew") represent perhaps Conrad's highest achievement in the classical mode of social realism and with the classical subject of money, manners, and morals. (The large philosophical sweep of *Nostromo,* the ironic distortions of *The Secret Agent,* the tragic character of *Under Western Eyes* put them into very different categories.) H. G. Wells may have suggested the image of a financial structure built on advertising alone, but de Barral evokes the more considerable names of Dickens and Faulkner.

De Barral is briefly and remarkably presented: a man without talent or imagination, who is "unable to organize anything, to promote any sort of enterprise if it were only for the purpose of juggling with the shares"; who has nothing in fact but the word *Thrift* to sell. At the bankruptcy proceedings "it was discovered that this man who had been raised to such a height by the credulity of the public was himself more gullible than any of his depositors. He had been the prey of all sorts of swindlers, adventurers, visionaries, and even lunatics." Only the great de Barral in his "unmeasurable conceit" does not laugh at his own folly as it emerges under questioning; he needed only time, he insists, for the enterprise to succeed. The figure is distinctly less symbolic than that of Holroyd, but taken with Holroyd's begins to fill out a meaningful image of one aspect of capitalism. By "a sort of mystical persuasion" de Barral had come to regard the investors' monies as his own. Yet he cries out indignantly that he has had nothing out of these immense sums:

> "It was perfectly true. He had had nothing out of them—nothing of the prestigious or the desirable things of the earth, craved for by predatory natures. He had gratified no tastes, had known no luxury; he had built no gorgeous palaces, had formed no splendid galleries out of these 'immense sums'. He had not even a home. He had gone into these rooms in an hotel and had stuck there for years, giving no doubt perfect satisfaction to the management." [12]

The emergence from prison occasions (pages 354–369) another excellent scene, once again narrated retrospectively. De Barral speaks of the trial and of his lost assets as though no years had intervened. But in the seclusion of prison he has thought himself into an extreme "sense of ownership of that single human being he had to think about." Flora's obligation to reveal her marriage to her obsessed father during that first cab-ride occasions some of Conrad's best dramatic dialogue. And he who has sought none of the gratifications can still speak with a passion:

"My girl, I looked at them making up to me and I would say to myself: What do I care for all that! I am a business man. I am the great Mr. de Barral (yes, yes, some of them twisted their mouths at it, but I was the great Mr. de Barral) and I have my little girl. I wanted nobody and I have never had anybody." [13]

The fourth chapter, with its acid story of Flora's betrayal by the governess and the ambiguous nephew is even more impressive. On first hearing rumors of the bankruptcy they carefully and quickly lay their plans to salvage what they can. The situation pushes to their limits the governess's active evil and the nephew's timid rascality and Flora's total innocence. The governness cannot forego a systematic attempt to damage Flora's mind before leaving. The material of this chapter is the great classical material of the ugly *revanche,* the humble and subservient showing their true feelings and colors when they discover the wealth is gone.

The account of the morning of ruin is exceptionally convincing, down to the last fine details of the drawing-teacher turning up for the usual lesson in water colors, or the butler remaining on the doorstep to look "down the street in the spirit of independent expectation like a man who is again his own master." Throughout this great controlled dramatic chapter, incidentally, we are often at a second or third remove from the scene: listening it may be to Marlow's speculations on Flora's report to Mrs. Fyne, itself made years after the event. The importance of such distancing to Conrad himself is an old story. But in this chapter its usefulness to the reader too cannot be questioned. The reader's experience is simultaneously to feel the full dramatic force of the scene and to speculate on its meanings. The method, we shall see, marks a slight extension over that of *Lord Jim* in the degree to which scenes are vivified through Marlow's speculations on them; conjecture replaces hearsay. Thus the slighter *Chance,* rather than *Lord Jim* or *Nostromo,* anticipates the full Faulknerian extension of the impressionistic method. The amount of meditative comment screening the naked scene, the degree and amount of interposition, gives Marlow at times the very accent and rhythm of a Faulknerian overriding voice. Only the second sentence below brings in a more conventional authorial consciousness. Flora

"stood, a frail and passive vessel into which the other went on pouring all the accumulated dislike for all her pupils, her scorn of all her employers (the ducal one included), the accumulated resentment, the infinite hatred of all these unrelieved years of —I won't say hypocrisy. The practice of hypocrisy is a relief in itself, a secret triumph of the vilest sort, no doubt, but still a way of getting even with the common morality from which some of us appear to suffer so much. No! I will say the years, the passionate, bitter years, of restraint, the iron, admirably mannered restraint at every moment, in a never-failing correctness of speech, glances, movements, smiles, gestures, establishing for her a high reputation, an impressive record of success in her sphere. It had been like living half strangled for years.

"And all this torture for nothing, in the end! What looked at last like a possible prize (oh, without illusions! but still a prize) broken in her hands, fallen in the dust, the bitter dust, of disappointment, she revelled in the miserable revenge — pretty safe too — only regretting the unworthiness of the girlish figure which stood for so much she had longed to be able to spit venom at, if only once, in perfect liberty. The presence of the young man at her back increased both her satisfaction and her rage. But the very violence of the attack seemed to defeat its end by rendering the representative victim as it were insensible." [14]

These chapters, then, are first-rate: very different from what we have come to expect from Conrad at his best, but by no means disgracing that Conrad. Flora de Barral is one of the most convincing of Conrad's bruised young women, and the first important scene between her and Captain Anthony (Chapter 7 of Part I) is possibly the most plausible love-scene in his work. It reaches us, it is worth noting, at third remove. But the remainder of the novel — all, that is, but a hundred pages give or take a few — is inferior: not absurdly inferior, as are parts of *The Rover* and *Victory,* but drably inferior: sentimental, overextended, inert, commonplace. The real interest, as Henry James perceived in his famous commentary, becomes technical:

It literally strikes us that his volume sets in motion more than anything else a drama in which his own system and his combined eccentricities of recital represent the protagonist in face of powers leagued against it, and of which the dénouement gives us the system fighting in triumph, though with its back desperately to the wall, and laying the powers piled up at its feet. This frankly has been *our* spectacle, our suspense and our thrill.[15]

Yet the system did not represent, for Conrad, a stubbornly sought hardest way. For the method was congenial. Someone is talking throughout the novel, after the opening pages, and all the storytelling is therefore retrospective. The novel simply does not have to face those conditions of presentness (present time and place, objective reporting, and impersonal exposition) which so often occasion a clumsy prose. So too the method invites a frank exposure rather than artful concealment of the temperamental evasiveness. But the number and quality of the speaking voices does raise serious questions, for the reader if not for the author. Some of these appear with the first chapter, which was written at least four years before the rest. This opening is very uncertain. It would seem to promise a retrospective novel of Powell's life, but *Chance* never develops into that. Powell exists only to observe matters on the *Ferndale,* and most fortuitously to save Captain Anthony's life, and ultimately to provide Marlow with his authority. If we are not uneasy about Powell's presence, at a first reading of that chapter, we may yet wonder about Marlow's, and even more about that of the original and unnamed "I." He at least (if not the whole frame of a dinner at the riverside inn) seems superfluous.

The clumsiness of the first chapter comes from something more than uncertainty of story line. It also seems to derive from a hesitant author-identification with all three of his speakers: with the "I" tentatively, with Marlow by old habit, and at least nominally with young Powell, since he lives through Conrad's own examination experience. As the novel develops the "I" moves into a very modest interlocutor's role. He is there to interrupt Marlow's flood of speech, to ask pertinent questions, and sometimes to protest against the glib editorials on women. This slight role may suggest Shreve McCannon, Quentin Compson's outraged listener. But Shreve (himself the weakest and least essential component of *Absalom, Absalom!*) and Quentin point to the one glaring fault of Conrad's "system." For those conversations in the Harvard room are debates, as between two parts of a single mind, carried on without trivial chatter, at a high level of intensity. At first Quentin, then both men are personally involved in the story they tell. But neither the "I" of *Chance* nor Marlow is personally involved in this history of fine consciences; and Powell, who will ultimately be involved enough, does not understand what he looks at.

An even more important difference, the great difference after all, is that Shreve McCannon and Quentin Compson and finally all of the subnarrators of *Absalom, Absalom!* are endowed with the author's elaborate rhetoric. They have their individual differences. Yet all speak a "Faulknerese" approximately as far elevated above standard colloquial English as is Elizabethan blank verse. This further step away from ordinary realism was the next and natural one for the meditative, impressionist novel to take. But Conrad was not ready to take it. Thus in the interests of realism both Powell and the "I" use a loose, unenriched, and hence inefficient language. So too does Marlow himself much of the time, and he is finally the greatest of *Chance*'s several disappointments. He has simply been borrowed from the earlier novels, but in name only. His manner has become urban, polite, jocular, chatty, feminine, and vulgarly "literary." Significantly this new Marlow's powers of speech and analysis are so weakened that Conrad feels obliged to apologize (" 'You seem to have studied the man,' I observed") for his eloquent summary of de Barral.

The vulgarity is most gross where faint echoes exist of the

speculative prose of *Lord Jim:* "a delicious day, with the horror of the Infinite veiled by the splendid tent of blue; a day innocently bright like a child with a washed face, fresh like an innocent young girl," etc. A moment of unconscious humor juxtaposes the trivial new Marlow and the old Marlow at his most pretentious: "I became conscious of a languid, exhausted embarrassment, bowed to Mrs. Fyne, and went out of the cottage to be confronted outside its door by the bespangled, cruel revelation of the Immensity of the Universe." And even the most unabashed admirer of *Chance* must recognize that Marlow's editorials on women are boring. His uneasy comments on his own narrative authority are as tiresome. "—You understand . . . that in order to be consecutive in my relation of this affair I am telling you at once the details which I heard from Mrs. Fyne later in the day, as well as what little Fyne imparted to me with his usual solemnity during that morning call." The "I" asks the one question that should not be asked: "How do you know all this?"

Yet the important experiment remains: the surprising adumbration of *Absalom, Absalom!*'s method. And Marlow notably recovers a great deal of his lost rhetorical power whenever he anticipates the Faulknerian device of narration through speculative commentary, of reporting disguised as conjecture. The method involves a nominal freeing of narrative consciousness and loosening of logical restrictions (since a speculating mind may move where it pleases); in practice it may also permit a convenient limiting. Where authority is so slight, reporting of detail may be kept to a minimum! In conveying the "evening confabulation" between the governess and the nephew Marlow seizes both advantages, very much in the manner of Quentin Compson. The limitations permit him to cut dialogue to a few lines. But the broadened authority of conjecture permits him to evoke the unspoken conflict of their thoughts. They say, after all, very little. The highly verbal method (which at a glance might seem unsuited to any situation of inarticulateness) is doubtless the best suited to save such a situation. Two passages will suggest how it is used.

"And we may conjecture what we like. I have no difficulty in imagining that the woman — of forty, and the chief of the enterprise — must have raged at large. And perhaps the other did not rage enough . . .

". . . Meantime returning to that evening altercation in deadened tones within the private apartment of Miss de Barral's governess, what if I were to tell you that disappointment had most likely made them touchy with each other, but that perhaps the secret of his careless, railing behaviour, was in the thought, springing up within him with an emphatic oath of relief, 'Now there's nothing to prevent me from breaking away from that old woman.' And that the secret of her envenomed rage, not against this miserable and attractive wretch, but against fate, accident and the whole course of human life, concentrating its venom on de Barral and including the innocent girl herself, was in the thought, in the fear crying within her, 'Now I have nothing to hold him with . . .' "[16]

In a few places Marlow, again like Quentin Compson, combines in the same sentences the immediacy of the present tense and the detachment of cool ironic categorizing. The conjectural method is particularly useful where the narrator does not want to report a scene at length, or cannot, and where it is desirable for the reader to do a good deal of active imagining. Thus the screens which stand between us and the interview of Anthony and little Fyne are useful in several ways. Marlow's report, finally, of Flora going to meet her father coming out of prison again takes us close to Quentin Compson's manner: to his fascinated yet detached attention, and to his rhetoric combining immediate rendition and distant ironic meditation:

"No. I suppose the girl Flora went on that errand reasonably. And then, why! This was the moment for which she had lived. It was her only point of contact with existence. Oh, yes. She had been assisted by the Fynes. And kindly. Certainly. Kindly. But that's not enough . . ."

"She was there in good time. I see her gazing across the road at these walls which are, properly speaking, awful. You do indeed seem to feel along the very lines and angles of that unholy bulk, the fall of time, drop by drop, hour by hour, leaf by leaf, with a gentle and implacable slowness. And a voiceless melancholy comes over one, invading, overpowering like a dream, penetrating and mortal like a poison.

"When de Barral came out she experienced a sort of shock to see that he was exactly as she remembered him. Perhaps a little smaller. Otherwise unchanged. You come out in the same clothes, you know. I can't tell whether he was looking for her. No doubt he was. Whether he recognized her? Very likely. She crossed the road and at once there was reproduced at a distance of years, as if by some mocking witchcraft, the sight so familiar on the Parade at Brighton of the financier de Barral walking with his only daughter." [17]

There are times in *Chance* when the techniques of *Lord Jim* seem borrowed for no good reason, as Moser has observed. But here at least method realizes the material, and makes meditation dramatic. Whatever Conrad's failure to use all the dramatic advantages of his "system," and however seriously irony has been weakened by a new tenderness, *Chance* remains a serious and important novel. It is not major Conrad, but it is the work of a mind still capable of significant invention.

There is much less to say, unfortunately, for *Victory*. It would be tempting to pass over it in silence, could one only be sure that readers would eventually reach the excellent critiques of Douglas Hewitt and Thomas Moser. For this is one of the worst novels for which high claims have ever been made by critics of standing: an awkward popular romance built around certain imperfectly dramatized reflections on skepticism, withdrawal, isolation. A study of the history of individual critical and especially professorial responses to *Victory* could well be illuminating. The rudimentary but exciting adventure story, the romantic pose of world-weary detachment, the simple yet vague erotic fantasy of the island shared with a grateful uneducated girl — all these are naturally pleasing materials to the adolescent mind. How many of the professorial admirers of *Victory* have not reread it since adolescence? Or how many, taking its story for granted, have reread it with eye fixed only on symbol and theme?

The questions raised by *Victory* are indeed interesting, Douglas Hewitt observes — "so long as we are discussing only a paraphrase of the book, the theme in isolation, an abstraction from the total effect of the work." [18] Again we have, but much less firmly even than in *Chance,* a critique of suspect pity, and the skeletal data for an interesting study of psychic coldness and withdrawal. But the view of Heyst is entirely too blurred to make these interests meaningful, and the moral melodrama too degraded. The presence or absence of secret symbolic patterns in *Victory* is a question of little more importance than would be their presence or absence in a good adventure story for boys. I do not find these symbolic subtleties in *Victory,* but for the sake of the argument am willing to concede that they may exist. For we may say of the "injection" of a symbol what Hewitt says of the invention of a fable posing a moral problem: that this in itself is "neither difficult nor important. It is the embodiment of this . . . in a series of concrete situations, in the detailed creation of character, in the flow of the narration and imagery which is significant." [19]

Why is there so much more awkward prose than in *Chance?* One reason is technical. *Victory* begins with an unidentified crude jocular narrator who presently calls in the no less commonplace Davidson. The narrative difficulties, once Heyst reaches his island, are theoretically insoluble. For the protagonists are secluded on that island, hundreds of miles from the narrator, and with Davidson as the only possible intermediary. He calls by the island every twenty-three days in his steamer, but does not stop unless signaled. It would be harder to imagine Conrad carrying further than this his habitual evasion of the immediate and dramatic. But this is only in theory, and the pretense of a narrator is soon dropped. The limited view gives way abruptly to standard omniscient narrative with Heyst as the usual post of observation. The story takes on, then, that presentness Conrad found so hard to manage. An occasional sentence suggests that he tried to view or imagine his material retrospectively. But he obviously did not succeed. The improbable appearance of Davidson at the end could be accepted with amused tolerance had it granted Conrad the detachment he needed. So far as the reader is concerned, there is no reason at all for Davidson to appear. The omniscient and certainly uninhibited narrator of the heart of the book could have described the holocaust just as well.

The merits of *Victory* as popular romantic fiction are obvious ones, though the exciting story gets under way rather slowly; the unholy trio reaches Samburan only on page 225. There are, moreover, a few good fictional "ideas" possessing some seriousness. And there are occasional good paragraphs. The opening image of Heyst smoking his cigar in the face of an indolent volcano conveys his isolation impressively, the volcano's glow "expanding and collapsing spasmodically like the end of a gigantic cigar puffed at intermittently in the dark." The whole first chapter has a casual, easy, professional finish. And the first conceptions of character are presented vividly enough — especially the brief suggestion of Heyst as an island adventurer now held, enchanted, in a magic circle of islands. The second chapter introduces Morrison as another Tom Lingard, trading with "God-forsaken villages up dark creeks and obscure bays" and benevolently extending credit.

This material, though far from new, has its proved excellence. But Morrison dies. And Heyst changes suddenly and radically into a meditative distruster of action, movement, life. The contradictions of this new withdrawn Heyst have a potential thematic interest, though it is by no means certain that Conrad was aware of them as contradictions. The novel remains ambivalent or perhaps only uncertain concerning a tenderness to be distinguished from love; and does not do much with the faint suggestion that the psychic and spiritual failure is also sexual. (The psychological disarming would be more significant if Heyst were not, also, literally disarmed.) And little of all this leads to good, energized writing — which must be, as usual, our final test of material and method. The most memorable pages are rather those evoking the influence of the dead father-philosopher: the years they spent together, and the father's chilling influence still working through the printed page.

The dramatic confrontation of Heyst and Mr. Jones makes serious psychological claims. For Mr. Jones (in an open recasting of the Lord Jim–Gentleman Brown incident) seeks to paralyze Heyst by insisting that they have much in common. Yet this scene, using again one of Conrad's most striking psychological intuitions, seems untrue or at least unimportant. The essence of Gentleman Brown's power lay in his shrewd appeal to a common guilt. The only genuine identification in *Victory* would connect Heyst's diffidence with Mr. Jones's "horror of feminine presence." Mr. Jones's pathological misogyny, on which the plot turns, is one of Conrad's more interesting conceptions. But the misogynist's rhetoric in a moment of crisis is almost as implausible as Ricardo's: "I have a good mind to shoot you, you woman-ridden hermit, you man in the moon, that can't exist without — no, it won't be you that I'll shoot. It's the other woman-lover — the prevaricating, sly, low-class, amorous cuss!" The neurotic element is entirely too explicit and unqualified.

The Mr. Jones, Ricardo, and Pedro of earlier chapters, who threaten to take over Schomberg's hotel, are fictionally more successful. Yet the quality of Mr. Jones's language suggests that the critic's one obligation, as things stand now with *Victory*, is to quote from it fairly liberally. To argue with Leavis about seriousness of theme or with Zabel about parabolic movements or with Stallman and others about secret symbolic intent is to postpone the essential considerations: the quality of the fictional imagination at work, and the quality of the prose. These qualities are such as to make other forms of analysis irrelevant. The time has come to drop *Victory* from the Conrad canon, at least to the degree that *The Trumpet-Major*, once so widely admired, has at last been dropped from Hardy's.

The prose of *Victory* is often flat and unenergized rather than grotesquely bad. It would be characterized, had it been written by an unknown, as the work of an earnest man who is "not a writer"; that is, of one who regardless of talent or lack of it shows no desire to give words something more than their everyday resonance:

> For instance, she could never perceive the prodigious improbability of the arrival of that boat. She did not seem to be thinking of it. Perhaps she had already forgotten the fact herself. And Heyst resolved suddenly to say nothing more of it. It was not that he shrank from alarming her. Not feeling anything definite himself he could not imagine a precise effect being produced on her by any amount of explanation.[20]

The brief passages to follow stand for many which read as though they had been dictated for future reference, or casually jotted down in a notebook. The structure of the sentence is presumably the leisurely one that came first to mind.

> That the hotel-keeper was capable of a great moral effort was proved by a gradual return of his severe, Lieutenant-of-the-Reserve manner.
>
> He proposed that his guest should start from town in his boat, as if going for an excursion to that rural spot. The custom-house people on the quay were used to see his boat go off on such trips.
>
> It was so extraordinary that nobody could possibly appreciate how extraordinary it was but himself. His mind was full of mere exclamations, while his feet were carrying him in the direction of the jetty.[21]

The normal symptoms of fatigue may suggest, too, a loss of imaginative rapport with one's subject. In one curious passage it is possible to watch the tiring mind at work. Here apparently Conrad took very literally a crude figure of speech; then, in afterthought, blamed Heyst for this literalism; then tried to rationalize his momentary lapse of common sense as a rare ("was not used to") but defensible occurrence. My distinct impression is that Conrad found it easier to blunder ahead, apologizing, than to strike out the original figure and begin anew:

Heyst sat down under his father's portrait; and the abominable calumny crept back into his recollection. The taste of it came on his lips, nauseating and corrosive like some kinds of poison. He was tempted to spit on the floor, naïvely, in sheer unsophisticated disgust of the physical sensation. He shook his head, surprised at himself. He was not used to receive his intellectual impressions in that way — reflected in movements of carnal emotion.[22]

But something else occurs in an occasional passage which may indicate a still more serious fatigue. This is a momentary loss of touch with English idiom, and the kind of trouble with prepositions that becomes pronounced toward the end of *Suspense*. Schomberg

could not believe that the creature he had coveted with so much force and with so little effect, was in reality tender, docile to her impulses, and had almost offered herself to Heyst without a sense of guilt, in a desire of safety, and from a profound need of placing her trust where her woman's instinct guided her ignorance.[23]

And there is the language of passion. The sentimentality and vagueness are not new, but the author's efforts seem more desperate than before. The third passage below asks us to consider, with Moser, how much of Conrad's admiring treatment of Lena and other late heroines was not secretly misogynous:

The indefinable emotion which certain intonations gave him, he was aware, was more physical than moral. Every time she spoke to him she seemed to abandon to him something of herself — something excessively subtle and inexpressible, to which he was infinitely sensible, which he would have missed horribly if she were to go away.

He jumped up and began to walk to and fro. Presently his hidden fury fell into dust within him, like a crazy structure, leaving behind emptiness, desolation, regret. His resentment was not against the girl, but against life itself — that commonest of snares, in which he felt himself caught, seeing clearly the plot of plots and unconsoled by the lucidity of his mind.

A great vagueness enveloped her impressions, but all her energy was concentrated on the struggle that she wanted to take upon herself, in a great exaltation of love and self-sacrifice, which is woman's sublime faculty; altogether on herself, every bit of it, leaving him nothing, not even the knowledge of what she did, if that were possible. She would have liked to lock him up by some stratagem. Had she known of some means to put him to sleep for days she would have used incantations or philtres without misgivings. He seemed to her too good for such contacts, and not sufficiently equipped.[24]

This is the language of *Victory*. On no theoretical or pragmatic basis can a novel containing this language, with all that it implies of blurred human understanding, be defended as deserving "classical standing."

The temptation, after leaving the grossly overvalued *Victory,* is to make too strong a case for *The Arrow of Gold*. And of course the novel has its great biographical and extra-literary interest, whether as true confession or as intricately contrived evasion of such confession. Did Conrad, like the Monsieur George of this novel, fight a duel with one J. K. M. Blunt, or was the wound in his left side self-inflicted? The matter (as one considers the various concealed crimes in Conrad's novels, and the various forms of self-destruction) is not a slight one. *The Arrow of Gold* may continue to be read, if only as a possible key to this enigma. Still it must be stated at once that this entertaining quasi-autobiographical novel belongs with the other works of the decline, and is far inferior to any of the novels from *The Nigger of the "Narcissus"* through *Chance*.

It is markedly superior, on the other hand, to the *Sisters* fragment of 1896, which distantly approached some of the same materials of the Marseilles romance. The detachable theme of initiation into the life of passion does not take us very far, since the initiate remains so inert and his passion so vague. A mere summary of the two novels would suggest that *Victory* deals with graver issues. And doubtless it is a more successful popular entertainment. But *The Arrow of Gold* is a less primitive, less sentimental, more adult novel, and it is quickened by one of Conrad's very few heroines worth listening to: Rita de Lastaola. The environing interests too, and the atmosphere of Marseilles (at times recalled in the aimlessness of actuality) have a certain maturity of appeal. Only the false center of M. George's passion is trivial or hopelessly blurred.

The rich material in a way seems Proustian rather than Conradian: a story of passions and reticences in a vivid setting of Legitimist conspirators and against a *mondain* past of successful artists and wealthy, corrupt aristocrats. Proust might have taken us at his snail's pace through the salons Conrad barely glances at; might have substituted long flights of analysis for Conrad's incisive five-page glimpse of the Marquis de Villarel. Conceivably he would have attempted, in place of Conrad's excellent minor ones, major portraits of Henry Allègre, Doyen, Mrs. Blunt, and Therese. And for Proust the central consciousness would not have been a false center. Presumably he would not have permitted the awkward discrepancy — hiatus, rather — between the very young M. George who acts his story blindly, and the evasive narrator who tells it. "And I can hardly remember my own feelings." M. George means very much less when he says this than does the Proustian narrator who says comparable things.

These references to Proust, otherwise impertinent, suggest how far afield Conrad went, fictionally, when he tried to dramatize (or tried to understand) the most "romantic" moment of his youth. The surprising thing is that he managed as well as he did, and that Rita is such an imaginative and credible creation. Even the dark matter of her psycho-sexual persecution by Ortega, in childhood and in the present, is handled with more firmness than one might have expected — the story culminating with the impotent Ortega baffled outside the locked room containing Rita and M. George, then wounding himself with the symbolic Nubian knife, "the clumsiest thing imaginable." The scene is awkwardly written. But at least it has the merit of imaginative audacity, and very nearly brings into the open interests only suggested before. Conrad wrote in response to a female reader that the "inner truth of the scene in the locked room is only hinted at," [25] referring presumably to Ortega's impotence but perhaps to the consummation of a love. Or is the "inner truth" rather M. George's own passivity? He too has his symbolic object to be retrieved. He knocks over a six-branched candlestick, which rebounds on the floor and comes to rest with the candles extinguished. This is a pattern we have seen before, and it may be connected in this scene with the feeling "that I dare not touch her." M. George, at several passionate moments of the story, feels a great fatigue, is aware of an ominous stillness. The creative imagination, that is, may have its secret and doubtful view of M. George too, not merely of Ortega. But the question is not an important one, or is important only insofar as it bears on the narrator's efforts to capture the language of passion. The deficiency of M. George that signifies is his deficiency as a narrator.

For *The Arrow of Gold* demonstrates as forcefully as any of the other novels the primary importance of congenial method and material. The ultimate difficulties may be directly biographical, as Conrad found it hard to dramatize either the success of this love affair or its final ruin, and found it hard to dramatize a duel reflecting or concealing a most ambiguous moment in his own life. The relationship of Conrad to M. George is never satisfactorily resolved. And for this reason we can say that nearly everything rendered by M. George himself — nominally recalling his youth but also trying to create an exciting fictional present — is unsuccessful: clumsily introduced and vaguely outlined, invertebrately phrased. This narrator too simply "cannot write," and it is reasonable to suppose that he is considerably more imperceptive than Conrad intended him to be. By the same token nearly everything memorable reaches us through some other character speaking, and telling a story retrospectively.

J. K. M. Blunt (whose prototype did or did not wound Conrad in a duel) gives a first and impressionistic yet economical account of Rita's liaison with Henry Allègre: of the tattered girl found in the great man's garden, presently to emerge on horseback at his side, and in his pavilion where the eminent of Paris meet. Rita herself, who is certainly the book's real "subject," speaks more forcefully than anyone else; she is also one of Conrad's very few charming and mature women. She can evoke vividly her childhood experience tending goats in the mountains, to be alternately kissed and stoned by the child José; and her life as mistress of Allègre, feeling as protected as a nun; and her sense of disarray when he dies, leaving her a fortune; and even her shadowy relationship with His Majesty Don Carlos. She speaks with remarkable frankness for her time. She has both wit and humor, and evokes as brilliantly her uncle, a snuff-loving peasant priest, and Azzolati, a rich and desperate seducer. There is both humor and pathos in her vivid pictures of the hangers-on after Allègre's death.*

All this is retrospective. But even her dramatic dialogue is excellent. She is created, as a person, by her rhetoric: by the economy and biting precision and intelligence of her diction, by her often elaborate sentence-structures and by the speeding rhythms of her occasional passionate outbursts. The character of Rita may have been largely supplied by life itself, but recalled reality seldom has this vividness. The successful portrait reminds us that audacious creation and rich imaginative dialogue may prove more plausible than cautious imitation of dull everyday speech and dull everyday reality. The major rule observed is that the fictional character who speaks a great deal must be allowed some vivacity and freshness, must not talk "like everyone else."

This is precisely the rule ignored with M. George, who nearly always writes badly. The rest of the novel is about him

* Pierre Benoit's *Pour Don Carlos* (Paris, 1920) presents a vivacious and wealthy young woman, formerly a mistress of the Pretender, who now loyally recruits young men for the cause, using her person as well as her fortune. It would be amusing to believe that the same historical personage lies behind both characterizations. But the first name of Benoit's heroine — Allegria — suggests, rather, that Benoit had read *The Arrow of Gold.*

and that rest is commonplace. Even the dramatic climax of the *Tremolino* story, which provided such moving pages in *The Mirror of the Sea,* is omitted. It is impossible to know whether Conrad, continuing his reduction of the narrator, deliberately made M. George's language dull and imprecise for purposes of realism. It may be he did not face the problem in exactly these terms, but simply tried to become, again, that bewildered uninitiated self of some forty years before. "But how and why did he get so far from the scene of his sea adventure was an interesting question. And I put it to him with most naïve indiscretion which did not shock him visibly." Such writing as this would suggest a deliberate coarseness, were it not scattered through the late novels. More probably Conrad simply could not make that bridge between his tired aging and perhaps at last forgiven self and the young dazed guilty adventurer of under twenty; and so had to make his youthful hero tired as well as dazed. All we can say is that the creative situation — the relationship of author to narrator-self to material — was unsatisfactory.

How much of the problem is biographical: recollected duel, or fictional duel to cover attempted suicide? Ambiguous love affair in fiction to cover a disastrous one in real life? These questions are perhaps unanswerable. Fictionally, the most important fact may well be that Rita gives life to the book. Thus the first serious signs of rhetorical collapse (after the excellent first two sections) occur in the third part, when M. George is frequently separated from Rita and when, on the other hand, he has come to know he is in love with her. That is, we have lost her energizing witty presence and been left with the dreary serious "subject" of his passion. Is Conrad trying to remember and dramatize incoherence, or is he simply and helplessly, for reasons we cannot entirely know, incoherent? "My emotions and sensations were child-like and chaotic inasmuch that they were very intense and primitive, and that I lay very helpless in their unrelaxing grasp." Rita, luckily, has more command of the language than this.

The most obvious failure of *The Arrow of Gold* is, not unexpectedly, with the language of passion; or, more exactly, with the rhetoric of uncertainty. The Doña Rita who speaks so vividly of her own life and of the great world becomes, in M. George's loving eyes, a mysterious woman of "all time." As such he can address her, during an intimate conversation, as follows: "Don't think I am reproaching you, O blind force!" His rhetoric is not only sentimental, but sentimental at times in a very peculiar way, and one that associates love and death. Rita has not the "gross immobility of a Sphinx proposing roadside riddles but the finer immobility, almost sacred, of a fateful figure seated at the very source of the passions that have moved men from the dawn of ages." And a period of enrapt gazing induces in M. George "a feeling of deep content, something like a foretaste of a time of felicity which must be quiet or it couldn't be eternal." He can, in his efforts to convey the nuances of passion, combine all of the following vagueness in a single sentence: "inconceivable intimacy . . . the closest embrace . . . indeterminate tenderness . . . infinite depths . . . unsuspected soul of peace."

Language is the key to all mysteries. Can we finally determine from the rhetoric of *The Arrow of Gold* whether Conrad was wounded in a duel or wounded himself? I am afraid not. On page 256, the wrecking of the ship "left in me the memory of a suicide"; on page 305 "I came here to face calmly the necessity of doing away with a human life." But this, presumably, was Ortega's life. The actual account of the duel is extremely blurred. But this could be the uncertainty and confusion of recall, or it could be the uncertainty and confusion of crucial experience evaded. To approach one's subject too close, or to keep it at the wrong distance, may alike produce dull writing. And this writing (for such a climax) is of course extraordinarily dull. Captain Blunt — and let us remember that such a man did exist — didn't open his lips,

> but only made a little bow. For the rest he was perfectly ruthless. If he was utterly incapable of being carried away by love there was nothing equivocal about his jealousy. Such psychology is not very rare and really from the point of view of the combat

itself one cannot very well blame him. What happened was this. Monsieur George fired on the word and, whether luck or skill, managed to hit Captain Blunt in the upper part of the arm which was holding the pistol. That gentleman's arm dropped powerless by his side. But he did not drop his weapon. There was nothing equivocal about his determination. With the greatest deliberation he reached with his left hand for his pistol and taking careful aim shot Monsieur George through the left side of his breast. One may imagine the consternation of the four seconds and the activity of the two surgeons in the confined, drowsy heat of the walled garden." [26]

One may imagine indeed! This passage betrays all the irrelevance of the *vécu,* the underdramatized quality of real recollection. Or does it betray rather the uncertain rhetoric of concealment? Perhaps we shall never know. But these questions remind us again that the interest of the novel — in spite of one fine creation of character — is extra-literary. It is, above all, material for the gossip of biographers.

The Rover, begun as a short story when plans for *Suspense* refused to develop, is presumably the slightest of the full-length novels. Conrad was shocked to find it reviewed in America under the "ominous" caption "A Popular Novel," and he outlined the seriousness of his aims in a long interesting letter to Edward Garnett. "This is perhaps my only work in which brevity was a conscious aim. I don't mean compression. I mean brevity *ab initio,* in the very conception, in the very manner of thinking about the people and the events." [27] The last sentence appears to imply a willed simplification of the artistic process; or, a determination not to be waylaid by subtleties and refinements. And in a sense the aim was accomplished too well. For *The Rover,* at its best a true adventure story for boys, is at its worst a coarse-grained study of feeble-minded and inarticulate people. The novel has no narrator, and in fact has no narrative method. But the dull consciousness of Peyrol gives most of the pages their tone.

Several of the feeble-minded persons we have seen under different names: the stiff reticent lover Réal; the girl half-crazed by traumatic experience; the husband Scevola, a literally impotent rival. The turning-point of the affair recalls the climax of "A Smile of Fortune." Réal regards Arlette as "untouchable" and goes back to the farm only for the pleasure of looking at her: at this "distracted girl, mysterious, awful, pale, irresistible in her strangeness . . ." But an inadvertent kiss changes their relationship for good. The older Peyrol stands outside the triangle. His own interest in the girl is so undramatized that it scarcely seems to exist. He sacrifices himself for the young lovers by replacing the Lieutenant on a dangerous mission. But to argue that Peyrol thus accomplishes (or that the novel "proves") a victory of the normal over the abnormal is to take simple matters very seriously. The story of the surviving lovers and the story of the returned patriotic seaman are essentially separate. And it is the second story that engaged Conrad more deeply.

"I am glad you think well of *The Rover,*" Conrad wrote to Galsworthy. "I have wanted for a long time to do a seaman's 'return' (before my own departure) and this seemed a possible peg to hang it on." [28] The personal correspondences are poignant, though slight. The aging "rover" Peyrol — a one-time mildly lawless Brother of the Coast, unable "to give a clear account of himself" — returns to the French region of his boyhood to settle down for a quiet old age. He acquires a tartane to give him a reassuring connection with the sea, and feels the normal reaction of travelers returning home after many years. "The thought that if he had remained at home he would have probably looked like that man crossed unbidden the mind of Peyrol." And he "felt the grip of his origins from the crown of his head to the soles of his feet while he clambered on board the tartane as if for a long and distant voyage." The simple Peyrol is momentarily endowed with "a drop of universal scorn, a wonderful sedative," and thus takes an unexpected place with Heyst, Decoud, and other skeptical intellectual author-projections. But the strongest evidence for arguing an intimate projection involving Poland lies in the brief grudging admission that Peyrol had been a deserter from the Navy. His defense is that this happened "in the time of kings and aristocrats."

Is France of the *ancien régime* then to be equated with Poland occupied by Russia? If so, the moving end of the story reconciles all conflicts. For Peyrol dies his hero's death after a deliberately losing fight with the British *Amelia* (losing, so that planted messages will be captured and read). He and his tartane are then given ceremonial burial at sea by the admirable officers of Nelson's fleet. Honor has thus been won on all sides. A successful return to land has been accomplished, and a successful return to the sea. Réal delivers the final judgment on this equivocal man: ". . . the only certain thing we can say of him is that he was not a bad Frenchman."

Unfortunately these authorial correspondences seem more interesting and more substantial in such a summary than they do in the novel itself. The very real recovery of energy and style that occurs in the final pages, as the tartane puts out to sea, may be due to technical rather than subjective reasons. The novel has escaped its narrow scene and constricted point of view, and has escaped its uncongenial lovers. It now has something worth writing about (a running fight at sea) and it can describe it from a distance of space, time, and cold nautical knowledge. From the vantage of these final pages, in fact, the clumsiness of the rest of the novel seems astonishing. For elsewhere Conrad has all the usual troubles with point of view which occur when he dispenses with a narrator, yet seems unaware that he is having them. "For an hour or so Captain Vincent mused a bit on his real home, on matters of service and other unrelated things, then getting into motion in a very wide-awake manner, he superintended himself the dispatch of that boat the existence of which had been acutely surmised by Lieutenant Réal and was a matter of no doubt whatever to old Peyrol." This is not uncongenial or imperfect method but rather a total absence of method or total indifference to it. The willed simplicity, if that is what it is, has certainly been achieved.

For this reason the recovery at the end of *The Rover,* after two hundred and fifty pages of extreme dullness and ineptitude, provides a very moving experience for the lover of Conrad's work. Even in those earlier pages the style achieved some firmness and variety when, momentarily, a retrospective view permitted genuine organization of the material; or when, very occasionally, Conrad allowed himself to step back from it and speak with expository authority. The narrative of the final chase, on the other hand, and the account of Peyrol's death and ceremonial burial, result in good narrative and descriptive prose carried for more than twenty pages. The style remains evocative and under firm control even for those final moments of Peyrol's life which posed acute problems of point of view and of pathos alike. The voice heard by Peyrol at the moment of his death echoes strangely the ending of *A Personal Record,* where Conrad tells of hearing himself addressed in English for the first time in his life: "Look out there."

> Peyrol, sinking back on the deck in another heavy lurch of his craft, saw for an instant the whole of the English corvette swing up into the clouds as if she meant to fling herself upon his very breast. A blown seatop flicked his face noisily, followed by a smooth interval, a silence of the waters. He beheld in a flash the days of his manhood, of strength and adventure. Suddenly an enormous voice like the roar of an angry sea-lion seemed to fill the whole of the empty sky in a mighty and commanding shout: "Steady!" . . . And with the sound of that familiar English word ringing in his ears Peyrol smiled to his visions and died.[29]

Suspense, conceived as early as 1907, poses special problems and demands particular caution, since Conrad left it unfinished at his death. We do not know how the story would have ended, and very possibly Conrad didn't know either. He spoke of it to Richard Curle the day before he died, and at that time could see five or six different lines of treatment.[30]

Cosmo is on his way to Elba when the long fragment breaks off; presumably he was to have worked on Napoleon's behalf. But the solution of the possible incestuous situation could have raised more difficult problems than the political one. There might well have been, if we accept the hint that Cosmo and Adèle had the same father,[31] two successive versions of the familiar Conradian triangle. In one Cosmo is the reticent lover, Adèle the persecuted victim, and Count Helion her husband the impotent and sadistic rival. In the second, Count Helion (now uncle not husband) would remain the rival, but Adèle would be replaced by the savage and unruly sixteen-year-old Clelia, another avatar of Alice Jacobus. Conceivably Clelia could have been cured of her bad manners by kindness and a decent British lover such as Cosmo, who would turn to her on discovering Adèle was his half-sister. But this is the purest conjecture, and it may be to the credit of Conrad's plotting that we cannot be more definite. At least it is safe to say that Conrad had here undertaken something more than an ordinary historical romance and adventure story for boys.

We can only conjecture, moreover, how or whether Conrad would have revised away what appears to be an excessive dependence on the memoirs of the Comtesse de Boigne. But it is possible to discern what materials, irrespective of source or of conceivable revision, were congenial, and what materials stultifying. Once again the great obstacle was proving to be the hero: a young man as dazed and passive as the M. George of *The Arrow of Gold,* he too incomprehensibly tired. He is not, luckily, a narrator. But the authorial summary—"Cosmo had no inborn aptitude for mere society life," etc. —indicates how little equipped he is even to occupy an important post of observation. The most awkward pages of *Suspense* are those which carry Cosmo through a fully reported fictional present time—whether as a jaded traveler in his hotel room, or as a dazed observer of the Montevesso household, or as accidental participant in an Elban conspiracy. Like most of his predecessors after Razumov, he is a hero incapable of action.

There is no good purpose to be served by seeking out and quoting the worst passages of inept, unidiomatic, or ungrammatical prose. Conceivably Conrad might have improved or eliminated them in preparing the final version. For this book had long been an important one for him, and even in its present state shows an intelligence and maturity of conception far beyond *The Rover*. The Montevesso household is vividly presented, even when Cosmo is our post of observation: the vast *palazzo* hired by a wealthy and brutal adventurer, and housing both his aristocratic wife and father-in-law and certain peasant relations; the corrupted servant Bernard hired to spy on Adèle and quietly accepted by her in this role; the cold formal relations of husband and wife; the strange unkempt and insubordinate figure of Clelia wandering in and out. We see these in the present. Otherwise, the best pages of *Suspense* are retrospective. The second and third chapters cover a period of years efficiently and with crisp historical irony. And Adèle's long surview of her married life, however bookish in tone or dependent on the Comtesse de Boigne, is a good piece of Conradian impressionism. Doctor Martel's brief evocation of the siege of Genoa shows the same power and assurance built on swiftness of pace and on rigid selection.

The strangest and loveliest page comes near the beginning, and is unlike anything Conrad had written before. The context and occasion are most improbable. Attilio, whom Cosmo has just met — and the reader never really knows who and what he is — casually mentions an old man who once said the English were a lordly nation. Cosmo takes this as a cue to ask about the old man's "wisdom," and so prompts the strange paragraph. Its quality is at once dreamlike and, in its elisions of thought, metaphysical:

"The wisdom of a great plain as level almost as the sea," said the other gravely. "His voice was as unexpected when I heard it as your own, signore. The evening shadows had closed about me just after I had seen to the west, on the edge of the world as it were, a lion miss his spring on a bounding deer. They went right away into the glow and vanished. It was as though I had dreamed. When I turned round there was the old man behind me no farther away than half the width of this platform. He only smiled at my startled looks. His long silver locks stirred in the breeze. He had been watching me, it seems, from folds of ground and from amongst reed beds for nearly half a day, wondering what I might be at. I had come ashore to wander on the plain. I like to be alone sometimes. My ship was anchored in a bight of this deserted coast a good many miles away, too many to walk back in the dark for a stranger like me. So I spent the night in that old man's ranch, a hut of grass and reeds, near a little piece of water peopled by a multitude of birds. He treated me as if I had been his son. We talked till dawn and when the sun rose I did not go back to my ship. What I had on board of my own was not of much value, and there was certainly no one there to address me as 'My son' in that particular tone—you know what I mean, signore." [32]

There is little in this passage to attach it to the personage of Attilio, or to attach it to anything else in the novel, unless perhaps to the strange old steersman who appears at the very end. Presumably it is a passage originating in some personal feeling not developed in the novel. But at the very end of the book Attilio prompts a long sentence echoing it. The prose here is of considerably less originality, but possesses the same gravity and exhibits too some of the old extended rhythms: "Attilio, the wanderer of the seas along the southern shores of the earth and the pupil of the hermit of the plains that lie under the constellation of the southern sky, smiled in the dark, a faint friendly gleam of white teeth in an over-shadowed face."

Is this briefly seen and enigmatic Attilio a final dramatization of Dominic Cervoni, as Jean-Aubry conjectures? The last pages of *Suspense* would in that event bring Conrad around and back to the greatest of his personal adventures and to some of the most durable of his literary materials. But the young Cosmo Latham watched over by Attilio is a much older man than the Conrad who sailed with Cervoni. "Come to sit at the stern, signore. I can find a rug to throw over a coil of rope for a seat." He is, in fact, a very tired old man. Those strange final pages, inevitably colored by our awareness of Conrad's death, seem in some sense to dramatize its approach. It is possible that this is true in something more than a metaphorical sense; possible that the unconscious and preconscious, which are capable of symbolizing and so betraying still undiscovered sexual longings, can also symbolize and convey a recognition of death and its coming. The conscious intent of these final pages, taking Cosmo and Attilio out to sea, was to carry them toward exciting youthful adventure in Elba. But the pages are profoundly dreamlike. The rowboat carrying them hovers near shore; it is being hunted by a dark galley at the harbor mouth, in an archetype of the crossing into death. At the brink of the adventure, Cosmo still nominally has a free choice to make: he can wade ashore and go back to his hotel, or he can advance into the unknown with Attilio. And they move toward the open sea and an awaiting felucca:

After the first few strokes Cosmo felt himself draw back again to the receding shore. But it was too late. He seemed to feel profoundly that he was not — perhaps no man was — a free agent. He felt a sort of fear, a faltering of all his limbs, as he swung back to his oar. Then his eyes caught the galley, indeed everybody's eyes in the boat were turned that way except the eyes of the ancient steersman, the white-headed figure in an unexpectedly erect attitude who, with hardly any breath left in his body and a mere helpless victim of other men's will, had a strange appearance of the man in command.[33]

On board the felucca, Cosmo feels "neither sleepy nor tired, nor even curious, as if altogether freed from the weaknesses of the body, and not indifferent but without apprehensions or speculations of any sort to disturb his composure as if of a fully informed wisdom." And this is the last we know of this now composed hero. He does not die. But the ancient steersman does, and at this point *Suspense* breaks off.

The early work of Conrad had a dreamlike quality, as a large proportion of truly original writing does. It is somehow pleasing to see his very last fiction return to that exciting and unstable element. There are moments of confusion and ineptitude as great as in the other late novels, but the ambition is on the whole a finer one. *Suspense* is the work of an exceedingly tired writer who was also a great one, and who exhibits signs and fragments of greatness at the last.

He was a very great novelist. And perhaps the chief reason for examining these final works is to remind ourselves of the sometimes dark senses in which this was so. Certain readers have applauded Conrad's movement toward the normal and affirmative, and his belated triumph over eccentricity, tragic inwardness, and despair. Even Morton D. Zabel speaks with sympathy and respect of a "final release of his spirit into reconciliation." But this movement, whatever comforts it brought the now famous and at last almost solvent man, either damaged his fiction or coincided with its destruction by some other agency. The imagined world no longer seemed so imperiled morally, and its heroes were now more innocent and less introspective. But also this imagined world had ceased to be meaningful and its heroes had become merely commonplace. The last works should be restudied especially by those who admire the early novels, yet regret their pessimism and corrosive analytic bent and austere moralism, and resent their complexity of method. For these qualities were essential rather than incidental to the success. A simple and serene Conrad could not have written *Lord Jim*.

The fictional world of the late novels is not as normal as it may seem at a first glance. The old triangle with its implications of voyeurism and impotence remains; so too does the unconscious association of sex and death. And the serenity is often that of a sad, tired resignation. The great difference is that the later Conrad (perhaps only half-consciously, but perhaps even by an act of will) assumed a more sociable pliant ethic and a more generous estimate of human character. Did he do so because age or a therapeutic art, or both, had now calmed his own tensions and conflicts? To cease to kick against the traces, to accept imperfection quietly, may be a sign of mature wisdom. But it can also be the sign of an indifference bred of fatigue. Perhaps Conrad had said what he needed to say. The impulse to dramatize certain loyalties and betrayals, realized fully in such great and in a sense "complete" works as *Lord Jim,* "The Secret Sharer" and *Under Western Eyes,* may have been virtually satisfied; i.e., exhausted.

There may occur, too, that other exhaustion in which one yields up moral questions in despair. Or, as Hewitt puts it: ". . . seeing no positive values to counter the force of his negative criticism, he took refuge in the unreal and unquestioned goodness of Lena and old Peyrol." [34] To this we may relate Moser's solid conviction that the unconscious mind could itself do no little questioning. The art stumbles because it tries to express a confident, genial ethic the artist in his deepest being cannot accept. We shall see this very strikingly illustrated in the Gidean trilogy of *L'Ecole des Femmes, Geneviève,* and *Robert.* The creative imagination simply refuses the "dishonest" task that a socially conscious intellect assigns it. And there are other ways for the spirit to become exhausted than these. One must insist again on the effect of physical fatigue; and, so far as failing syntax and diction are concerned, on the pernicious effect of dictation. But the mysteries of words cannot be wholly solved at this distance and so long after the event. Friends have reported that Conrad's foreign accent increased in his last years, and certain locutions toward the end of *Suspense* suggest that he may have been thinking at least intermittently in French.

Such is the later work. But it would be disheartening to end thus, pawing over the slackened will and imperfect unrevised writings of a very tired man. And misleading too, since last impressions receive disproportionate attention. The decline of Conrad — insofar as it was accelerated by a conscious effort to become a more positive and more "normal" writer — provides a useful warning lesson for fellow novelists. But under the aspect of eternity and in that long run which finally concerns criticism, this lesson may not matter very much to readers who are not novelists. What matters are Conrad's best works, not the order in which he wrote them. It would therefore seem fairer to ignore chronology at the last, and to conclude with a brief glance at some major full-length novel written at the turn of the century or shortly afterward, when Conrad was in the fullness of his powers. Unfortunately no such full-length novel exists, between *Lord Jim* and *Nostromo*.

But *Typhoon* (1902) exists, a short novel nearly all readers admire. It stands almost alone among Conrad's better books as a work whose preoccupations are nearly all on the surface, and in which the devil's share of unconscious creation was very slight. It is not concerned with a man's dark traffic with himself, nor with the drama of personal loyalty to an outlaw brother. Its matter is rather that of character and conscience facing more outward challenges. Thus *Typhoon* requires no elaborate interpreting. But it is the work of a true professional, professional seaman and professional writer both. The story says what it intended to say, and moves as it intended to move.

Typhoon therefore corresponds more closely than most of the works do to the accepted older view of Conrad: a simple rational man possessed of a simple forthright ethic, and who liked to write about ships and the sea. It also corresponds to the image Conrad sometimes thought he wanted to leave behind him. He resented being classified as a novelist of the sea. But more than once he apparently longed to be thought of as a reliable, normal Captain MacWhirr. "MacWhirr is not an acquaintance of a few hours, or a few weeks, or a few months. He is the product of twenty years of life. My own life." [35]

Thus *Typhoon* is a fine example of "shipshape" Conrad for the critic who likes to see the artist in total and planned control of his material. It is also, for the critic of any stripe, a fine and moving achievement, based on a true respect for both material and form.

The story has at least two intentions, as Conrad suggests in his evasive Author's Note. One of these obviously was to tell a story of hardship and courage at sea, this story based on a real occurrence involving returning coolies, an event well-known among ship captains of the time. What must it have been like, Conrad surely asked himself, to take a ship through a typhoon while one's desperate, clawing human cargo in the hold shifted in a howling mass with each roll of the ship, the sea chests split open and hard-earned dollars rolling loose? The writing of the "storm-piece," as Conrad calls it, is lucid and vivid, seemingly exact without excess detail, very obviously expert. At first there is only the heat and a lurid sunshine that casts "faint and sickly shadows," as the sea swell rises. But the barometer is falling very fast. And presently the ship is moving toward a dense bank of cloud with a sinister dark olive tint, lying as "a solid obstacle in the path of the ship. She went floundering towards it like an exhausted creature driven to its death."

The approach to the storm is conveyed in economical and evocative prose. And even under the full stress of the storm the style remains in splendid control, the very rhythms reflecting the crashing and receding waters, the plungings and risings of the ship:

> It suffocated them, and with eyes shut they tightened their grasp. What from the magnitude of the shock might have been a column of water running upright in the dark, butted against the ship, broke short, and fell on her bridge, crushingly, from on high, with a dead burying weight.
>
> A flying fragment of that collapse, a mere splash, enveloped them in one swirl from their feet over their heads, filling violently their ears, mouths, and nostrils with salt water. It knocked out their legs, wrenched in haste at their arms, seethed away swiftly under their chins; and opening their eyes, they saw the piled-up masses of foam dashing to and fro amongst what looked like the fragments of a ship. She had given way as if driven straight in. Their panting hearts yielded too, before the tremendous blow; and all at once she sprang up again to her desperate plunging, as if trying to scramble out from under the ruins.[36]

The success of the storm-piece is universally recognized. The second large intention was to test, under conditions of extreme stress, certain types of human character. The helmsman who "can steer for ever if nobody talks to me" is of Singleton's heroic mold, and the second mate shares Donkin's squalid destiny. He is without Donkin's vicious gregariousness, however, and isolates himself in his cabin, there to lie on his bed and soiled pillow; he has no connections on shore. These seamen behave in crisis exactly as we would expect them to. But the portraits are slighter than the corresponding ones in *The Nigger of the "Narcissus."* In *Typhoon,* the main interest is in the officers.

The essential contrast is between the sensitive, imaginative, thoughtful, vulnerable mate Jukes and the stolid unimaginative Captain MacWhirr, who can't see what people find to talk about. The typical Conradian protagonist of the early work is haunted by the past and either longs for or dreads the future. Therefore he betrays the present. But for MacWhirr the past was "done with, and the future not there yet." The introspective brooding captains of "The Secret Sharer" and *The Shadow Line* were the ones with whom Conrad identified most deeply. But MacWhirr exhibits an extrovert simplicity Conrad envied and at times even idealized, and a natural easy heroism free from guilt or fear. He is the unconscious servant and product of a certain training and tradition, and builds his ethic on fairness or justice not sentiment.

The two men and the two ethics come into full contrast in response to the plight of the coolies. In the first hours of the rising storm Jukes proposes changing the course of the ship to reduce its roll, and so that the Chinese can ride more comfortably. But later, in an hour of real danger, he would have been willing to let them fight for the dollars. This critique of a sentimental ethic is not entirely convincing, however, since Jukes was merely "clutching at a straw" when he proposed that change of course. He had come to Captain MacWhirr to express his anxiety, and hoping to be reassured; the coolies were an afterthought. Thus Jukes seems less a typical sentimentalist than a man of good intentions who is also a "worrier," and meets trouble half-way. He is not an egoist or egotist of Lord Jim's magnitude, is perhaps not even capable of Lord Jim's glamorous dreams. He is simply a poor officer: a man who, if finally he does his duty, at once wants to be praised.

As for Captain MacWhirr — nothing could better dramatize the quiet heroism of "fairness" than his conduct toward the coolies. He insists that the fighting be stopped, the money picked up and distributed in the only equitable way. Perhaps we must add that he sees these coolies as a white man's burden? MacWhirr shares none of Jukes's (and Conrad's) sentimental attachment to the British flag as symbol. But he is an Englishman of his time and of his calling in his refusal to think of the Chinese coolies as "passengers."

The characterization of Captain MacWhirr moves with assurance, from its first note of faint contempt and first glance at his "ordinary, irresponsive, and unruffled" face to its final heroic image of the exhausted and perspiring man in his shirt-sleeves, paying out the dollars to the Chinese. This movement is certainly calculated. Yet how far does Conrad mean to carry this celebration of the uncomplicated and unintellectual man? Is it even a celebration at all? The famous statement at the end of the first chapter should not be regarded as definitive. It concerns a Captain MacWhirr who had not yet been tested, who

> had sailed over the surface of the oceans as some men go skimming over the years of existence to sink gently into a placid grave, ignorant of life to the last, without ever having been made to see all it may contain of perfidy, of violence, and of terror. There are on sea and land such men thus fortunate — or thus disdained by destiny or by the sea.[37]

In the test itself, facing an extraordinary violence, MacWhirr is at first wholly contemptuous of the "storm strategy" outlined in books. And perhaps he is so to the end. "A gale is a gale, Mr. Jukes . . . and a full-powered steam-ship has got to face it. There's just so much dirty weather knocking about the world, and the proper thing is to go through it." It is not clear whether this blunt innocence and ignorance — this refusal to profit from man's accumulated knowledge of what typhoons can do — is responsible for his later moment of astonished and failing confidence, as he sits "apart from the sea, from his ship, isolated, as if withdrawn from the very current of his own existence." But it is entirely clear what saves him: the meticulous attention to order and detail, and his submission to "all these little habits that chain us to the weary round of life."

He is saved, specifically, in the darkness of his cabin and in the hour of his demoralization, by finding a towel in the place it is supposed to be. So reassured that his world is in place, he at once goes back on deck to continue his stubborn fight with the sea. This humble moment is the story's climax. It occurs during the calm before the worst of the storm — that worst which, André Gide remarked, Conrad was so wise to omit.

Captain MacWhirr was trying to do up the top button of his oilskin coat with unwonted haste. The hurricane, with its power to madden the seas, to sink ships, to uproot trees, to overturn strong walls and dash the very birds of the air to the ground, had found this taciturn man in its path, and, doing its utmost, had managed to wring out a few words. Before the renewed wrath of winds swooped on his ship, Captain MacWhirr was moved to declare in a tone of vexation, as it were: "I wouldn't like to lose her."

He was spared that annoyance.[38]

Some of these materials may seem familiar. The choice between pity and justice; the plight of the untested and innocent man in a storm having its center of strange calm; that other choice between brutal and devious means, will and intelligence; a situation of underdeck chaos to be subdued; the moment of isolated communion with self and the moment of recognition in a dark cabin — all this might suggest that *Typhoon* belongs with "The Secret Sharer" and the other symbolic night journeys. Not impossibly it was intended to carry such overtones. But I think it can carry them importantly only for a reader who likes his symbols and meanings put very bluntly, or who pays a great deal of attention to a few general statements, or who bases his entire interpretation on the phrase "disdained by destiny or by the sea." There is a very good and simple reason why *Typhoon* cannot become such a symbolic descent into self and into the preconscious. This is that Captain MacWhirr remains to the end incapable of genuine introspection. So this storm at least cannot be called an inward one.

For somewhat the same reason the superbly written scene of the boatswain's descent into the bunker (where a sliding and clattering iron bar threatens to kill him in the dark) and his appalling vision of the shifting mass of coolies cannot carry the subjective meanings of James Wait imprisoned below decks. But this does not mean that the scene from *Typhoon* is in any way deficient, is not in its own way a triumph. These are, simply, two different modes of fiction. It is proper and even necessary to draw a line between the very complex *Nigger of the "Narcissus"* and the relatively simple *Typhoon*. And in our age of anxiety and analysis there may be a natural preference for the more difficult and more psychological story. But explicit even transparent ethic may also have its claims, if built on a solid enough base. And so too, if only on stylistic grounds, may such a powerful evocation of storm at sea.

The prose of *Typhoon* at least is not that of a man thinking in French. Between the younger Conrad and the genius of the English language there was, as he claimed, "a subtle and unforeseen accord." [39] The rhythms of the language responded to nervous energies, and to the needs of a rich style combining to a remarkable degree written and spoken effects. Even at its most elaborate that style expresses a personal voice. It has a somber authority and grace of cadence possessed by no earlier English novelist, and is not like anyone else's style. Otherwise too Conrad stands a little apart, with his European intelligence and sensibility.

Hence to try to "place" Conrad as a novelist, seems an unrewarding task. A critic may, according to his relative valuation of fantasy and intelligence, creativity and control, place either Dickens or James at the summit of the English novel. Conrad certainly lacked Dickens' compulsive terrible comic strangeness and astounding creative power, and on the whole lacked James's full devotion to fiction as a conscious fine art. But he had a kind of inward seriousness Dickens and even James lacked, provoked subtler conflicts of feeling in his readers, and dramatized certain psychic processes beyond their ken. He could conceive better than they the tragic boundary-situation, where choice is virtually impossible. He is more interesting than the grave primitive Hardy, if only to the extent that he is more aware of inward crisis, and substitutes a stern for a tender outlook. It is hard to see with whom else he may be compared. Certainly not with Bennett, Galsworthy, Wells, and his other "engaged" Edwardian friends, nor with the delicate noncommittal E. M. Forster. He was less changeful than George Moore and less conscious of technique than Ford Madox Ford, but far more original than either.

He seems closer to the present — to Faulkner, Graham Greene, Malcolm Lowry, and others — than to the major figures who emerged just before and after the First World War. It was understandably hard, in the early 1920's, to recognize how original he was, or even to remember his greatness. For the historical fact is that he published his worst and least original books during those crucial and exciting postwar years; that he finished *The Rover* in the year of *Ulysses*. But today in perspective, and in spite of the popularity finally achieved, he occupies an advanced place in the movement of the novel toward a more meditative and less popular form. That such a movement has been and is still going on is obvious enough. So too it is obvious that the best writers will not soon return, if ever, to the very ample methods and large social aims of the nineteenth-century and Edwardian realists. But Conrad's early fiction reminds us that the novel can move toward this subtler, more difficult, more thoughtful, more poetic form without becoming trivial or decadent. The novel can still to its advantage tell great human stories, though it may be unable or unwilling to tell them simply. And it can still speak, and with a personal voice that more popular forms lack, of perils of the spirit both public and intimate.

It is tempting to suppose that Conrad would have been a still more original and even greater writer had he been freed from commercial pressures and ambitions; had he shared, for instance, Gide's money and Gide's literary connections. In that event he would almost certainly not have written certain pot-boiling short stories; it is even possible, since composition became so difficult, that he would have written little or nothing after *The Shadow Line*. But it is doubtful whether the great early work through *Nostromo* would have been substantially changed; or that he would have advanced toward some still more radical form of the novel. He came too late to literature to join consciously a destructive *avant-garde*. And it was not within the scope of his self-protective temperament to manage such a movement as Joyce made between *Dubliners* and *Finnegans Wake*, or even as Gide between *Le Voyage d'Urien* and *Les Faux-Monnayeurs*.

He did of course argue the possibilities of the "new novel" with Ford, and he was professionally and passionately concerned with style. But he was even more concerned, as he insisted repeatedly, with sincerity of expression — which means, among several other things, writing as one feels compelled to write. His highly original structures and methods were, possibly, the ones he would have used under any circumstance. For they were necessary to "sincerity": they responded to certain peculiarities of temperament and they managed to organize and express the essential Conradian dreams. Hence the striking fact that Conrad — trying for "sincerity" but trying also for a larger public — was so much more original than the Moores and Wildes who moved in more advanced circles. He was, behind his mask of a hard conservative ethic, the most personal of the great English novelists. And his method respects that fact.

The human materials explored by both short and long novels were the essential ones of human beings in crisis, facing the testing moments of their lives; and the central impulses of loyalty to the community, to the "outlaw" brother, to oneself. The later works (with their conflict between innocent hero and pathological villain) are melodramatic or pathetic, not tragic. But the great early novels — dramatizing conflicts between "good" or defensible loyalties, and knowing that even the best intentions are menaced by inward forces — show a tragic understanding such as few other English novels have shown before or since. The world of the early novels is a dark one; its demands on human beings are extreme. But there is rare consolation in the thoroughness and lucidity with which Conrad saw that there was no easy way out. And his honest pessimist's universe is a moral one in which all conduct signifies.

APPENDIX

The most important part of the letter from Tadeusz Bobrowski to Stefan Buszczyński, as translated in Jocelyn Baines, "The Young Conrad in Marseilles" (*Times Literary Supplement,* December 6, 1957), is subjoined. The letter, I am informed by Professor Edmund Ordon of Wayne State University, appeared in the Cracow weekly *Życie literackie* for October 6, 1957, as part of a chapter from Zdzisław Najder's forthcoming book on Conrad. The original of the letter is located in the library of the Polish Academy of Sciences in Cracow: Ms. 2064, vol. 2, pp. 693–696. The letter is dated March 24 (New Style), 1879.

Mr. Baines, who has graciously permitted me to quote from this translation of the letter, will doubtless record the steps leading to this important discovery in his own forthcoming biography of Conrad. Mr. Baines informs me that he expressed to Mr. Najder, who was visiting England, his belief — based on a forgotten article and on references made by Bobrowski to suicide — that Conrad did not fight a duel but instead tried to kill himself. He persuaded Mr. Najder to look for the lost letter, on his return to Poland, and this led to the discovery (letter to the author, March 7, 1958).

What you have heard of my journey to Marseilles, and perhaps even of its causes, is unfortunately true! But, as you have lost touch with Conrad's activities, I must briefly outline everything. During 1875/76 and 1877, Conrad made four voyages on French merchant vessels belonging to one and the same shipowner though under various captains: to Guadeloupe, Martinique, the St. Thomas Islands, Haiti and New Orleans, in each case sailing from Marseilles and in consideration of an annual premium of 2,000–24,000 (*sic*) francs. It came as a great shock to me when, in 1876, he committed an escapade; he collected his half-yearly allowance in a lump sum from the Bank, and, he said, lent the money to acquaintances in which young Chodzko, his co-protector, participated. I had no reason to doubt that this is what happened, and to this day do not doubt it; I patched up the gap, gave him a good scolding — and he sailed off again. I may add that his employer and the captain wrote to me reporting most favourably on his application to work and his conduct.

At the beginning of 1877, just before embarking on a fresh voyage, he was laid up with an anal abscess for four weeks. The ship left port and, to the great regret of Captain Escarras (who even wrote to me about this), Conrad was left behind. Not wishing to sail under another captain, he remained in Marseilles to pursue theoretical studies while awaiting the return of his captain, with whom he hoped to circumnavigate the globe. In October, 1877, on his urgent demand and as he was to be away between eighteen months and two years, I sent him over and above his allowance an extra 2,000 francs, together with my blessing. I was quite sure he was somewhere in the Antipodes when, suddenly, while engaged in business at the Kieff Fair in 1878, I received a telegram reading: "Conrad blessé envoyez argent — arrivez." Naturally, I could not fly off at once like a bird, so, after concluding my business and having received a reply that Conrad was recovering, I left Kieff on 24th February (Old Style) and arrived in Marseilles on the 27th. On arrival I found that Conrad was already able to walk, and, after a previous talk with his friend Mr. Richard Fecht (a very prudent and decent young man), I visited the delinquent. This is what had happened. When Captain Escarras returned, Conrad was quite certain he would sail under him; but the Bureau de l'Inscription forbade this as he was an alien, aged twenty-one, and liable to military service in his country. Moreover, it was discovered that Conrad had never received permission from his Consul, so the former Inspector of the Port of Marseilles was summoned to explain why he had noted on the lists that such permission had been granted. He was reprimanded and very nearly lost his post. As could be expected, this was very painful for Conrad. The whole affair became too widely known — all the efforts of the Captain and the shipowner were in vain (Monsieur Delestang, the shipowner, told me all this), and Conrad had to stay ashore, without any hope of serving as a seaman in French vessels. Before all this happened, however, another catastrophe, a financial one, had overtaken him. Having the 3,000 francs I sent him for the voyage, he met a former captain of his, a Monsieur Duteil, who persuaded him to participate in some affair on the coast of Spain — simply, some kind of smuggling. He invested 1,000 francs and made a profit of over 400 francs; this pleased them greatly, so he thereupon engaged all he had in a second venture — and lost all. This Monsieur Duteil consoled him with a kiss, and departed for Buenos Aires, while Conrad remained, unable to sign up as a sailor, penniless (literally, "naked as a Turkish saint") and moreover in debt. For while speculating, he had lived on credit, had ordered things necessary for the voyage, and so on. Faced by such a situation, he borrowed 800 francs from his friend, Mr. Fecht, and set off for Villa-Franca (Villefranche), where an American squadron was anchored, with the intention of entering American naval service. Nothing came of this, and, wishing to repair his finances, he tried his luck in Monte Carlo, where he lost the borrowed 800 francs at the gaming tables. Having so excellently managed his affairs, he returned to Marseilles, and one fine evening he invited the aforesaid friend to tea; but, before the time fixed, he attempted to kill himself with a revolver shot. (Let this detail remain between us; for I have told everyone that he was wounded in a duel. In this matter I do not want and should not want to keep this a secret from you.) The bullet went *durch und durch* near the heart, not injuring any important organ. Luckily he had left all his addresses on top — so that good Mr. Fecht could immediately notify me and even my brother who, again, bombarded me in turn. That is the whole story.

I spent a fortnight in Marseilles, first studying the whole affair and then the Individual. Apart from those lost 3,000 francs, I had to pay off debts for a like sum. I would not have done this for a son of mine, but, for the son of my dear Sister, I confess, I was weak enough to act contrary to my principles.

Nevertheless, I took an oath that even if I knew he should shoot himself again, he could not count on a repetition of this weakness.

. . . . .

. . . He seems to know his job well and likes it very much. I suggested that he return to his country — he flatly refused; I suggested that he return to Galicia, get naturalized and seek a career there — he refused this, too, stating that he loves his profession, does not want to change it, and will not do so. . . . I have more than once seen what cordial greetings were exchanged between him and sailors, who call him Monsieur Georges.

. . . . .

POSTSCRIPT TO THE SECOND PRINTING. Jocelyn Baines's biography, *Joseph Conrad* (New York, 1960) provides no definite answer to the questions raised on page 11 above, "Did Conrad lie to his uncle? Or did he prefer to lie to posterity most intricately?" Mr. Baines is wholly committed to the hypothesis of attempted suicide. But the following considerations seem to leave the matter open:

(1) The "web of proof" for the official, public story of a duel wound was woven *after* Bobrowski's death.

(2) Mr. Baines reveals that almost four years later than the Marseilles wound Conrad lied to Bobrowski, "in a "desperate letter," in appealing for £10. He claimed to have lost all his kit in the sinking of a ship named *Anna Frost*. This appears to have been a fabricated disaster. An *Annie Frost* did sail from London on July 31, 1881, but Conrad was not on the crew's list, and this ship did not sink until just over a year *after* Conrad's appeal. (See Baines, pp. 68–69.)

(3) Mr. Baines again brings Conrad's veracity into question with his allegation that César Cervoni (whose death is recounted in *The Mirror of the Sea*) in fact lived to serve a long career in the French merchant marine. (See Baines, p. 47 n.) It is to be noted that Conrad claimed to have been unconscious, knocked out by the tiller, at the time César was swept into the sea by Dominic's blow, the body fatally weighted by Conrad's stolen money belt. (See *Mirror*, p. 180.) Did Dominic lie to Conrad about César's disappearance? Was he even in league with the nephew to secure the contents of the money belt? (He parted from Conrad at once.) Or shall we, more simply, acknowledge that many novelists have notoriously inventive memories?

A conjectural identification of Doña Rita has been made by Jerry Allen in *The Thunder and The Sunshine* (New York, 1958). She is said to be one Paula de Somogyi, mistress of Don Carlos. Baines argues (p. 57) that Paula arrived on the scene much too late to be the "Rita" in Conrad's life, but he acknowledges that Conrad may have had her in mind in writing his novel *The Arrow of Gold*.

NOTES

The "Kent Edition" of Conrad's collected works, published by Doubleday, Page in 1926, has been used throughout, unless otherwise indicated. Other Doubleday and British Dent editions follow the same pagination.

Chapter 1. THE JOURNEY WITHIN

1. Ford Madox Ford, *Joseph Conrad: A Personal Remembrance* (Boston, 1924), p. 167. Ford's testimony is never to be considered wholly reliable.
2. G. Jean-Aubry, *Joseph Conrad: Life and Letters* (2 vols.; New York, 1927), I, 37–38. Hereafter cited as *Life and Letters.* See also Gérard Jean-Aubry, *The Sea Dreamer* (New York, 1957), pp. 65–66. The true name of the author of these volumes was Jean Aubry; he added the initial "G." and hyphenated his two names to avoid confusion with another writer. The "G." — which actually stood for nothing — was commonly accepted as standing for "Georges." But there is no justification, according to his widow, for the "Gérard" supplied by his publisher for this translation of the *Vie de Conrad.* See also Jocelyn Baines, "The Affair in Marseilles," *The London Magazine,* IV (November 1957), 41–46, and editor's foreword, *ibid.,* p. 11, and especially Baines, "The Young Conrad in Marseilles" (*Times Literary Supplement,* December 6, 1957); and see Appendix to this book.
3. *A Personal Record,* pp. 111–112.
4. "No epithet could be more inapplicable to a man with such a strong sense of responsibility in the region of ideas and action and so indifferent to the promptings of personal ambition as my father. Why the description 'revolutionary' should have been applied all through Europe to the Polish risings of 1831 and 1863 I really cannot understand. These risings were purely revolts against foreign domination. The Russians themselves called them 'rebellions', which, from their point of view, was the exact truth. Amongst the men concerned in the preliminaries of the 1863 movement my father was no more revolutionary than the others, in the sense of working for the subversion of any social or political scheme of existence. He was simply a patriot in the sense of a man who believing in the spirituality of a national existence could not bear to see that spirit enslaved" (Author's Note, *A Personal Record,* pp. ix–x).

   But see Gustav Morf, *The Polish Heritage of Joseph Conrad* (London, n.d.), pp. 27–30, 37–39.

5. "Prince Roman," *Tales of Hearsay,* p. 48.
6. *A Personal Record,* p. 35. In 1899 an article in the Polish newspaper in St. Petersburg provoked a controversy over Conrad's emigration, and one Elise Orzeszko "declared flatly that Joseph Conrad had betrayed the cause of Poland and was no better than a renegade." According to Jean-Aubry, Conrad's lines refer to these later accusations. See *The Sea Dreamer,* pp. 237–238.
7. *A Personal Record,* p. 121.
8. *Ibid.,* p. 110.
9. "A Familiar Preface," *ibid.,* p. xxi.
10. *The Mirror of the Sea,* pp. 139–140, 54–55.
11. *Ibid.,* p. 159.
12. *Life and Letters,* II, 228.
13. See note 2 above, and Appendix.
14. Conrad by no means discouraged the impulse to connect the two books, or to connect the historical Blunt with the fictional Blunt who fights a duel.
15. *The Sea Dreamer,* p. 200. Dr. Ernest Kahn of Cambridge, Massachusetts, called my attention to the possible significance of Conrad being able to finish his book at this time.
16. The conservativism and the cosmic skepticism find their extreme expression in Conrad's letters to R. B. Cunninghame Graham. Conrad dismisses contemptuously the socialist ideals of Jaurès, Liebknecht, etc.: "Fraternity means nothing unless the Cain-Abel business. That's your true fraternity. *Assez* . . . L'homme est un animal méchant. Sa méchanceté doit être organisée. Il faut un principe défini. Si l'idée nationale apporte la souffrance et son service donne la mort, ça vaut toujours mieux que de servir les ombres d'une eloquence qui est morte, justement parce qu'elle n'a pas de corps" (February 8, 1899, *Life and Letters,* I, 269). Certain letters to Cunninghame Graham suggest the excesses to which one may be driven by a stubborn opponent. But Conrad's distrust of social democracy was sincere and long-lived. He writes to Spiridion Kliszczewski in 1885: "The great British Empire went over the edge, and yet on to the inclined plane of social progress and radical reform . . . Where's the man to stop the rush of social-democratic ideas? . . . Socialism must inevitably end in Caesarism" (*ibid.,* I, 84). The Russia of 1920 is (in a letter to John Quinn) "an enormous seething mass of sheer moral corruption" (*ibid.,* II, 237). In 1919 Conrad writes to Sir Hugh Clifford, deploring British appeasement of Russia: "In a class contest there is no room for conciliation. The attacked class cannot save itself by throwing honesty, dignity and convictions overboard. The issue is simply life and death, and if anything can save the situation it is only ruthless courage" (*ibid.,* II, 217). In November 1922, to be sure, he writes

Elbridge L. Adams that the "only class really worth consideration is the class of honest and able men to whatever sphere of human activity they may belong — that is, the class of workers throughout the nation" (*ibid.*, II, 285).

The cosmic skepticism of the letters to Cunninghame Graham takes on an end-of-century eloquence, the tones of Hardy and Arthur Balfour: "The attitude of cold unconcern is the only reasonable one. Of course reason is hateful, — but why? Because it demonstrates (to those who have the courage) that we, living, are out of life, — utterly out of it. The mysteries of a universe made of drops of fire and clods of mud do not concern us in the least. The fate of a humanity condemned ultimately to perish from cold is not worth troubling about" (*ibid.*, I, 222). Or, ". . . the most withering thought is that the infamous thing has made itself: made itself without thought, without conscience, without foresight, without eyes, without heart. It is a tragic accident, — and it has happened. You can't interfere with it. The last drop of bitterness is in the suspicion that you can't even smash it" (*ibid.*, I, 216).

17. The examples are Conrad's own. Letter to Richard Curle, July 14, 1923, *Life and Letters,* II, 316.
18. Preface, *The Nigger of the "Narcissus."*
19. ". . . for me writing — *the only possible writing* — is just simply the conversion of nervous force into phrases" (letter to H. G. Wells, November 30, 1903, *Life and Letters,* I, 321).
20. See *The Mirror of the Sea,* pp. 141, 142, 148.
21. *Youth,* p. 32.
22. See especially "Falk," *Typhoon,* pp. 188–189.
23. *Life and Letters,* I, 100.
24. *The Mirror of the Sea,* pp. 54–55.
25. *Lord Jim,* pp. 11–14.
26. "The Secret Sharer," *'Twixt Land and Sea,* pp. 118–119.
27. Boston, 1924.
28. These lines from Baudelaire furnish the epigraph to *The Shadow Line* and an important clue to its meaning.
29. Jean-Aubry, *Life and Letters,* I, 141, and *The Sea Dreamer,* p. 175. Reportedly said to Edward Garnett. In his *Joseph Conrad in the Congo* (London, 1926), p. 73, Jean-Aubry gives a slightly different wording: "Before the Congo I was only a simple animal."
30. *Life and Letters,* I, 121, 124; *The Sea Dreamer,* pp. 154–159.
31. *Life and Letters,* I, 137; *The Sea Dreamer,* p. 171.
32. F. R. Leavis, *The Great Tradition* (London, 1948), p. 183.
33. Lilian Feder finds a number of parallels with the sixth book of the *Aeneid* in "Marlow's Descent into Hell," *Nineteenth-Century Fiction,* IX (March 1955) 280–292; Robert O. Evans finds chiefly the influence of Dante's *Inferno* in "Conrad's Underworld," *Modern*

Fiction Studies, II (May 1956), 56–62. My views on literary influence differ from those of Miss Feder and Mr. Evans. But echoes and overtones may exist. We may apply to "Heart of Darkness" Thomas Mann's words on *Death in Venice:* a little work of "inexhaustible allusiveness."

34. "Heart of Darkness," *Youth,* pp. 92–93.
35. *Life and Letters,* I, 148. *The Sea Dreamer,* p. 183, offers a slightly different translation of these lines.
36. *An Outcast of the Islands,* p. 250.
37. Morf, *Polish Heritage,* p. 169; his italics. In *The Sea Dreamer,* p. 218, Jean-Aubry relates the story to Conrad's illness in France in 1896: "Mrs. Conrad . . . speaking almost no French, with an old navy doctor who knew almost no English, while Conrad was raving in Polish."
38. *Life and Letters,* I, 113.
39. *The Sea Dreamer,* pp. 139–148. As often, the bibliography is detailed and at a glance persuasive, but the text exceedingly vague and with few specific references to these many sources of information. How far is Jean-Aubry's informant — one Auguste Esnouf of Curepipe, Mauritius (penname, Savinien Mérédac) — to be trusted to discover the truth of this affair more than forty years after the event?
40. "A Smile of Fortune," *'Twixt Land and Sea,* p. 62.
41. *Ibid.,* p. 79.
42. Ford, *Joseph Conrad,* pp. 111–112.

Chapter 2. THE DISCOVERY OF A FICTIONAL WORLD

1. *The Nigger of the "Narcissus,"* p. 89.
2. *The Sisters,* pp. 22–23.
3. *A Personal Record,* p. 68.
4. Jean-Aubry, *Life and Letters,* I, 193.
5. Carlier not Conrad was given command of the Katanga Expedition's ship; a Kayaerts was on board the *Roi des Belges.* Jean-Aubry, *Joseph Conrad in the Congo,* pp. 61, 71.
6. Letter to Richard Curle, July 14, 1923. *Life and Letters,* II, 317.
7. In *A Christmas Garland.*
8. "The Lagoon," *Tales of Unrest,* p. 193.
9. *Ibid.,* p. 192.
10. Harvard College Library, MS Eng. 46.5.
11. See Thomas Moser, "The Rescuer MS.: A Key to Conrad's Development — and Decline," *Harvard Library Bulletin,* Autumn 1956, pp. 325–355; also Moser's *Joseph Conrad: Achievement and Decline,* pp. 145–148, 172–178. See also Vernon Young, "Joseph Conrad: Lingard's Folly: the Lost Subject," *Kenyon Review,* XV (Autumn 1953), 522–539.

12. *The Rescue,* p. 102.
13. *An Outcast of the Islands,* p. 200.
14. *A Personal Record,* p. 18.
15. *Almayer's Folly,* pp. 88–89.
16. *Ibid.,* p. 5.
17. Author's Note, *An Outcast of the Islands.*
18. *An Outcast of the Islands,* p. 161.
19. *Ibid.,* pp. 5, 54.
20. *Ibid.,* pp. 53, 54.
21. *Ibid.,* pp. 213–250.
22. Letter to publishers, April 9, 1896. *Life and Letters,* I, 164 n.
23. *The Rescue,* pp. 19–20, for instance.
24. *Ibid.,* p. 94 (corrected version).
25. My colleague Professor Alfred Harbage suggested to me the possible relevance of Stevenson's work to that of the early Conrad.
26. "Karain," *Tales of Unrest,* pp. 25–26.
27. Introduction, *The Sisters,* pp. 2–3, 16.
28. *The Sisters,* pp. 41.
29. *Ibid.,* p. 47.
30. Author's Note, *Tales of Unrest.*
31. "The Idiots," *Tales of Unrest,* p. 67.
32. Introduction, *The Sisters.*
33. "The Return," *Tales of Unrest,* p. 176.
34. *Ibid.,* pp. 129–130.

Chapter 3. *THE NIGGER OF THE "NARCISSUS"*

1. Preface, *The Nigger of the "Narcissus."*
2. John D. Gordan, *Joseph Conrad: The Making of a Novelist* (Cambridge, Mass., 1941), pp. 141–144.
3. "To My Readers in America" (Preface of 1914), *The Nigger of the "Narcissus."*
4. Gordan, *Joseph Conrad,* pp. 289, 286.
5. *The Nigger of the "Narcissus,"* p. 172.
6. Preface, *The Nigger of the "Narcissus."*
7. Vernon Young, "Trial by Water," *Accent* (Spring 1952), pp. 80–81.
8. *The Nigger of the "Narcissus,"* pp. 138, 139.
9. This was called to my attention by Mrs. Elizabeth Von Klemperer, who is preparing a dissertation on James and Conrad in France.
10. "To My Readers in America."
11. Henry James, Preface to *The Aspern Papers.*
12. *The Nigger of the "Narcissus,"* p. 90. My italics.
13. *Ibid.,* pp. 8, 22, 24.
14. *Ibid.,* p. 145.
15. *Ibid.*, p. 76. My italics.

16. *Ibid.*, pp. 14–15. My italics.
17. *Ibid.*, p. 172.

Chapter 4. *LORD JIM* (I)

1. *The Critic,* XXXVIII (1901), 438, quoted in Gordan, *Joseph Conrad,* p. 297.
2. *The English Novel: Form and Function,* p. 234.
3. November 3, 1900, quoted in Gordan, *Joseph Conrad,* pp. 294–295.
4. *Lord Jim,* p. 14.
5. *Times Literary Supplement,* October 11, 1923, p. 670, quoted in Gordan, *Joseph Conrad,* p. 63.
6. *Lord Jim,* p. 132.
7. *Ibid.*, pp. 247–248.
8. *Ibid.*, p. 416.
9. *Ibid.*, pp. 303–304.
10. *Ibid.*, p. 51.
11. *Ibid.*, p. 93.
12. *Ibid.*, p. 152.
13. *Ibid.*, p. 58.
14. Morf, *Polish Heritage,* p. 158.

Chapter 5. *LORD JIM* (II)

1. *Lord Jim,* pp. 98–99.
2. *Ibid.*, p. 140. For instance, the arrow wound of the count in *The Sun Also Rises.*
3. *Ibid.*, p. 139.
4. *Ibid.*, p. 209.
5. *Ibid.*, p. 148.
6. Van Ghent, *The English Novel,* p. 237. This may be true, though the split hill exists in the "source" of Brooke's memoirs. The imagination makes its significant selections from reality.
7. *Lord Jim,* p. 215.
8. *Ibid.*, p. 214.
9. *Notes on Life and Letters,* p. 33.
10. *Life and Letters,* I, 298.
11. *Lord Jim,* pp. 136–137.
12. *Ibid.*, pp. 226–227.
13. Gordan, *Joseph Conrad,* pp. 57–73.
14. *Lord Jim,* pp. 323–324.
15. *Ibid.*, p. 47.
16. *Ibid.*, pp. 162–163.
17. *Ibid.*, p. 163.

Chapter 6. *NOSTROMO*

1. *The Great Tradition,* p. 190.
2. R. P. Warren, Introduction, *Nostromo* (Modern Library edition), p. xxxix. Page references to the text are, as usual, to the Kent edition.
3. *Nostromo,* p. 102.
4. *Ibid.,* pp. 17–18.
5. *Ibid.,* pp. 62, 63.
6. *Ibid.,* p. 55.
7. *Ibid.,* p. 367.
8. *Ibid.,* pp. 160–161.
9. *Ibid.,* pp. 398–399.
10. *Ibid.,* pp. 214–215, 218.
11. *Ibid.,* pp. 317–318.
12. Warren, Introduction, p. xxii.
13. *Nostromo,* p. 77.
14. *Ibid.,* p. 84.
15. *Ibid.,* p. 511.
16. *Ibid.,* p. 521.
17. Warren, Introduction, p. xxx.
18. *Nostromo,* p. 166.
19. *Ibid.,* pp. 496–501.
20. *Ibid.,* p. 171.
21. Leavis, *The Great Tradition,* p. 190.
22. See Author's Note.
23. *Nostromo,* pp. 331, 417, 419–420, 428.
24. *Ibid.,* p. 393.
25. Warren, Introduction, p. xi.

Chapter 7. TWO VERSIONS OF ANARCHY

1. These stories were written before *The Secret Agent,* although the volume *A Set of Six* was not published until 1908.
2. Author's Note.
3. See Morton D. Zabel's excellent introduction to the New Directions edition (New York, 1951).
4. Letter to John Galsworthy, September 12, 1906. *Life and Letters,* II, 37.
5. Letter to (Sir) Algernon Methuen, November 7, 1906. *Ibid.,* II, 38.
6. *The Secret Agent,* p. 139.
7. *Ibid.,* p. 303.
8. *Ibid.,* pp. 69, 92.
9. *Ibid.,* pp. 262–263.
10. *Ibid.,* p. 311.
11. *Ibid.,* pp. 118, 149.

12. *Under Western Eyes,* pp. 228–229.
13. *Ibid.,* p. 298.
14. *Ibid.,* p. 299.
15. *Ibid.,* p. 380.
16. *Ibid.,* pp. 359–360.
17. Letter to John Galsworthy, January 6, 1908. *Life and Letters,* II, 65.
18. *Under Western Eyes,* p. 66.
19. *Ibid.,* pp. 67, 104.
20. *Ibid.,* p. 175.
21. "Joseph Conrad: Order and Anarchy: The Political Novels," *Kenyon Review,* (Autumn 1953), 505–521.
22. *Under Western Eyes,* pp. 305–306.
23. *Ibid.,* p. 162.
24. Author's Note.

Chapter 8. *CHANCE* AND AFTER

1. *The Great Tradition,* p. 209.
2. *Life and Letters,* II, 200.
3. *Ibid.,* 47.
4. *Chance,* p. 144; see also p. 281.
5. *Ibid.,* p. 56.
6. *The Rover,* p. 122.
7. *Suspense,* pp. 76–77.
8. *Victory,* pp. 288–289.
9. *Chance,* pp. 426–427.
10. *Ibid.,* p. 348. My italics.
11. *Ibid.,* p. 331.
12. *Ibid.,* p. 84.
13. *Ibid.,* p. 362.
14. *Ibid.,* pp. 119–120.
15. "The New Novel," in *Notes on Novelists.*
16. *Chance,* pp. 101, 102–103.
17. *Ibid.,* pp. 353, 354.
18. Douglas Hewitt, *Conrad: A Reassessment* (Cambridge, 1952), pp. 103–104.
19. *Ibid.,* p. 104.
20. *Victory,* p. 248.
21. *Ibid.,* pp. 159, 166, 225.
22. *Ibid.,* p. 218.
23. *Ibid.,* p. 95.
24. *Ibid.,* pp. 188, 215, 317.
25. *Life and Letters,* II, 232.
26. *The Arrow of Gold,* p. 346.
27. *Life and Letters,* II, 326.
28. *Ibid.,* 339.

29. *The Rover,* p. 269.
30. Introduction, *Suspense.*
31. See, for instance, *Suspense,* p. 18.
32. *Ibid.,* p. 6.
33. *Ibid.,* pp. 270–271.
34. Hewitt, p. 131.
35. Author's Note, *Typhoon.*
36. *Ibid.,* pp. 46–47.
37. *Ibid.,* p. 19.
38. *Ibid.,* p. 90.
39. Letter to Hugh Walpole, June 7, 1918. *Life and Letters,* II, 206. In this letter Conrad discounts the legend that he had hesitated between English and French, and claims he read *Madame Bovary* only after finishing *Almayer's Folly*. But Jean-Aubry properly calls attention to a letter of April 6, 1892, in which Conrad speaks of "re-reading *Madame Bovary* with an admiration tinged with respect" (*The Sea Dreamer,* p. 185).

INDEX

INDEX